HISTORY OF THE

NIAGARA RIVER

View of Horseshoe Falls from the Canadian Side

From a Photograph

HISTORY OF
THE NIAGARA RIVER

By
Archer Butler Hulbert

With 67 Maps and Illustrations

HARBOR HILL BOOKS
Harrison, N. Y.
1978

Library of Congress Cataloging in Publication Data
Hulbert, Archer Butler, 1873-1933.
  History of the Niagara River.

  Reprint of the 1908 ed. published by Putnam, New York under title: The Niagara River.
  Includes index.
  1. Niagara River. 2. Niagara frontier--History. I. Title.
F127.N6H8   1978   974.7'99   78-12656
ISBN 0-916346-29-3

Reprinted from the edition
published by G. P. Putnam's Sons
New York 1908
with the title
THE NIAGARA RIVER

Harbor Hill Books, P.O. Box 407, Harrison, N. Y. 10528

Manufactured in the United States of America

TO
HENRY CARLTON HULBERT
IN
APPRECIATION OF ENCOURAGEMENT AND FRIENDSHIP
AND AS A TOKEN OF
ESTEEM

Note

In the endeavour to gather into one volume a proper description of the various interests that centre in and around the Niagara River the author of this book felt very sincerely the difficulties of the task before him. As the geologic wonder of a continent and the commercial marvel of the present century, the Niagara River is one of the most remarkable streams in the world. In historic interest, too, it takes rank with any American river. To combine, then, into the pages of a single volume a proper treatment of this subject would be a task that perhaps no one could accomplish satisfactorily.

Works to which the author is most indebted, especially the historical writings of Hon. Peter A. Porter, Severance's *Old Trails of the Niagara Frontier*, *The Niagara Book*, and the writings of the scholar of the old New York frontier, the late O. H. Marshall, and the collections of the historical societies along the frontier, are indicated frequently in footnotes and in text. The author's particular indebtedness to Mr. Porter is elsewhere described; he is also in the debt of F. H. Mautz, Henry Guttenstein, Superintendent Edward H. Perry, whose kindness to the author was so characteristic of his treatment of all comers to the shrine over which he presides, E. O. Dunlap, and many others mentioned elsewhere. He has appreciated Mr. Howells's characteristic conscientiousness when he wrote concerning Niagara, "I have always had to take myself in hand, to shake myself up, to look twice, and recur to what I have heard and read of other people's impressions, before I am overpowered by it. Otherwise I am simply charmed." The author has laboured under the difficulty of attempting to remain "overpowered" during a period of several years. That there have been serious lapses in the shape of lucid intervals, the critic will find full soon!

It has seemed best to treat of modern Niagara under what might have been called "Part I." of this volume. The history of the Niagara region proper begins in Chapter VII., the problems of present-day interest occupying the preceding six chapters.

A. B. H.

MARIETTA COLLEGE, MARIETTA, OHIO,
January 26, 1908.

Contents

CHAPTER		PAGE
I.—Buffalo and the Upper Niagara		1
II.—From the Falls to Lake Ontario		23
III.—The Birth of Niagara		52
IV.—Niagara Bond and Free		72
V.—Harnessing Niagara Falls		99
VI.—A Century of Niagara Cranks		123
VII.—The Old Niagara Frontier		153
VIII.—From La Salle to De Nonville		171
IX.—Niagara under Three Flags		196
X.—The Hero of Upper Canada		231
XI.—The Second War with England		263
XII.—Toronto		292
Index		315

List of Illustrations

	PAGE
VIEW OF HORSESHOE FALLS FROM THE CANADIAN SIDE From a photograph. *Frontispiece*	
A GLIMPSE OF BUFFALO HARBOR	4
LAFAYETTE SQUARE	5
ST. PAUL'S CHURCH, BUFFALO	12
NIAGARA FALLS	13
From the original painting by Frederick Edwin Church, in Corcoran Gallery.	
THE AMERICAN RAPIDS	16
THE VIEW FROM PROSPECT POINT	17
From a photograph by Notman, Montreal.	
GOAT ISLAND BRIDGE AND RAPIDS	24
HORSESHOE FALLS FROM BELOW	25
"THE SHORELESS SEA"	28
From a photograph by Notman, Montreal.	
RUSTIC BRIDGE, WILLOW ISLAND	29
THE CAVE OF THE WINDS	32
THE AMERICAN FALL	33
From a photograph by Notman, Montreal.	
REMAINS OF STONE PIERS OF THE "FIRST RAILWAY IN AMERICA"—THE BRITISH TRAMWAY UP LEWISTON HEIGHTS, 1763	38

Illustrations

	PAGE
AMID THE GOAT ISLAND GROUP	39
From a photograph by Notman, Montreal.	
HORSESHOE FALLS FROM THE CANADIAN SHORE	44
From a photograph by Notman, Montreal.	
LOOKING UP THE LOWER NIAGARA FROM PARADISE GROVE	45
From a photograph by Wm. Quinn, Niagara-on-the-Lake.	
THE MOUTH OF THE GORGE	48
From a photograph by Notman, Montreal.	
THE WHIRLPOOL RAPIDS	49
THE AMERICAN FALL, JULY, 1765	54
From an unsigned original drawing in the British Museum.	
THE HORSESHOE FALL, JULY, 1765	55
From an unsigned original drawing in the British Museum.	
ICE MOUNTAIN ON PROSPECT POINT	64
CAVE OF THE WINDS IN WINTER	65
"MAID OF THE MIST" UNDER STEEL ARCH BRIDGE	70
BEACON ON OLD BREAKWATER AT BUFFALO	71
WINTER SCENE IN PROSPECT PARK	74
BATH ISLAND, AMERICAN RAPIDS, IN 1879	75
From New York Commissioners' Report.	
PATH TO LUNA ISLAND	86
GREEN ISLAND BRIDGE	87
BIRD'S-EYE VIEW OF THE CANADIAN RAPIDS AND FALL	100
From a photograph by Notman, Montreal.	
AMERICAN FALLS FROM BELOW	101
THE RIVERSIDE AT WILLOW ISLAND	118

Illustrations

	PAGE
GOAT ISLAND BRIDGE, SHOWING NIAGARA'S FAMOUS CATARACT AND INTERNATIONAL HOTELS	119
THE PATH TO THE CAVE OF THE WINDS . . . From a photograph by Notman, Montreal.	130
AMERICAN FALLS FROM GOAT ISLAND	131
HORSESHOE FALLS FROM GOAT ISLAND	142
ICE BRIDGE AND AMERICAN FALLS	143
COLONEL RÖMER'S MAP OF THE COUNTRY OF THE IROQUOIS, 1700	154
CHAMPLAIN	155
MAP OF FRENCH FORTS IN AMERICA	164
NIAGARA FALLS BY FATHER HENNEPIN . . . . The first known picture of Niagara, dated 1697.	165
R. RÉNÉ CAVELIER, SIEUR DE LA SALLE . . .	172
FRONTENAC, FROM HÉBERT'S STATUE AT QUEBEC . .	173
LUNA ISLAND BRIDGE	184
"CARTE DU LAC ONTARIO." A SPECIMEN FRENCH MAP OF THE NIAGARA FRONTIER DATED OCTOBER 4, 1757 From the original in the British Museum.	185
STONES ON THE SITE OF JONCAIRE'S CABIN UNDER LEWISTON HEIGHTS, WHERE THE "MAGAZINE ROYALE" WAS ERECTED IN 1719	198
SPECIMEN MANUSCRIPT MAP OF NIAGARA FRONTIER OF EIGHTEENTH CENTURY . . . . . . From the original in the British Museum.	199
A DRAWING OF FORT NIAGARA AND ENVIRONS SHOWING PLAN OF ENGLISH ATTACK UNDER JOHNSON . .	208

Illustrations

	PAGE
A Sketch of Fort Niagara and Environs by the French Commander Pouchot Showing Improvements of 1756–1758	209 and 210
Canadian Trapper, from La Potherie	211
Youngstown, N. Y., from Paradise Grove	214
The Stone Redoubt at Fort Niagara, Built in 1770	215
From the original in the British Museum.	
Pfister's Sketch of Fort Niagara and the "Communication," Two Years before the Outbreak of the Revolutionary War	220
Fort Erie and the Mouth of the Niagara, by Pfister, in 1764	221
From the original in the British Museum.	
Major-General Brock	232
A Plan of Fort Niagara after English Occupation, by Montresor	233
"Navy Hall Opposite Niagara"	244
A drawing on bark by Mrs. Simcoe.	
Queenston and Brock's Monument	245
From a photograph by Wm. Quinn, Niagara-on-the-Lake.	
Brock's Monument	260
"Queenston or Landing near Niagara"	261
A drawing on bark by Mrs. Simcoe.	
Lieutenant Pierie's Sketch of Niagara, 1768	272
From an old print.	
Old View of Fort Missisagua	273
Monument at Lundy's Lane	284
Lieutenant-General Simcoe	285

Illustrations

	PAGE
"York Harbor"	296
A drawing on bark by Mrs. Simcoe.	
"The Garrison at York"	297
A drawing on bark by Mrs. Simcoe.	
Captain Sowers's Drawings of Fort Niagara, 1769 .	308
From the original in the British Museum.	

The Niagara River

Chapter I

Buffalo and the Upper Niagara

THE Strait of Niagara, or the Niagara River, as it is commonly called, ranks among the wonders of the world. The study of this stream is of intense and special interest to many classes of people, notably historians, archæologists, botanists, geologists, artists, mechanics, and electricians. It is doubtful if there is anywhere another thirty-six miles of riverway that can, in this respect, compare with it.

The term "strait" as applied to the Niagara correctly suggests the river's historic importance. The expression, recurring in so many of the relations of French and English military officers, "on this communication" also indicates Niagara's position in the story of the discovery, conquest, and occupation of the continent. It is probably the Falls which, technically, make Niagara a river; and so, in turn, it is the Falls that rendered Niagara an important strategic key of the vast waterway stretching from the mouth of the St. Lawrence to the head of Lake Superior. The lack —so far as it does exist—of historic interest in the immediate Niagara region, the comparative paucity of military events of magnitude along that stream during the old French and the Revolutionary wars proves, on the one hand, what a wilderness separated the English on the South from the French on the North, and, on the other, how strong "the communication" was between Quebec and the French posts in the Middle West. It does not prove that Niagara was the less important.

The Falls increased the historic importance of Niagara because it limited navigation and made a portage necessary; the purposes of trade and missionary enterprise, as well as those of conquest, demanded that this point be occupied, and occupation necessarily meant defence. Here, from Lewiston and Queenston to Chippewa and Port Day (to use modern names) ran the two most famous portage paths of the continent. Here were to be seen at one time or another the footprints of as famous explorers, noble missionaries, and brave soldiers as ever went to conquest in history.

The Niagara River was important in the olden time to every mile of territory drained by the waters that flowed through it. What an empire to hold in fee! Here lies more than one-half the fresh water of the world—the solid contents being, according to Darby 1,547,011,792,300,000; it would form a solid cubic column measuring nearly twenty-two miles on each side.

The most remote body of water tributary to Niagara River is Lake Superior, 381 miles long and 161 miles broad with a circumference of 1150 miles. The Niagara of Lake Superior is the St. Mary's River, twenty-seven miles in length, its current very rapid, with water flow-

Buffalo and the Upper Niagara

ing over great masses of rock into Lake Huron. Lake Huron is 218 miles long and 20 miles wider than Lake Superior, but with a circumference of only 812 miles. Lake Michigan is 345 miles long and 84 broad and enters Lake Huron through Mackinaw Straits which are four miles in length, with a fall of four feet. In turn Lake Huron empties into the St. Clair and Detroit rivers which, with a total fall of eleven feet in fifty-one miles, forms the Niagara of Lake Erie. This sheet of water is 250 miles long and 60 miles broad at its widest part. The area drained by these lakes is as follows, including their own area:

Lake Superior...............	85,000 sq. m.
" Huron.................	74,000 "
" Michigan..............	70,040 "
" Erie...................	39,680 "
Total................	268,720 "

Considering this as a portion of the St. Lawrence drainage, we have the marvellous spectacle of a navigable waterway from the St. Louis River, Lake Superior, to Cape Gaspé at the mouth of the St. Lawrence, of twenty-one hundred miles in length, the Niagara River being paralleled to-day by the Welland Canal, and lesser canals affording a passageway around the rapids of the St. Mary's in the West and the St. Lawrence in the East. In a previous volume in the present series [1] it was seen that the improved rivers in the Ohio basin now offered a navigable pathway over four thousand miles in length; how insignificant is that prospect in view of this great transcontinental waterway two thousand miles in length but including the 268,000

[1] *The Ohio River; A Course of Empire*, p. 359.

square miles in the four great lakes alone! Well does George Waldo Browne in his beautiful volume on this subject, *The St. Lawrence River*, say:

Treated in a more extended manner, according to the ideas of the early French geographers, and taking either the river and lake of Nipigon, on the north of Superior, or the river St. Louis, flowing from the south-west, it has a grand total length of over two thousand miles. With its tributaries it drains over four hundred thousand square miles of country, made up of fertile valleys and plateaux inhabited by a prosperous people, desolate barrens, deep forests, where the foot of man has not yet left its imprint.

Seldom less than two miles in width, it is two and one-half miles wide where it issues from Ontario, and with several expansions which deserve the name of lake it becomes eighty miles in width where it ceases to be considered a river. The influence of the tide is felt as far up as Lake St. Peter, about one hundred miles from the gulf, while it is navigable for sea-going vessels to Montreal, eighty miles farther inland. Rapids impede navigation above this point, but by means of canals continuous communication is obtained to the head of Lake Superior.

If inferior in breadth to the mighty Amazon, if it lacks the length of the Mississippi, if without the stupendous gorges and cataracts of the Yang-tse-Kiang of China, if missing the ancient castles of the Rhine, if wanting the lonely grandeur that still overhangs the Congo of the Dark Continent, the Great River of Canada has features as remarkable as any of these. It has its source in the largest body of fresh water upon the globe, and among all of the big rivers of the world it is the only one whose volume is not sensibly affected by the elements. In rain or in sunshine, in spring floods or in summer droughts, this phenomenon of waterways seldom varies more than a foot in its rise and fall.

The history of the Niagara is so closely interwoven with that of the great "Queen City of the Lakes,"

A Glimpse of Buffalo Harbor.

Lafayette Square.

Buffalo, that it would seem as though the famous waterway was in the suburb of the city and its greatest scenic attraction. However true this is to-day, it was very far from the case a century ago, for though the site of Buffalo was historic and important, the city, as such, is of comparative recent origin, coming to its own with giant strides in those last decades of the nineteenth century. Writes Mr. Rowland B. Mahany in his excellent chapter on "Buffalo" in *The Historic Towns of the Middle States:*

> Few cities of the United States have a history more picturesque than Buffalo, or more typical of the forces that have made the Republic great. At the time of the adoption of the Federal constitution, in 1787, not a single white settler dwelt on the site of what is now the Queen of the Lakes; and it was not until after the second presidency of Washington, that Joseph Ellicott, the founder of Buffalo, laid out the plan of the town, which he called New Amsterdam.

On February 10, 1810, the "Town of Buffaloe" was created by act of the State Legislature, a name originally given to the locality by the Seneca Indians, who, we shall see, dominated the old Niagara frontier; it is believed that the name came from the animals which visited the neighbouring salt licks; and the name therefore may be much older than any settlement or even camping site. The village of New Amsterdam was now merged into the town of Buffalo, which boasted a newspaper in the second year of its existence, 1811. The story of the following years falls naturally into that of the disastrous war with England from 1812 to 1814, in which Buffalo suffered severely. As Mr. Mahany suggests, the story of Buffalo is characteristically American, and its phases, as such offer an inviting field, but one too wide for full examination in the present history.[1]

The important position of the city with reference to the Great Lakes was very greatly increased with the building of the Erie Canal from 1817 to 1825. It is interesting to recall the fact that it was in reality fear of the possibility of another war with England that caused the deciding vote for the Erie Canal project to be cast in its favour.[2] In the proper place we shall have impressed upon us the great distance that separated the Niagara frontier from the inhabited portion of the Republic at this early period, the great length of the land route and the difficulty of it; it was said to be far more than a cannon was worth to haul it to the frontier during the War of 1812. All this shows very distinctly the early condition surrounding the rise of the metropolis of the Niagara country, and, from being strange that little Buffalo did not grow faster, it is amazing to find such rapid growth during the first twenty-five years of her life.

With the opening of the canal in 1825 a new era dawned; the work of the great land companies in northeastern New York drew vast armies of people thither, and the canal proved to be the great route for a much longer migration from the seaboard to the further north-west, to Michigan and Wisconsin, as well as to neighbouring Ohio. All this helped Buffalo. Numbers of travellers arriving at the future site of the Queen

[1] Frank H. Severance in his delightful *Old Trails of the Niagara Frontier* has several most interesting chapters relating to the Buffalo neighbourhood. Mr. Severance has done, through the Buffalo Historical Society, much good work in keeping warm the affection of the present generation for the memory of the past, its heroes and its sacrifices.

[2] See A. B. Hulbert, *The Great American Canals*, vol. ii., p. 111.

City of the Lakes at once decided that they could at least go farther and fare very much worse, and so sat down to grow up with the Niagara frontier. The proximity of the Falls had something to do, of course, with bringing increasingly larger numbers of travellers and transients to the Lake Erie village. But it was slow work, this building up a great city, and no doubt the very fact that the stones of the mighty edifice one finds beside that beautiful harbour to-day were laid slowly accounts for the solidity of the structure; Buffalo was not built on a boom.

From James L. Barton's reminiscences, for instance, we have clear pictures of the early struggle for business in this frontier town, which prove it to have been typically American. Mr. Barton owned a line of boats on the Lakes and canal but found it very difficult to find freight for the boats to carry down the State;

> A few tons of freight [he writes], was all that we could furnish each boat to carry to Albany. This they would take in, and fill up at Rochester, which place, situated in the heart of the wheat-growing district of Western New York, furnished nearly all the down freight that passed on the canal. Thus we lived and struggled on until 1830. Our population had increased largely, and that year numbered six thousand and thirty-one. In the fall of 1831, I received from Cleveland one thousand bushels of wheat. . . . The next winter I made arrangement with the late Colonel Ira A. Blossom, the resident agent of the Holland Land Company, to furnish storage for all the wheat the settlers should bring in, towards the payment on their land contracts with the company. The whole amount did not exceed three thousand bushels. . . . In 1833 the Ohio canal was completed, which gave us a little more business. Northern Ohio was then the only portion of the great West that had any surplus agricultural products to send to an eastern market. In 1833 a little stir commenced in land operations, which increased the next year, and in 1835 became

a perfect fever and swallowed up almost everything else. Nearly every person who had any enterprise got rich from buying and selling land; using little money in these transactions, but paying and receiving in pay, bonds and mortgages to an illimitable amount.

In 1837 the panic affected the young lake city as it did all parts of the land, but by 1840 the population of Buffalo had swelled to over eighteen thousand. The record of growth of the past century is a matter of figures strung on the faith of a great company of active, enterprising, far-sighted business men, until Buffalo ranks among the cities of half a million population, with a future unquestionably secure and brilliant.

The Niagara River is some nineteen hundred feet in width at its mouth here at Buffalo and forty-eight feet deep; the average rate of current here is under six miles per hour, but when south-west gales drive the lake billows in gigantic gulps down the river's mouth the current sometimes races as fast as twelve miles per hour. Old Fort Erie, built here at the mouth of the Niagara immediately after England won the continent from France, in 1764, was formerly the only settlement hereabouts, Black Rock, now part of Buffalo, at the mouth of the Erie Canal, was not settled until near the close of that century. It is believed that five forts have guarded the mouth of this strategic river, all known as Fort Erie. When the people of the opposite sides of the river were in conflict in 1812, Black Rock was the rival of Fort Erie. The large black rock which formed the landing-place of the ferry across the river here, and which gave the hamlet its name, was destroyed when the Erie Canal was built. Black Rock was formally laid out in 1804 and in 1853 was incorporated with the city of Buffalo.

The upper Niagara with its even current and low-lying banks is not specially attractive. Grand Island, two miles below the mouth, divides the river into two narrow arms. This beautiful island, the Indian name of which was Owanunga, so popular to-day as a summering place, is remembered in history especially as the site selected in 1825 for Major M. M. Noah's "New Jerusalem," the proposed industrial centre of the Jews of the New World, but nothing was accomplished on the island itself toward the object in view.

At Buffalo, however, Noah took the title "Judge of Israel," and held a meeting in the old St. Paul's Church, where remarkable initiatory rites took place. In resplendent robes covered by a mantle of crimson silk, trimmed with ermine, the Judge held what he termed "impressive and unique ceremony," in which he read a proclamation to "all the Jews throughout the world," bringing them the glad tidings that on the ancient isle Owanunga "an asylum was prepared and offered to them," and that he did "revive, renew, and establish (in the Lord's name), the government of the Jewish nation, . . . confirming and perpetuating all our rights and privileges, our rank and power, among the nations of the earth as they existed and were recognised under the government of the Judges." Mr. Noah ordered a census of all the Hebrews in the world to be taken and did not forget, incidentally, to levy a tax of about one dollar and a half on every Jew in order to carry on the project. A "foundation stone" was prepared to be erected on the site of the future New Jerusalem; the following inscription was engraved upon it:

Hear, O Israel, the Lord
is our God—the Lord is one.

ARARAT,
A CITY OF REFUGE FOR THE JEWS,
FOUNDED BY MORDECAI MANUEL NOAH,
IN THE MONTH OF TISRI 5586—SEPT. 1825
IN THE FIFTIETH YEAR OF
AMERICAN INDEPENDENCE.

At the lower extremity of Grand Island is historic Burnt Ship Bay, made famous, as hereafter related, in the old French War.

The little town of Tonawanda, with its immense lumber interests, and La Salle, famous in history as the building site of the *Griffon*, elsewhere described, lie opposite Grand Island on the American shore, the former at the mouth of Cayuga Creek. On the opposite shore, a little below the beautiful Navy Island, is the historic town of Chippewa.

Below Navy Island the river spreads out to a width of over two miles; it has fallen twenty feet since leaving Lake Erie, and now gathers into a narrower channel for its magnificent rush to the falls one mile below. In this mile the river drops fifty-two feet, through what are known as the American and Canadian Rapids, on their respective sides of the river.

From a scenic standpoint it is questionable whether any of the delights of Niagara surpass those afforded by this beautiful series of cascades; sightseers are prepared from their earliest days for the magnificent beauty of the Falls themselves, but of the Rapids above little is known until their insidious charm gradually works its way into the heart to remain forever an image of beauty and rapture that cannot be effaced. Guide books will give adequate advice as to the best points of vantage from which to view the various rifts and cascades.[1]

Some years ago [writes Mr. Porter], Colin Hunter, then an Associate, now a Royal Academician, came over from London to paint Niagara. Of all the points of view he selected the one as seen up stream from the head of the Little Brother Island. A temporary bridge was built to it, and here, with a guard at the bridge, so as to be secure from intrusion, he painted his grand view, looking up stream. The upper ledge of rocks, with its long, rapid cascade, was his sky-line; in the foreground were the tumbling Rapids; far to the right of the picture the tops of a few trees appearing on the Canada shore above the waters alone showed the presence of any land. We advise . . . the visitor to clamber over the rocks on the Canadian shore of the Island . . . go out as near the water's edge as possible, and you will appreciate the difference that a few feet in a point of observation may make in what is apparently the same scenery. Just before you reach the foot of the island a gnarled cedar tree and a rock, accessible by leaping from stone to stone, gives you access to a point of observation than which there is nothing more beautiful at Niagara. Do not fail to get this view, for it is the Colin Hunter view, as nearly as you can get it, and you will appreciate the artistic sense of the great painter who chose this incomparable view in preference to the Falls themselves for a reproduction of the very best at Niagara.

Another beautiful point from which to view the Rapids is on Terrapin Rocks, the so-called scenic and geographical centre of Niagara. Here the power of

[1] Congressman Peter A. Porter's Guide Book may be recommended highly; its use to the present writer, taken in addition to its author's personal assistance and advice, must be acknowledged in the most unreserved way. Numerous references to Mr. Porter's various monographs, especially his *Old Fort Niagara* and *Goat Island*, in addition to his Guide, will be met with frequently in this volume. To one really interested in Niagara history *Old Fort Niagara* will be found most attractive and comprehensive; its numerous references to authorities put it quite in a class by itself among local histories.

the magnificent river, the "shoreless sea" above you, the clouds for its horizon, grows more impressive with every visit. By day the sight is marvellously impressive; by night, under some circumstances, it is yet more wonderful. Of this night view Margaret Fuller wrote, most feelingly:

> After nightfall as there was a splendid moon, I went down to the bridge and leaned over the parapet, where the boiling rapids came down in their might. It was grand, and it was also gorgeous; the yellow rays of the moon made the broken waves appear like auburn tresses twining around the black rocks. But they did not inspire me as before. I felt a foreboding of a mightier emotion to rise up and swallow all others, and I passed on to the Terrapin Bridge. Everything was changed, the misty apparition had taken off its many coloured crown which it had worn by day, and a bow of silvery white spanned its summit. The moonlight gave a poetical indefiniteness to the distant parts of the waters, and while the rapids were glancing in her beams, the river below the Falls was as black as night, save where the reflection of the sky gave it the appearance of a shield of blue steel.

As the Falls of Niagara slowly creep backward in tune to their stupendous recessional toward Lake Erie they encroach more and more on the magnificent domain of the Rapids, nor will their gradual increase in height atone for this savage invasion nor palliate the offence committed. A thousand years more, we are told, and the visitor will view the "Horseshoe" Fall from the upper end of the Third Sister Island, and the marvellous canvas of Colin Hunter will be as meaningless as Hennepin's picture of two centuries and more ago. The American Fall, receding much more slowly than the Horseshoe Fall, will invade the beautiful rapids above Goat Island bridge at a very much later date, for, as we shall see, the greater fall recedes almost as many

St. Paul's Church, Buffalo.

Niagara Falls.

From the original painting by Frederick Edwin Church, in Corcoran Gallery.

feet per year as the lesser recedes inches. And in this connection it is interesting to note that if the recession continued to Lake Erie and onward into that lake until the line of fall was a mile long at its crest, with the water falling 336 feet, Victoria Falls in the Zambesi River would still exceed their American rival by sixty-four feet in height!

The accessibility of the Niagara Rapids, because of the fortunate location of the Goat Island group is, in itself, one of the great charms of the region, and this may explain in part the insuppressible desire of early visitors to reach these glorious points of vantage. The view of the rapids from the Goat Island bridge to-day is said to be the source of chief pleasure "to half the visitors to Niagara." [1]

George Houghton's beautiful lines on "The Upper Rapids" express with fine feeling the effect of these racing cascades on the sensitive mind:

Still with the wonder of boyhood, I follow the race of the Rapids,
Sirens that dance, and allure to destruction,—now lurking in shadows,
Skirting the level stillness of pools and the treacherous shallows,
Smiling and dimple-mouthed, coquetting,—now modest, now forward;

Tenderly chanting, and such the thrall of the weird incantation,
Thirst it awakes in each listener's soul, a feverish longing,
Thoughts all absorbent, a torment that stings and ever increases,
Burning ambition to push bare-breast to thy perilous bosom.

[1] Frederick Almy in *The Niagara Book*, p. 51. This volume has been of perennial interest to the author because of the contributions of the venerable William Dean Howells and E. S. Martin. No one who in early life has essayed the life of journalist and correspondent can read Mr. Howells's article in this little book without immense relish; its humour is contagious, and its descriptions of Niagara in 1860, fascinating.

Thus, in some midnight obscure, bent down by the storm of
    temptation
(So hath the wind, in the beechen wood, confided the story),
Pine-trees, thrusting their way and trampling down one another,
Curious, lean and listen, replying in sobs and in whispers;

Till of the secret possessed, which brings sure blight to the hearer,
(So hath the wind, in the beechen wood, confided the story),
Faltering, they stagger brinkward,—clutch at the roots of the
    grasses,
Cry,—a pitiful cry of remorse,—and plunge down in the darkness.

Art thou all-merciless then,—a fiend, ever fierce for new victims?
Was then the red-man right (as yet it liveth in legend),
That, ere each twelvemonth circles, still to thy shrine is allotted
Blood of one human heart, as sacrifice due and demanded?

Butterflies have I followed, that leaving the red-top and clover,
Thinking a wind-harp thy voice, thy froth the fresh whiteness
    of daisies,
Ventured too close, grew giddy, and catching cold drops on their
    pinions,
Balanced — but vainly,—and falling, their scarlet was blotted
    forever.

When, about 1880, William M. Hunt was commissioned to decorate the immense panels of the Assembly Chamber of the Capitol at Albany, N. Y., he chose, with true artistic feeling, the view of the rapids above Goat Island bridge as the choice picture to represent the great marvel and chief wonder of the Empire State —Niagara. It is generally conceded that Church's *Horseshoe Falls* takes rank over all other paintings of Niagara, but Colin Hunter's *Rapids of Niagara* excel any other view of either the Falls, Gorge, or Rapids on canvas to-day.

But we must observe here that these Rapids were something aside from beautiful to the French and English officers whose duty it was to defend and supply "the communication" from Fort Frontenac to Fort Chartres; they probably seemed very "horrid," in the old time sense, to those who struggled under the burdens of the ancient portage path. The southern termini of the two pathways—one on either side of the river—were Chippewa and Port Day, respectively. The route from Lewiston to Port Day was evidently the common portage until after the War of 1812 when the Canadian path was opened. A little below what is known as Schlosser Dock stood the French fort guarding this end of their old portage path, Fort du Portage or Little Fort Niagara, built about 1750, nine years before England conquered the region. Near by stands the one famous relic of the old régime, the Old Stone Chimney of Fort du Portage, later a chimney of the English mess-house at Fort Schlosser. As will be noted later Fort du Portage was destroyed by the retreating French, after the capture of Fort Niagara by Sir William Johnson; to guard that end of the portage the English under Colonel Schlosser built Fort Schlosser in 1761. The road occupying the course of the ancient portage does not extend to the river now, but it bears the old name, and on it you may see, not half a mile back, outlines of the earthen works of one of the eleven block-houses built in 1764 by Captain Montresor the first of which was erected on the hill above Lewiston; these block-houses guarded the important roadway from the assaults of Indians such as the famous Bloody Run Massacre of 1763. Frenchman's Landing is the modern name for the cove below the Old Stone Chimney where was the terminus of the earliest portage path guarded by the block-house known as the first Little

Fort Niagara. This whole district is now the site of the power-houses and mills that are making Niagara a word to conjure with in the centres of trade as certainly as in the ancient day it was a mesmeric word in the courts and camps of the Old World.

The thunder of Niagara Falls reaches our ears even amid the music of these beautiful Rapids, and we are drawn on to the marvellous group of islands that impinge upon the cataract.

What is commonly known as the Goat Island group consists of the island of that name, containing some seventy acres of land, and sixteen other islands or rocks contiguous thereto. Without undertaking to dispute or defend many of the extravagant assertions made in behalf of Goat Island, to which have been given the titles "Temple of Nature," "Enchanted Isles," "Isle of Beauty," "Shrine of the Deity," "Fairy Isles," etc. it would, I think, be difficult to disprove the statement often made that no other seventy acres on the continent are more interesting than these bearing this homely name. From the standpoint of the artist and naturalist this statement would probably pass unquestioned. The views already alluded to of the American and Canadian rapids to be gained from this delightful vantage point are probably unparalleled. To the botanist Goat Island is a paradise. Sir Joseph Hooker affirmed that he found here a greater variety of vegetation within a given space than he had found in Europe or in America east of the Sierras, and Dr. Asa Gray confirmed the extravagant statement. Wrote Frederick Law Olmsted:

> I have followed the Appalachian chain almost from end to end, and travelled on horseback "in search of the picturesque"

The American Rapids.

The View from Prospect Point.
From a photograph by Notman, Montreal.

over four thousand miles of the most promising parts of the continent without finding elsewhere the same quality of forest beauty which was once abundant about the Falls, and which is still to be observed on those parts of Goat Island where the original growth of trees and shrubs has not been disturbed, and where from caving banks trees are not now exposed to excessive dryness at the root.

In a report, prepared by David F. Day for the New York State Reservation Commissioners, we find explained, in part, the notable fertility of this little plot of ground, although the oft-returning misty rain from the Falls, and the fact that Goat Island never experiences the dangers of a "forward" spring have much to do in preserving its beautiful robe of colours:

A calcareous soil enriched with an abundance of organic matter like that of Goat Island would necessarily be one of great fertility. For the growth and sustentation of a forest and of such plants as prefer the woods to the openings it would far excel the deep and exhaustless alluvians of the prairie states.

It would be difficult to find within another territory so restricted in its limits so great a diversity of trees and shrubs and still more difficult to find in so small an area such examples of arboreal symmetry and perfection as the island has to exhibit.

The island received its flora from the mainland, in fact the botanist is unable to point out a single instance of tree, shrub, or herb, now growing upon the island not also to be found upon the mainland. But the distinguishing characteristic of its flora is not the possession of any plant elsewhere unknown, but the abundance of individuals and species, which the island displays. There are to be found in Western New York about 170 species of trees and shrubs. Goat Island and the immediate vicinity of the river near the Falls can show of these no less than 140. There are represented on the island four maples, three species of thorn, two species of ash, and six species, distributed in five genera, of the cone-bearing family. The one species of basswood belonging to the vicinity is also there.

Mr. Day has a catalogue of plants in his report to the Reservation Commissioners, giving 909 species of plants to be found on the Reservation, of which 758 are native and 151 foreign. Wrote Margaret Fuller:

> The beautiful wood on Goat Island is full of flowers, many of the fairest love to do homage there. The wake robin and the May apple are in bloom, the former white, pink, green, purple, copying the rainbow of the Falls, and fit it for its presiding Deity when He walks the land, for they are of imperial size and shaped like stones for a diadem. Of the May apple I did not raise one green tent without finding a flower beneath.

Explaining the climatic advantages of the island Mr. Olmsted remarks:

> First, the masses of ice which every winter are piled to a great height below the Falls and the great rushing body of ice cold water coming from the northern lakes in the spring prevent at Niagara the hardship under which trees elsewhere often suffer through sudden checks to premature growth. And second, when droughts elsewhere occur, as they do every few years, of such severity that trees in full foliage droop and dwindle and even sometimes cast their leaves, the atmosphere at Niagara is more or less moistened by the constantly evaporating spray of the Falls, and in certain situations bathed by drifting clouds of spray.

It is a very irony of fate that this marvellous gem among the islands of earth could not bear a name befitting its place in the admiration and esteem of a world; it was, I believe, Judge Porter himself that named this beautiful spot "Iris Island," a name altogether fitting in both wealth of suggestion and beauty of association. One John Steadman, remembered as a contractor to widen the old portage path from Lewiston to Fort Schlosser, and former owner of the island under a

Buffalo and the Upper Niagara

"Seneca patent," planted some turnips here, we are told, in the year 1770 A.D., and in the following autumn placed here "a number of animals, among them a male goat," to get them out of the reach of the bears and wolves that infested the neighbouring shore near his home two miles up the river. In the spring of 1771 it was found that the severe winter had been too much for all but the "male goat," who, unfortunately, survived the ordeal, and by so doing bids fair to hand his name down through the centuries attached to the most beautiful island in the world. In the Treaty of Ghent, which set our boundary line here, the island bears the name "Iris." Mr. Porter has stated that even if it were desirable to change the name now "it would seem impossible now to do so." [1] Is this the truth? Could not the commissioners who have the matters in hand do a great deal toward inaugurating a change to the old official name that would in the long run prove effective? The present writer is most positive that this could be done and that it is a thing that ought certainly to be attempted immediately. It would be surprising how much the change would be favoured if once attempted, if guide books and maps followed the new nomenclature. The only possible satisfaction that one can have in the present name is in the horrifying reflection that if the male goat had died the island would probably have been "Turnip Island" if not "Colic Island."

Below the islands resound the Falls. Perhaps there

---

[1] *Goat Island*, p. 28. This most interesting pamphlet by Mr. Porter will be found quite a complete guide to a study of Niagara Falls, and is most worthy the perusal of those who care to examine more than the mere surface of things at Niagara.

is no better method of describing this almost indescribable wonder than by taking the familiar walk about them beginning at the common point of commencement, Prospect Point.

It is important on visiting the Falls for the first time to obtain as good a view as possible, as the first view comes but once. Many are somewhat disappointed with it, since from a distance the Falls give the idea of a long low wall of water, their great height being offset by their great breadth of almost a mile. The best view is from the top of the bank on the Canadian side; but as most of the tourists reach the American side first it is from this standpoint that most visitors gain their first impression. No better vantage ground can be gained on the American side than Prospect Point. Here, placed at the northern end of the American cataract, is the best position to make a study of the geography of Niagara. Stretching from your feet along the line of sight extends the American Fall to a distance of 1060 feet. At the other side of the American Fall is the Goat Island group. This group stretches along the cliff for a distance of 1300 feet more. Beyond this extends the line of the Horseshoe Fall for a further distance of 3010 feet, making in all a total of slightly over a mile. To the right, down the river is the gorge which Niagara has been chiseling and scouring for unnumbered centuries; this chasm extends almost due north for a distance of seven miles to Lewiston. Down the gorge the gaze is uninterrupted for a distance of nearly two miles, almost to the Whirlpool where the river turns abruptly to the left on entering this whirling maelstrom, issuing again almost at right angles to continue its mad plunges.

To the left, up the river lie the American Rapids, where the water rushes on in its madness to hurl its volume over the 160 feet of precipice and into the awful chasm below. Just below Prospect Point and somewhat higher in altitude than it, is what has been called Hennepin's View, so named after Father Hennepin, who gave the first written description of the Niagara. Here one sees not only the Horseshoe Fall in the foreground, as at Prospect Point, but the American Fall also, which lies several feet lower than our point of vantage.

Proceeding up the river the next point of interest reached is the steel bridge to Goat Island. The first bridge to this island was constructed by Judge Porter in 1817 about forty rods above the site of the present one. In the spring of the next year this bridge was swept away by the large cakes of ice coming down the river. It was rebuilt at its present site, its projector judging that the added descent of the rapids would so break up the ice as to eliminate any danger to the structure; and the results proved his theory true. This structure stood until 1855 when its place was taken by a steel arch bridge, which served the public until 1900. In that year the present structure authorised by the State of New York took its place.

Looking upon this structure, one wonders how the foundations could possibly have been laid in such an irresistible current of water. First, two of the largest trees to be found in the vicinity were cut down and hewn flat on two sides. A level platform was erected on the shore at the water's edge and on this the hewn logs were placed about eight feet apart, supported on rollers with their shore ends heavily weighted with stone. These logs were then run as far out over the river as possible, and a man walked out on each one armed with an iron pointed staff. On finding a crevice in the rock forming the bottom of the river, these staffs were driven firmly into the rock and then lashed to the ends of the timbers, thus forming a stay to them and furnishing the means necessary for beginning the construction of the crib. The timbers were planked, and the same process was pursued until the island was reached.

While the second bridge was under construction, the famous Indian chieftain and orator, Red Jacket, visited the Falls. The old veteran is said to have sat for a long time watching the process of bridging the angry waters, the transforming power of the white man at work, conquering a force which to him appeared more than able to baffle all the ingenuity of man. On being asked by a bystander what he thought of the work of construction he seemed mortified that the white man's hand should so desecrate these sacred waters; folding his blanket slowly about him, with his eyes fixed upon the works, he is said to have given forth the stereotyped Indian grunt, adding " D——n Yankee!"

Upon this bridge we find one of the best positions, as we have noted, from which to view the Rapids. From the point of their beginning, about a mile above the Falls to the crest of the cliff the descent is over fifty feet. Here, standing upon what seems in comparison but a frail structure, one can realise the grandeur of the Rapids. In the terrible race they seem to be trying to tear away the piers of the bridge which are fretting their current.

Chapter II

From the Falls to Lake Ontario

THESE American rivers of ours have their messages, historical, economic, and social, to both reader and loiterer. And, too, are not these streams so very much alive that through the years their personalities remain practically unchanged, while generations of loiterers come and go on forever? Are not the eccentricities of these great living forces forever recurrent, however whimsical they may seem, to us as we stop for our brief instant at the shore?

The word Niagara stands to-day representing power; the most common metaphor used, perhaps, to represent perpetual irresistible force is found in the name Niagara. Now it is admitted that nothing is more interesting than to observe the contradictions noticeable in most strong personalities. View the Niagara from this personal standpoint. I think its most attractive features may be summed up in a catalogue of its eccentric contradictions. It is famous as a waterfall, yet its greatest beauty is to be found in its smallest rapids. Its thundering fall outrivals all other sounds of Nature, yet you can hear a sparrow sing when the spray of the torrent is drenching you; the "noise" of Niagara is often spoken of as the greatest sound ever heard, yet most of the cataract's music has never been heard because it is pitched too low for human ears. Niagara's Whirlpool is a placid, mirrored lake compared to the rapids above and below it and brings from the lips of the majority of sightseers, looking only at the surface of things, words of disappointment. The great message and influence of the foaming cataract and rapids and terrible pool, to all awake to the finer meanings, as has been so beautifully brought out by Mr. Howells, should be one of singular repose. The louder the music the more certain the strange influence of this message of quiet and calm.

Take, for instance, what is so commonly called the roar of Niagara, but which ought to be known as the music of Niagara, first at the Rapids and then the Falls.

There is sweet music in Niagara's lesser rapids. Mrs. Schuyler Van Rensselaer observes, most felicitously:

It is a great and mighty noise, but it is not, as Hennepin thought, an "outrageous noise." It is not a roar. It does not drown the voice or stun the ear. Even at the actual foot of the falls it is not oppressive. It is much less rough than the sound of heavy surf—steadier, more homogeneous, less metallic, very deep and strong, yet mellow and soft; soft, I mean, in its quality. As to the noise of the rapids, there is none more musical. It is neither rumbling nor sharp. It is clear, plangent, silvery. It is so like the voice of a steep brook—much magnified, but not made coarser or more harsh—that, after we have known it, each liquid call from a forest hillside will seem, like the odour of grapevines, a greeting from Niagara. It is an inspiriting, an exhilarating sound, like freshness, coolness, vitality itself made audible. And yet it is a lulling sound. When we have looked out upon the American rapids for many days, it is hard to remember contented life amid motionless surroundings; and so, when we have slept beside them for many nights, it is hard to think of happy sleep in an empty silence.

A most original and interesting study of the music

Goat Island Bridge and Rapids.

Horseshoe Falls from Below.

of the great Falls was made some years ago in a more or less technical way by Eugene Thayer.[1] It had been this gentleman's theory that Niagara had never been heard as it should be heard, and his mission at the cataract was accomplished when there met his ears, not the "roar," but, rather, a perfectly constructed musical tone, clear, definite, and unapproachable in its majestic proportions; in fact Mr. Thayer affirms that the trained ear at Niagara should hear "a complete series of tones, all uniting in one grand and noble unison, as in the organ, and all as easily recognisable as the notes of any great chord in music." He had heard it rumoured that persons had been known to secure a pitch of the tone of Niagara; he essayed to secure not only the pitch of the chief or ground tone, but that of all accessory or upper tones otherwise known as harmonic or overtones, together with the beat or accent of the Falls and its rhythmical vibrations.

All the tones above the ground tone have been named overtones or harmonics; the tones below are called the subharmonics, or undertones. It will be noticed that they form the complete natural harmony of the ground tone. What is the real pitch of this chord? According to our regular musical notation, the fourth note given represents the normal pitch of diapason; the reason being that the eight-foot tone is the only one that gives the notes as written. According to nature, I must claim the first, or lowest note, as the real or ground tone. In this latter way I shall represent the true tone or pitch of Niagara.

How should I prove all this? My first step was to visit the beautiful Iris Island, otherwise known as Goat Island. Donning a suit of oilcloth and other disagreeable loose stuff, I followed the guide into the Cave of the Winds. Of course, the sensation at first was so novel and overpowering that the question of pitch

[1] *Scribner's Monthly*, vol. xxi., pp. 583–6.

was lost in one of personal safety. Remaining here a few minutes, I emerged to collect my dispersed thoughts. After regaining myself, I returned at once to the point of beginning, and went slowly in again (alone), testing my first question of pitch all the way; that is, during the approach, while under the fall, while emerging, and while standing some distance below the face of the fall, not only did I ascertain this (I may say in spite of myself, for I could hear but one pitch), but I heard and sang clearly the pitch of all the harmonic or accessory tones, only of course several octaves higher than their actual pitch. Seven times have I been under these singing waters (always alone except the first time), and the impression has invariably been the same, so far as determining the tone and its components. I may be allowed to withhold the result until I speak of my experience at the Horseshoe Fall, and the American Fall proper—it being scarcely necessary to say that the Cave of the Winds is under the smaller cascade, known as the Central Fall.

My next step was to stand on Luna Island, above the Central Fall, and on the west side of the American Fall proper. I went to the extreme eastern side of the island, in order to lose as far as possible the sound of the Central Fall, and get the full force of the larger Fall. Here were the same great ground tone and the same harmonics, differing only somewhat in pitch.

I then went over to the Horseshoe Fall and sat among the Rapids. There it was again, only slightly higher in pitch than on the American side. Not then knowing the fact, I ventured to assert that the Horseshoe Fall was less in height, by several feet, than the American Fall; the actual difference is variously given at from six to twelve feet. Next I went to the Three Sister Islands, and here was the same old story. The higher harmonics were mostly inaudible from the noise of the Rapids, but the same two low notes were ringing out clear and unmistakable. In fact, wherever I was I could not hear anything else! There was no roar at all, but the same grand diapason— the noblest and completest one on earth! I use the word completest advisedly, for nothing else on earth, not even the ocean, reaches anywhere near the actual depth of pitch, or makes audible to the human ear such a complete and perfect harmonic structure.

Remembering always that the actual pitch is four octaves lower, here are the notes which form this matchless diapason:

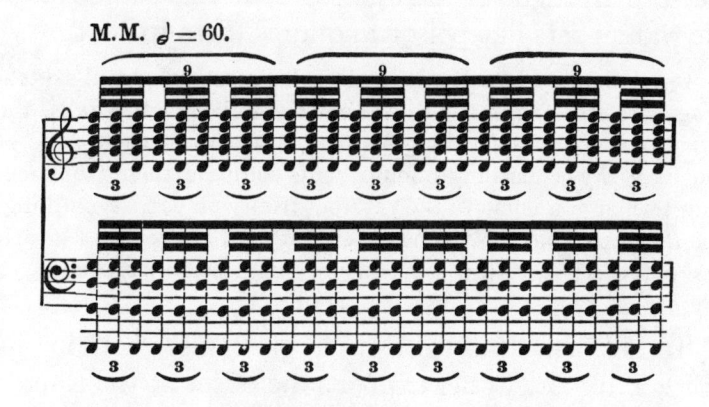

M.M. ♩ = 60.

Mrs. Van Rensselaer tells us there is yet another music at Niagara that must be listened for only on quiet nights. It is like the music of an orchestra so very far away that its notes are attenuated to an incredible delicacy and are intermittently perceived, as though wafted to us on variable zephyrs.

It is the most subtle, the most mysterious music in the world. What is its origin? Such fairy-like sounds are not to be explained. Their appeal is to the imagination only. They are so faint, so far away, that they almost escape the ear, as the lunar bow and the fluted tints of the American Fall almost escape the eye. And yet we need not fear to lose them, for they are as real as the deep bass of the cataracts.

Whether it be the resounding waterfall producing this wondrous harmony of the floods, or the most charming choral of the Rapids, the music of Niagara on the mind properly adjusted and attuned must create a most profound impression of repose. The exception to this rule, most terrible to contemplate, is certainly to be found in the cases of the unfortunates whose minds are so distraught or unbalanced that this same call of the waters acts like poison and lures them to death.

<blockquote>
I still think [wrote Mr. Howells in his most delightful sketch, *Niagara, First and Last*] that, above and below the Falls, the Rapids are the most striking features of the spectacle. At least you may say something about them, compare them to something; when you come to the cataract itself you can say nothing; it is incomparable. My sense of it first, and my sense of it last, was not a sense of the stupendous, but a sense of beauty, of serenity, of repose.
</blockquote>

In her beautiful description, given elsewhere in our story, Margaret Fuller explains the effect of the Rapids by moonlight on the heart of one who, during the day, had passed through the familiar throb of disappointment in the great spectacle at Niagara.

Now I take it one must see in Niagara this element of repose or find in it something less than was hoped for. To one who expects an ocean pouring from the moon, a rush of wind and foam like that to be met with only in the Cave of the Winds, there is bound to come that common feeling that the fact is not equal to the picture imagination had previously created. Take the Whirlpool; seen from the heights above, it

<blockquote>
has that effect of sculpturesque repose [writes Mr. Howells], which I have always found the finest thing in the Cataract itself. From the top the circling lines of the Whirlpool seemed graven in a level of chalcedony. . . . I have no impression to impart except this sense of its worthy unity with the Cataract in what I may call its highest æsthetic quality, its repose.[1]
</blockquote>

All this is most impressively true of the central won-

---

[1] *The Niagara Book*, p. 15.

"The Shoreless Sea."
From a photograph by Notman, Montreal.

Rustic Bridge, Willow Island.

From the Falls to Lake Ontario

der of the entire spectacle, the Falls themselves. That mighty flood of water, reborn as it dies, forms a marvellous spectacle. Writes Mrs. Schuyler Van Rensselaer:

> Very soon we realise that Niagara's true effect is an effect of permanence. Many as are its variations, it never alters. It varies because light and atmosphere alter. Tremendous movement thus pauseless and unmodified gives, of course, a deeper impression of durability than the most imposing solids. . . . As soon as this fact is felt, the Falls seem to have been created as a voucher for the permanence of all the world.[1]

But how conform this repose and spirit of permanency with the echoing tones of that never-ending, never-satisfied dominant chord? How reconcile the repose of those dropping billows with the tantalising unrest of that for ever incomplete, unfinished recessional that has been playing down this gorge since, perhaps, darkness brooded over the deep—that seems to await its fulfilment in the thunders of Sinai at that Last Day?

And what could be more human than this in any river—a seeming calm with over it all a never-ending cry of unrest, of wonder, of unsatisfied longing never to find repose until in that far resting-place of which Augustine thought when he wrote:

> Our hearts are restless until they rest in Thee.

Across the American Rapids lies the Goat Island group which divides the waters into the two falls. Goat Island is about half a mile long and half as wide at its broadest part, but slopes to a point at its eastern extremity. Its area is about seventy acres. Besides this there are a number of

[1] *The Century Magazine*, vol. xxxvi., p. 197.

smaller islands and rocks varying in diameter from four hundred feet to ten feet. Of these smaller islands five are connected with Goat Island by bridges, as are also the Terrapin Rocks.

At the end of the first bridge is situated Green Island, named after the first president of the Board of Commissioners of the New York Reservation. The former name was Bath Island because of the "old swimming hole"—the only place where one could dip in the fierce current of Niagara without danger. Just a short distance above Green Island are two small patches of land called Ship Island and Bird Island from supposed resemblances to these objects in general contour, the tall leafless trees in winter supposed to be suggestive of masts. These islands were formerly both connected with Goat Island by bridges; one, known as "Lover's Bridge," from its romantic name was so greatly patronised that both bridges were destroyed by the owners on account of danger.

On Green Island formerly stood the immense Porter paper-mill, which not only contributed its own ugliness to the beautiful prospect but also ran out into the current long gathering dams for the purpose of collecting water. All this was removed when the State of New York assumed control.

Passing from the bridge and ascending the steps which lead to the top of the bank, the shelter house is reached. All around and, in fact, covering nearly all the island, is the primeval forest in its ancient splendour—fit companion of the Falls, which defy the puny power of man.

Occasional glimpses of the river may be had through the dense foliage as one proceeds to Stedman Bluff, where one of the grandest panoramas to be seen anywhere on earth bursts upon the view. Here one appreciates the beauty of the American Fall better than at Prospect Point. Turning towards the American shore stone steps lead down to the water's edge, and thence a small bridge spans the stream separating Goat Island and Luna Island, so called from the fact that it has been considered the best place from which to view the lunar bow. The small stream dividing these islands in its plunge over the precipice forms the "Cave of the Winds." Half-way across Luna Island is to be seen a large rock on whose face have been carved by an unknown hand the following lines:

> All is change.
> Eternal progress.
> No Death!

The author of the sentiment is unknown, but no one has more truly voiced the spirit of the great cataract. From the edge of the cliff on Luna Island is to be obtained the finest view down the gorge. Along the front of the American Fall are to be seen the immense masses of wave-washed rocks which have fallen from the cliff above. From rock to rock stretch frail wooden bridges, the more important of which lead to the cave.

Luna Island is the last point which one can reach from Goat Island toward the American shore. Proceeding toward the Canadian Fall, one reaches at a short distance the Biddle Stairs. Here a break in the foliage reveals a grand view down the gorge with the Canadian Fall directly in front. A stairway leads to a wooden building down which runs a spiral stairway to the rocks below. This stairway received its name from

Nicholas Biddle, of old National Bank fame, who proposed this means of reaching the rocks below and offered a contribution for its construction. The offer was rejected, but his name was given to the structure. A trip to the rocks below this point is well worth while, difficult though it be; the descent of the spiral stairway is eighty feet. Turning to the right one comes out upon a ledge of rock with the roaring waters below and the line of the cliff above, along the top of which objects appear at only half their real size. Passing around a short curve there bursts upon one's view the fall which forms the Cave of the Winds—a most beautiful sheet of water. The passage of the cave can hardly be described by the pen. Here one is assailed on all sides by fierce storms and clouds of angry spray. The cave seems at first dark and repelling, for in this maddening whirl of wind and water one is at first almost blinded; but as soon as the eye becomes accustomed to the darkness, it can follow the graceful curve of the water to where it leaves the cliff above. The dark, forbidding, terraced rocks are seen dripping with water. The passage of the cave is too exciting to be essayed by persons with weak hearts, but the return across the rocks in front of it on a bright day is genuinely inspiring. Here the symbol of promise is brought down within one's very reach; above, around, on all sides are to be seen colours rivalling the conception of any artist—whole circles of bows, quarter circles, half circles, here within one's very grasp. The far fabled pot of gold is here a boiling, seething mass of running, shimmering silver. If possible, more glorious than all else, up above, along the sky-line, there appears the shining crest of the American Fall, glim-

The Cave of the Winds.

The American Fall.
From a photograph by Notman, Montreal.

From the Falls to Lake Ontario

mering in the sunlight like the silvery range of some snow-covered mountains.

In size the cave is about one hundred feet wide, a hundred feet deep, and about one hundred and sixty feet high. At one point in the cave, on a bright day, by standing in the very edge of the spray, one becomes the centre of a complete circle of rainbows, an experience probably unequalled elsewhere.

About half-way between the stairway and the cave is the point from which, in 1829, Sam Patch made his famous leap, elsewhere described.

On the side of the Horseshoe Fall is to be found a fine position from which to view the mighty force of the greater mass of waters. For some distance along the front of the fall immense masses of rock have accumulated. The trip over these rocks is fraught with danger and is taken by very few. For those who care to take the risk, the sight is well worth the effort. Just above at the crest are Terrapin Rocks, where formerly stood Terrapin Tower. Professor Tyndall went far out beyond the line of Terrapin Rocks to a point which has been reached by very few of the millions of visitors to this shrine. Passing along the cliff toward Canada, Porter's Bluff is soon reached, which furnishes one of the grandest views of the Horseshoe Fall. Fifty years ago, from this point one could see the whole line of the graceful curve of the Horseshoe; since that time the rapid erosion in the middle of the river (where the volume is greatest) has destroyed almost all trace of what the name suggests. The sides meet now at a very acute angle, the old contour having been entirely destroyed.

One of the most interesting experiments conducted

under these great masses of falling water was essayed by the well-known English traveller Captain Basil Hall in 1827. It seems that Babbage and Herschel had said that there was reason to expect a change of elastic pressure in the air near a waterfall. Bethinking himself of the opportunity of testing this theory at Niagara during his American tour, Captain Hall secured a mountain barometer of most delicate workmanship for this specific purpose. In a letter to Professor Silliman the experimenter described his experience as follows, the question being of interest to every one who has attempted to breathe when passing behind any portion of this wall of falling water:

I think you told me that you did not enter this singular cave on your late journey, which I regret very much, because I have no hope of being able to describe it to you. In the whole course of my life, I never encountered anything so formidable in appearance; and yet, I am half ashamed to say so, I saw it performed by many other people without emotion, and it is daily accomplished by ladies, who think they have done nothing remarkable.

You are perhaps aware that it is a standing topic of controversy every summer by the company at the great hotels near the Falls, whether the air within the sheet of water is condensed or rarefied. I have therefore a popular motive as well as a scientific one, in conducting this investigation, and the result, I hope, will prove satisfactory to the numerous persons who annually visit Niagara.

As a first step I placed the barometer at a distance of about 150 feet from the extreme western end of the Falls, on a flat rock as nearly as possible on a level with the top of the "talus" or bank of shingle lying at the base of the overhanging cliff, from which the cataract descends. This station was about 30 perpendicular feet above the pool basin into which the water falls.

The mercury here stood at 29.68 inches. I then moved the

instrument to another rock within 10 or 12 feet of the edge of the fall, where it was placed, by means of a levelling instrument, exactly at the same height as in the first instance.

It still stood at 29.68 and the only difference I could observe was a slight continuous vibration of about two or three hundredths of an inch at intervals of a few seconds.

So far, all was plain sailing; for, though I was soundly ducked by this time, there was no particular difficulty in making these observations. But within the sheet of water, there is a violent wind, caused by the air carried down by the falling water, and this makes the case very different. Every stream of falling water, as you know, produces more or less a blast of this nature; but I had no conception that so great an effect could have been produced by this cause.

I am really at a loss how to measure it, but I have no hesitation in saying that it exceeds the most furious squall or gust of wind I have ever met with in any part of the world. The direction of the blast is generally slanting upwards, from the surface of the pool, and is chiefly directed against the face of the cliff, which being of a friable, shaly character, is gradually eaten away so that the top of the precipice now overhangs the base 35 or 40 feet and in a short time I should think the upper strata will prove too weak for the enormous load of water, which they bear, when the whole cliff will tumble down.

These vehement blasts are accompanied by floods of water, much more compact than the heaviest thunder shower, and as the light is not very great the situation of the experimenter with a delicate barometer in his hand is one of some difficulty.

By the assistance of the guide, however, who proved a steady and useful assistant, I managed to set the instrument up within a couple of feet of the "termination rock" as it is called, which is at the distance of 153 feet from the side of the waterfall measured horizontally along the top of the bank of shingle. This measurement, it is right to mention, was made a few days afterward by Mr. Edward Deas-Thompson of London, the guide, and myself with a graduated tape.

While the guide held the instrument firmly down, which required nearly all his force, I contrived to adjust it, so that the spirit level on the top indicated that the tube was in the perpendicular position. It would have been utterly useless to have attempted any observation without this contrivance. I then secured all tight, unscrewed the bag, and allowed the mercury to subside; but it was many minutes before I could obtain even a tolerable reading, for the water flowed over my brows like a thick veil, threatening to wash the whole affair, philosophers and all, into the basin below. I managed, however, after some minutes' delay to make a shelf or spout with my hand, which served to carry the water clear of that part of the instrument which I wished to look at and also to leave my eyes comparatively free. I now satisfied myself by repeated trials that the surface of the mercurial column did not rise higher than 29.72. It was sometimes at 29.70 and may have vibrated two or three hundredths of an inch. This station was about 10 or 12 feet lower than the external ones and therefore I should have expected a slight rise in the mercury; but I do not pretend to have read off the scale to any great nicety, though I feel quite confident of having succeeded in ascertaining that there was no sensible difference between the elasticity of the air at the station on the outside of the Falls and that, 153 feet within them.

I now put the instrument up and having walked back towards the mouth of this wonderful cave about 30 feet, tried the experiment again. The mercury stood now at 29.68, or at 29.70 as near as I could observe it. On coming again into the open air I took the barometer to one of the first stations, but was much disappointed though I cannot say surprised to observe it full of air and water and consequently for the time quite destroyed.

My only surprise, indeed, was that under such circumstances the air and water were not sooner forced in. But I have no doubt that the two experiments on the outside as well as the two within the sheet of water were made by the instrument when it was in a correct state: though I do not deny that it would have been more satisfactory to have verified this by repeating the observations at the first station.

On mentioning these results to the contending parties in the controversy, both asked me the same question, "How then do you account for the difficulty in breathing which all persons experience who go behind the sheet of water?" To which I replied: "That if any one were exposed to the spouts of half a

From the Falls to Lake Ontario

dozen fire engines playing full in his face at the distance of a few yards, his respiration could not be quite free, and for my part I conceived that this rough discipline would be equally comfortable in other respects and not more embarrassing to the lungs than the action of the blast and falling water behind this amazing cataract."

It is almost impossible to conceive of the immense mass of water tumbling over this precipice. It has been estimated in tons, cubic feet, and horse-power, but the figures are so large as to stagger the human mind. Out there at the apex of the angle, the water, over twenty feet deep, is drawn from almost half a continent, forming a picture to make one's nerves thrill with awe and delight, where the international boundary line swings back and forth as the apex of the angle formed sways from side to side.

Just off the shore of the island are seen Terrapin Rocks. Why this name was applied is uncertain. These rocks are scattered in the flood to the very brink of the fall and in the titanic struggle with the rush of waters seem hardly able to maintain their position. Upon these rocks on the very brink of the Falls in 1833 was erected, by Judge Porter, Terrapin Tower, for many years one of the centres visited by every person journeying to the Falls. From its summit could be seen the wild rapids rushing on toward the precipice; below shimmering green of the fall. Down, far down, in the depths beneath was the boiling, seething caldron, from which arose beautiful columns of spray. From this position, forty-five feet above the surface of the water, probably a more comprehensive view of the many features of Niagara could be obtained than from any other point. Forty years later it was blown up, not because it was unsafe, as alleged, but that it might not prove a rival attraction to Prospect Point. Recently suggestions have been made looking toward the restoration of this ancient landmark, but no definite action has been taken.

Over a half-century ago, almost opposite this tower on the Canadian side, was to be seen the immense Table Rock hanging far out over the current below. On the 25th of June, 1850, this large mass of rock fell. Fortunately the fall occurred at noon with no loss of life; it was one of the greatest falls of rock known to have taken place at the cataract, for the dimensions of the rock were two hundred feet long, sixty feet wide, and a hundred feet deep. Like the roar of muffled thunder the crash was heard for miles around.

It was from the Terrapin Rocks to the Canadian side that Blondin wished to stretch his rope, elsewhere described, and it was over the very centre of Niagara's warring powers he desired to perform his daring feat, looking down upon that shimmering guarded secret of the "Heart of Niagara." The Porters, who owned Goat Island, however, refused to become parties to what they considered an improper exposure of life and Blondin stretched his cable farther down the river, near the site of the crescent steel arch bridge.

Standing upon these rocks and looking out over that hurrying mass of waters, it seems almost impossible to imagine any power being able to stop them; but on the 29th of March, 1848, the impossible happened, the Niagara ran dry. From the American shore across the rapids to Goat Island one could walk dry-shod. From Goat Island and the Canadian shore the waters were contracted to a small stream flowing

Remains of Stone Piers of the "First Railway in America"—
the British Tramway up Lewiston Heights, 1763.

Amid the Goat Island Group.
From a photograph by Notman, Montreal.

over the centre of what was then the Horseshoe; only a few tiny rivulets remained falling over the precipice at other points. The cause of this unnatural phenomenon was wind and ice. Lake Erie was full of floating ice. The day previous the winds had blown this ice out into the lake. In the evening the wind suddenly changed and blew a sharp gale from exactly the opposite direction, driving the mass of ice into the river and gorging it there, thus cutting off almost the whole water supply, and in the morning people awoke to find that the Niagara had departed. The American Fall was no more, the Horseshoe was hardly a ghost of its former self. Gone were the rapids, the fighting, struggling waters. Niagara's majestic roar was reduced to a moan. All day people walked on the rock bed of the river, although fearful lest the dam formed at its head should give way at any moment. By night, the warmth of the sun and the waters of the lake had begun to make inroads on the barrier and by the morning of the next day Niagara had returned in all its grandeur.

However cold Niagara's winter may be, the moan of falling water here can always be heard, though at times the volume is very small. The winter scenes here often take rank in point of wonder and beauty with the cataract itself. When the river is frozen over below the Falls the phenomenon is called an "Ice Bridge," the blowing spray sometimes building a gigantic sparkling mound of wonderful beauty. The island trees above the Falls, covered by the same spray, assume curiously beautiful forms which, as they glitter in the sun, turn an already wonder-land into a strange fairyland of incomparable whiteness and glory.

A short distance up the river along the shore a position just opposite the apex of the Falls is reached. Here, along the shore of the island, the waters are comparatively shallow, but toward the Canadian shore races the current which carries fully three fourths of Niagara's volume. Out in the very midst of the current is a small speck of land, all that is now left of what was once Gull Island, so named from its having been a favourite resting place for these birds, which can hardly find a footing now on its contracted shores. From what can be learned of the past history of this island, it must have occupied about two acres three quarters of a century ago. Its gradual disappearance shows to what degree the mighty forces of Niagara are removing all obstacles placed in their path. Goat Island is gradually suffering the same fate. At points the shore line has encroached upon the island to a distance of twenty feet in a half-century. At this point the carriage road used to run out beyond the present edge of the bluff.

Passing on along the shore of the island, Niagara's scenery is present everywhere. At quite a distance up stream the Three Sister Islands are reached. These islands were named from the three daughters of General P. Whitney, they being the first women to visit them, probably in winter when the waters were low.

To the first Sister Island leads a massive stone bridge. From this bridge is to be obtained a fine view of the Hermit's Cascade beneath. This little fall receives its name from having been the favourite bathing place of the Hermit of Niagara, a strange half-witted young Englishman by the name of Francis Abbott

From the Falls to Lake Ontario 41

who lived in solitude here for two years preceding his death by drowning in 1831, during his sojourn at the Falls.

These three islands are replete with small bits of scenery and overflowing with beauty. In them are to be found the smaller attractions of Niagara; not so much of the stern majesty and awful grandeur, but smaller and more comprehensible features come before the view following each other in rapid succession. On the second Sister Island is one point which should be visited by every one. Just before reaching the bridge to third Sister Island, by turning to the right and proceeding along a somewhat difficult path for a short distance one comes to a point at the water's edge and finds lying right below him the boiling waters with their white, feathery spray; here also is the small cataract between the second and third islands fed by the most rapid although small stream of Niagara. From this point is to be obtained one of the most varied of scenic effects of any point at the Falls. The scenery from the third Sister must be seen to be appreciated. From its upper end one looks directly at the low cliff which forms the first descent of the Rapids. Here the waters start from the peaceful stream above on their maddening race for the Falls. Out along the line of the cliff the waters deepen and increase in rapidity toward the Canadian shore. Just below this ledge, probably three hundred feet from the head of the island, the current is directed against some obstruction which causes it to spout up into the air, causing what is called the Spouting Rock.

Many have been the changes wrought by the waters themselves since white men knew the Falls; but a thousand years hence the visitor to Niagara will behold the main fall not from Terrapin Rocks or Porter's Bluff, but from this third Sister Island. The Rapids then shall have almost entirely disappeared, but their beauty will be compensated for by the additional grandeur of the fall itself. The gorge will have widened and the fall itself shall have added fifty feet to its height, making it two hundred feet high. Third Sister Island should be gone over thoroughly, for it offers some of the finest views, especially of colouring, above the Falls, and many of them.

Niagara owes its sublime array of colour to the purity of its water. Nothing finer has been written on this subject than the words of the artist Mrs. Van Rensselaer, whom we quote:

> To this purity Niagara owes its exquisite variety of colour. To find the blues we must look, of course, above Goat Island, where the sky is reflected in smooth if quickly flowing currents. But every other tint and tone that water can take is visible in or near the Falls themselves. In the quieter parts of the gorge we find a very dark, strong green, while in its rapids all shades of green and grey and white are blended. The shallower rapids above the Falls are less strongly coloured, a beautiful light green predominating between the pale-grey swirls and the snowy crests of foam—semi-opaque, like the stone called aquamarine, because infused with countless air-bubbles, yet deliciously fresh and bright. The tense, smooth slant of water at the margin of the American fall is not deep enough to be green. In the sunshine it is a clear amber, and when shadowed, a brown that is darker, yet just as pure. But wherever the Canadian fall is visible its green crest is conspicuous. Far down-stream, nearly two miles away, where the railroad-bridge crosses the gorge, it shows like a little emerald strung on a narrow band of pearl. Its colour is not quite like that of an emerald, although the term must be used because no other is more accurate. It is a

From the Falls to Lake Ontario 43

purer colour, and cooler, with less of yellow in it—more pure, more cool, and at the same time more brilliant than any colour that sea-water takes even in a breaking wave, or that man has produced in any substance whatsoever. At this place, we are told, the current must be twenty feet deep; and its colour is so intense and so clear because, while the light is reflected from its curving surface, it also filters through so great a mass of absolutely limpid water. It always quivers, this bright-green stretch, yet somehow it always seems as solid as stone, smoothly polished for the most part, but, when a low sun strikes across it, a little roughened, fretted. That this is water and that the thinnest smoke above it is water also, who can believe? In other places at Niagara we ask the same question again.

From a distance the American fall looks quite straight. When we stand beside it we see that its line curves inward and outward, throwing the falling sheet into bastion-like sweeps. As we gaze down upon these, every change in the angle of vision and in the strength and direction of the light gives a new effect. The one thing that we never seem to see, below the smooth brink, is water. Very often the whole swift precipice shows as a myriad million inch-thick cubes of clearest glass or ice or solidified light, falling in an envelope of starry spangles. Again, it seems all diamond-like or pearl-like, or like a flood of flaked silver, shivered crystal, or faceted ingots of palest amber. It is never to be exhausted in its variations. It is never to be described. Only, one can always say, it is protean, it is most lovely, and it is not water.

Then, as we look across the precipice, it may be milky in places, or transparent, or translucent. But where its mass falls quickly it is all soft and white—softer then anything else in the world. It does not resemble a flood of fleece or of down, although it suggests such a flood. It is more like a crumbling avalanche, immense and gently blown, of smallest snowflakes; but, again, it is not quite like this. Now we see that, even apart from its main curves, no portion of the swiftly moving wall is flat. It is all delicately fissured and furrowed, by the broken edges of the rock over which it falls, into the suggestion of fluted buttresses, half-columns, pilasters. And the whiteness of these is not quite white. Nor is it consistently iridescent or opalescent. Very faintly, elusively, it is tinged with tremulous stripes and strands of pearly grey, of vaguest straw, shell-pink, lavender, and green—inconceivably ethereal blues, shy ghosts of earthly colours, abashed and deflowered, we feel, by definite naming with earthly names. They seem hardly to tinge the whiteness; rather, to float over it as a misty bloom. We are loath to turn our eyes from them, fearing they may never show again. Yet they are as real as the keen emerald of the Horseshoe.[1]

One should walk through the New York State Reservation, which extends for some distance above the commencement of the Rapids, to get a more complete view of the scenery above the Falls, the wooded shores of Goat Island, the swiftly moving waters, the broad river, the beginning of the Canadian Rapids, and the Canadian shore in the distance. On up the river at a distance are to be seen those forest-clad shores of Navy Island and Grand Island.

On the Canadian side of the river, after crossing the steel arch bridge just below the Falls, beautiful Victoria Park is first reached. From this position a new and entirely different view of the American Fall is obtained from almost directly in front. Turning and going up the river a fine view of the Horseshoe is obtained from a distance. Just opposite the American Fall is Inspiration Point, from which the best view of the Falls is to be obtained. From here one can watch the little *Maid of the Mist* as she makes her trips through the boiling waters below.

On up the river one wanders, past Goat Island, whose cliff is seen from directly in front. Just before reaching the edge of the Horseshoe the position of

[1] *The Century Magazine*, xxxvi., 198–201.

Horseshoe Falls from the Canadian Shore.
From a photograph by Notman, Montreal.

Looking up the Lower Niagara from Paradise Grove.
From a photograph by Wm Quinn, Niagara-on-the-Lake.

From the Falls to Lake Ontario

old Table Rock is seen. Little is left of this old and once famous point for observing Niagara's wonders. Several different falls of immense masses of rock, one of which has been mentioned, have reduced it to its present state. Here the Indian worshipped the Great Spirit of the Falls, gazing across at his supposed home on Goat Island; and here comes the white man to look upon the wonders of that mighty cataract with a feeling almost akin to that of his red brother. Here one could stand with the maddening waters rushing beneath, the Falls near at hand, its incessant roar assailing the ears while the spray was wafted all round. Little wonder that the red man worshipped, or that the white man looks on with feelings of awe, admiration, and wonder.

Passing on up the river and around the pumping station for the neighbouring village, one reaches the point at the water's edge from which the "Heart of Niagara" can best be seen, where millions of tons of water are continually pouring over the cliff and causing some of the most beautiful effects produced by the spray called the "Darting Lines of Spray" to be seen anywhere at the Falls. From this point one sees up the river over a mile of the Rapids with their madly hurrying waters rushing on as if to engulf everything below.

Along the water's edge, the journey should be pursued. A short distance farther up stream, a crib work has been built as a protection to the bank. Here is to be gained one of the finest views of the Canadian Rapids, one feature of which can not be seen to so great advantage from any other point. The "Shoreless Sea," as this view has been called, is a grand and inspiring sight. Gazing up the stream the Rapids are seen tumbling on toward one, with no land in sight. The clouds form the sky-line and it is as if the very chambers of heaven had been opened for a second deluge. It is, indeed, a "Shoreless Sea," tumbling on, a grand and awful sight.

Pursuing one's way on up the river, Dufferin Islands are reached. These are formed by a bend in the current. Here is a sylvan retreat, full of lovers' walks and beauties of nature. Here is the burning spring—escaping natural gas from a rift in the rock. Not far from this point, on up the river, was fought the battle of Chippewa. About a mile above these islands, at the mouth of Chippewa Creek, stood Fort Chippewa, built by the British in 1790 to protect this, their most important portage.

To reach the points of interest, just mentioned, on the Canadian side, as well as those down the river, it is best to make the trip from one scenic position to another by electric car. Returning to the Horseshoe one will doubtless have called to his mind that about a mile back to the left occurred the famed battle of Lundy's Lane on July 5, 1814. At the edge of the cliff on the right was the position of the "Old Indian Ladder," by means of which the Indians used to descend to the lower level for the purpose of fishing. This ladder was only a long cedar tree, which had been deprived of its limbs and had been placed almost perpendicularly against the cliff. On down the way a short distance, the road which leads down the face of the cliff, to the *Maid of the Mist's* landing, is reached. Just beyond this point, at the top of the inclined railway, is to be obtained the best view of the steel arch bridge. Just below the bridge, opposite, on the American shore,

From the Falls to Lake Ontario

a maddened torrent comes pouring from the base of the cliff as if anxious to add its fury to that of the waters round. It is the outlet of the tunnel which disposes of the tail water from the electric powerhouse over a mile above, mentioned in our chapter on power development at Niagara. The manufacturing plants of the Hydraulic Company, the first to use Niagara's waters to any great extent for power, are situated just opposite.

A short distance on down the stream, and after descending a slight incline, the point where Blondin stretched his rope across the gorge in 1859 is reached.

Next on the journey the cantilever bridge is reached. This bridge was constructed in 1882. Just below this is the steel arch bridge, both being railroad bridges. The second one was first constructed as a suspension bridge by John A. Roebling, being the first railroad bridge of its kind in the country. It has been several times replaced, the present structure having been erected in 1897. Just below the railroad bridges several persons have made the trip across the gorge on ropes.

Soon the Whirlpool is reached, and the madly rushing waters are seen as at no other place on the surface of the earth. Rounding the rapids, the car runs over a trestle work in crossing the old pre-glacial channel of the river referred to in our geologic chapter. Here one can look down on the waters almost directly beneath him, with the forests covering the sloping incline of the ancient bed of the river stretching up to the level above. Just as the car finishes the rounded curve of the Whirlpool, at the point of the cliff at the outlet, one catches the best view of both inlet and outlet at the same time, flowing directly at right angles to each other. The car continues on its course, now near, now farther back from the edge of the gorge. One catches occasional glimpses of the bridge far below, over which the electric line passes back to the American shore. For over three miles the car continues its course along the cliff before the next point of special interest presents itself in Brock's monument.

From this monument one of the finest panoramic views of the surrounding regions can be obtained. The monument stands on Queenston Heights, with the remains of old Fort Drummond just back of it.

All about is historic ground. On the surrounding plain and slopes was fought the battle of Queenston Heights. Every inch of ground has some story to tell of that struggle. The car soon begins to descend the incline which, ages ago, formed the shores of Lake Ontario. Below, at the end of the gorge, the river seems to forget its tumultuous rush, and spreading out pursues a placid and well-behaved course to the lower lake.

About half-way down the descent, the point where General Brock fell is reached, which point is marked by a massive stone monument set in place in 1861 by King Edward VII., then Prince of Wales. Just below to the right is seen an old, ruined stone house which was General Brock's shelter after being wounded, and in which was printed, in 1792, the first newspaper of Upper Canada. The bridge is soon reached, in the crossing of which, a fine view of the last mad rush of the waters is gained as they issue from the gorge into the placid stream leading to the lake below. On they come with the waves piled high in the centre, tearing along in a mad fury, until they seem to be pacified by

The Mouth of the Gorge.
From a photograph by Notman, Montreal.

The Whirlpool Rapids.

From the Falls to Lake Ontario

a power stronger even than their own; and they glide smoothly along to the end of their course in the lower lake.

On the American heights stood old Fort Gray, connected with the history of the War of 1812. On the American shore was the head of navigation, and up the cliff all the freight sent over the old portage was hoisted by hand and later by machinery. High up on the American cliffs, half-way between the Whirlpool and Lewiston, is the famous "Devil's Hole," an interesting cave known among the Indians, we are told, as the "Cave of the Evil Spirit." Here, it has been stated, geologists find some of the clearest evidences of the former existence of the presence of the Falls in that far day when the migration had extended thus far up the river from the escarpment at Lewiston.

Much has been said about the rapids of the river below the Falls—the lesser Rapids of Niagara. What of this seething, spouting, tumbling mass that races along below these towering cliffs, maddening, ungovernable, almost horrifying to gaze upon? It is very singular how little is said about this torrent. They illustrate very significantly the fact that mere power has little of charm for the mind of man; it interests, but often it does not please or delight. In our chapter on the foolhardy persons to whom these bounding billows have been a challenge, and who have attempted to navigate or pass through them, are descriptions of their savage fury and wonderful eccentricities. The most interesting fact respecting these great rapids is the unbelievable depth of the channel through which they race, since it sometimes approximates, according to the best sources of information, the height of the towering cliffs that compose the canyon. By government survey we know that the depth of the river between the Falls and the cantilever bridge is two hundred feet. The Whirlpool is estimated as four hundred feet deep, and the rapids above the Whirlpool as forty feet deep; the rapids below the Whirlpool are thought to be about sixty.

The romantic situation of the two ancient towns, Lewiston and Queenston, at the foot of the two escarpments, on opposite sides of the river, is only equalled by the absorbing story of their part in history when they were thriving, bustling frontier outposts. The beauty of the locations of these interesting towns contains in itself sufficient promise of growth and prosperity equal to, or exceeding, that of beautiful Youngstown, near Fort Niagara, or Niagara-on-the-Lake on the Canadian shore. This lower stretch of river teems with historic interest of the French era and especially of the days when the second war with Great Britain was progressing; in our chapters relating to those days will be found references to these points of present-day interest in their relation to the great questions that were being settled by sword and musket, by friend and foe, who met beside the historic river that empties into Lake Ontario between old Fort George and old Fort Niagara.

For ease of access, romantic situation, historic interest, and many of the advantages usually desired during a hot vacation recess, these towns along the lower Niagara offer a varied number of important advantages; if by some magic touch a dam could be raised between Fort Mississagua and the American shore, rendering that marvellously beautiful stretch of river—unmatched in some ways by any American stream—slack water, one of the most lovely boating lakes on the Continent could be created, whereon international regattas in both winter and summer could be held of unusual interest. Is it supposable that this could be effected without great detriment to either the yachting fraternity, whose sails, from the verandah of the Queen's Royal, are always a delight, or the steamboat interests, which could land as well at Fort Niagara, perhaps, as at Lewiston, or at Niagara-on-the-Lake, which could be connected with the Gorge Route. The river's current is all now that keeps the lower Niagara from being as popular a resort of its kind as can be suggested. All the elements of popularity are in fair measure present here, and immensely enjoyed yearly by increasing multitudes.

A little beyond the mouth of the Niagara, just over those blue waves, rise the spires of the queen city of Canada, Toronto. To all practical purposes this beautiful city stands at one end of Niagara River, as Buffalo stands at the other. Historically and commercially this is altogether true, and we elsewhere weave its history into our record.

Chapter III

The Birth of Niagara

GEOLOGIC time presents to the scientist one of the most difficult problems with which he has to deal. When the different divisions into which he would divide the ages are numbered by thousands and even millions of years, the human mind is appalled at the prospect; and when the calculations of different geologists vary by hundreds of thousands of years, the lay mind can not help growing somewhat credulous, and at times be tempted to discard the whole mass of scientific data relating to the subject.

Niagara River forms one of the best, if not the best, means of studying the lapse of time since the Ice Age. Finding, as students do here, the best material in existence for this study, leads to exhaustive scientific analysis of every clue presented by the Cataract and the deep Gorge it has cut for itself through the solid lime rock and Niagara shale forming its bed.

We are prone to look upon the great wonders of the world as destined to last as long as the earth itself. We do not realise that the mountains, miles in height, are slowly crumbling before our eyes, or realise that the rivers are carrying them slowly toward the sea, filling the lakes and lower portions of land along their courses. These slow but ceaseless forces are con-

The Birth of Niagara 53

tinually at work, reducing the surface of the earth to that of a level plain and at the same time depriving the land of its lakes by filling their depressions with silt. The winds and the waters, together with the wearing power effected by frost, are the forces struggling at this great levelling task. The work is partly done; in many of the older regions the lakes and elevations have almost entirely disappeared. Other parts of the land are comparatively new; and it is here that one sees the rough mountain or the deep canyon of the river; sufficient time not having elapsed to wear away the elevation in the one case nor the steep banks in the other.

One needs but to look at a relief map of the Niagara district to note the Falls and the outline of the Gorge to see at once that this is a comparatively new region or, at least, that the formative forces which gave it its present characteristics were at the highest stage of their career when the lands to the south had almost reached their present stage. These facts can be observed by any person visiting the Niagara district; it does not require a geologist to trace roughly their course.

Questions naturally arise in calculating the age of Niagara. If, as all the facts seem to indicate, this river has had a very recent beginning, what then did it do before it occupied its present course? What will be its final destiny? What will happen when it has worn its Gorge back to Lake Erie? Or will the general level of the land be so changed that the Falls will never recede to the lake? The last and most important of all is: How long has it taken the Falls to grind out the Gorge thus far? This latter question, viewed in its relation to the first one, forms the basis of the present chapter. The great work of the Cataract is going on before our very eyes. The history of this great river is working itself out at the height of its glory, in an age when all can behold. It is the more interesting since it is the only example of the kind known. One can easily look back to the time when the water flowed along the top of the plateau to Lewiston and the Falls were situated at that point. This date, of course, witnessed the birth of Niagara, for, wherever the waters flowed before, they could not have taken this course before the Falls began their work. The day that witnessed the beginning of the one witnessed also the birth of the other. Likewise one can not help looking forward to the day when Niagara shall have accomplished its work, when its waters shall have completely ground the plateau in two, and so drained Lake Erie to its bottom.

What did the waters of the lakes do before the Niagara began its history? How long has it been at its present work? These are the questions interesting to every one; and by far more interesting to one who is making a study of the formative forces now contributing, and which have contributed to bring about the present characteristics of surface structure. A few important facts exist, and these now are beyond doubt, upon which rest the inferences concerning the age of the Falls. In ancient times the waters of Lake Erie did not find an outlet through Niagara River, so there was no channel ready made for the river when it began its present course. Even after the beginning of the river the upper lakes, Huron, Michigan, and Superior, did not discharge their waters through Niagara

The American Fall, July, 1765.
From an unsigned original drawing in the British Museum.

The Horseshoe Fall, July, 1765.
From an unsigned original drawing in the British Museum.

The Birth of Niagara 55

Until comparatively recent times only the waters from Lake Erie discharged through this channel and therefore for many ages only a small fraction of the present volume could possibly have been at work on the Falls.

The striking features of the Gorge are modern, and have been very little affected by those agencies which are continually moulding the contours of land surfaces. The inclination of the river's bed has varied greatly with the ages, due to gradual uplifting or depressing of the earth's crust; consequently the current has varied greatly in velocity with these changes. A calculation of the work done by the river during each epoch of its history is indeed fraught with many difficulties. Much investigation, however, has been made along this line and with a rather satisfactory degree of success.

Niagara appears to have had a life peculiar to itself; but what is unique in its history, is the presentation of characteristics which in the case of other rivers have long since passed away. Rivers, and especially very large ones, appeal to us as "unchangeable as the hills themselves"; but the truth is, that the very hills and mountains are changing as a result of the forces exerted by water. Niagara, as viewed by the geologist, is unique, not on account of its having a different history than any other river, but for the reason that it had a more recent beginning. The calculation of the life of such a stream is interesting in itself, besides the other great questions settled by the solution of such a problem as the probable number of years that the river shall exist in its present form, the centuries which have elapsed since the ice retreated from this region, and the ascertaining of certain facts concerning the antiquity of man. In order to make a thorough study of these topics, one must take a view of the relief features of the Niagara region, and make a careful review of what conditions existed at the time that this district was covered by the great ice sheet, together with the changes effected during the retreat of the Great Glacier to the north.

Niagara River has its origin in the eastern end of Lake Erie, about three hundred feet higher than the surface of Lake Ontario. Passing from Erie to the last-mentioned lake the descent is not gradual, but one finds a gently rolling plain with almost no slope for nineteen miles until almost at the very shore of Lake Ontario, where almost unexpectedly one comes upon a high precipice from which a magnificent view of the lower lake may be gained, only a narrow strip of beach intervening. This cliff is called by geologists the Niagara escarpment.

When the river leaves Lake Erie its waters are interfered with by a low ledge of rock running across its channel. After passing this its waters meet no more troublesome obstructions until coming to the head of Goat Island. The river can scarcely be said to have a valley. One is reminded more of an arm of the lake extending out over this region. The country from Lake Erie to near the head of the Rapids above the Falls rests on a stratum of soft rock; from the Falls northward the underlying stratum is formed by a ledge of hard limestone, and beneath this a shale and two thin strata of sandstone. By the descent of the Rapids and the Falls, the waters are dropped two hundred feet, and thence through the Gorge they rush along at an appalling rate over the descent, through the Whirlpool and on to Queenston for a distance of seven miles. From

The Birth of Niagara

this city to the lake there is little fall and so only a moderate current.

The deep, narrow gorge extending from the Falls to Lewiston is the especial subject of study to the geologist. This canyon is scarcely a quarter of a mile wide, varying little in the distance from cliff to cliff throughout most of its course. This chasm opens up before the student with almost appalling suddenness, while travelling over an otherwise regular plain. Its walls are so precipitous that few opportunities are offered for scaling them; and their height from the bottom of the river varies from two hundred to five hundred feet. An examination of both sides of the Gorge shows the same order in the layers of rock and shale on comparatively the same level, with the same thickness of each corresponding stratum. If a superstitious person had come unexpectedly upon this gigantic fissure ages ago, he might easily have imagined it to have been the work of some mighty mythological hero; but the modern scientist has reached a much better, as well as a much more satisfactory conclusion, namely, that this immense cleft has been sawed by the force of the water, from a structure whose features were continuous, as is manifest by the similarity of the exposed strata on the two sides of the stream. To be convinced of the fact that the Falls are gradually receding, it is only necessary to observe them closely for a few years. The breaking away of an immense mass of rock previously described is one of the recent events in the history of the river. This establishes the fact that the Gorge is growing longer from its northern end through the agency of the waterfall.

These facts show us the river working at a

monstrous task. Its work is only partly done. Two questions come to us almost immediately: When this work is done what will it do? and, What did it do before its present work begun? The waters of Lake Erie could never have flowed to Lake Ontario without wearing away at the Gorge we now see. The birth of the river and the cutting of the canyon were simultaneous. Of this much we are assured.

A superficial study of a map of North America will show at once a great difference in the northern and the southern sections. From the region of the Great Lakes northward the district is one continuation of lakes, ponds, swamps, and rivers with many rapids. South of the Ohio there are few lakes, and the rivers flow on with almost unbroken courses. Here is a region much older than that to the north; and its waters have had ages more in which to mould down elevations and fill up depressions. The cause of this difference in the characteristics of the streams of the North and those of the South is to be explained by the great Ice Age. As far as we now know there may have been little difference in relief forms between the two sections before the encroachment of the ice. During the glacial epoch the whole northern part of the continent was covered with a thick ice sheet, which was continually renewed at the north, and as continually drifted slowly in a general southerly direction. As this heavy ice cap passed over the surface, it acted somewhat like a river in its erosive power, only working much greater changes. It not only picked up loose particles, but also scoured and wore away solid rocks along its bed. Thus the whole configuration of the country was changed.

The Birth of Niagara

At the southern terminal of the glacier, where it ended in the ocean, the ice broke away in large bergs, as in the northern seas to-day; but where the advancing ice met the warmer climate on land, it was melted and thus deposited at its terminal all the material it carried. The eroding power of this ice sheet, together with the deposit of its materials on melting, brought about a great change in the configuration of the country. Many old valleys were obliterated, while a number of new ones were carved. As the ice retreated northward with the change of climate, new lakes and rivers were formed. Many times the streams escaping from the lower level of lakes were forced to find an entirely new course, and so to carve a new channel of their own. The region of the Great Lakes and the Niagara River is no exception to this rule; and it is with the ending of the Ice Age that the history of the river begins.

A glance at a map shows a low range of hills or rather a gentle swell in the land surface forming the watershed between the lakes and the streams flowing to the south. At the time of the farthest southerly extension of the glacier it reached beyond this elevation; and its waters were discharged into the rivers flowing to the south. When the southern terminal had retreated to the north of this divide, but still blocked all outlet to the north or east, there was doubtless a number of lakes here discharging their waters across the present low watershed to the south. Some of these ancient valleys can still be traced for long distances of their course. These lakes passed through their varying history as those of to-day, their surface troubled by wind and storm and their waves leaving indelible carvings upon their shores.

One of these lakes occupied what is now the western end of Lake Erie, shortly after the ice front had passed to the north of the watershed mentioned. There are still very definite markings which show that its waters were discharged across the divide by a channel into the present Wabash River and thence into the Ohio. This channel can be traced throughout most of its course very easily. There are at least four distinct shore lines preserved to us, which show four successive levels of the lake as it reached lower outlets before the Niagara River was born. All of these old shore lines can be traced throughout most of their courses.

As the ice continued to retreat, next we notice the greatest change in elevation of the surface of the water. The ice front finally passed to the north of the present Mohawk River, thus allowing the waters to escape by that outlet, and, as a consequence, lowering the surface of the lakes by over five hundred feet. This drained a great extent of land and dropped the surface of Ontario far below the present level of the Niagara escarpment. Then for the first time the Niagara began to flow, and its Falls began their work. Immediately upon the formation of this new, lower lake it began the work of leaving its history carved upon the rocks, sands, and gravels which formed its shores. Its first ancient beach is more easily traced for almost its entire course than any of the other old levels. It does not even take the trained eye of the scientist to see its unmistakable history written in the sands. The earliest western travellers describe the Ridge Road running along this old, deserted beach as showing unmistakable signs of having been an ancient shore line of the lake.

The Birth of Niagara

In following the course of this old shore line a gradual slope is noticed, and if this was a shore line, we must account for this variation in elevation, since the surface of the water is always level. The explanation is to be found in the fact that portions of the earth's surface are gradually rising while others are as gradually sinking. On comparing the old coast line with the level of the present one, we find that the lake has gradually inclined to the south and the west. This change in elevation had its share in determining the configuration of the lake as well as the relief features of the surrounding region. The point of discharge was at Rome, New York, as long as the barrier blocked the regions north of the Adirondack Mountains. As soon as the encroaching warmth of the south had removed this barrier to the level of the Rome outlet, the water began flowing by the St. Lawrence course. True the first outlet was not the same as the present one; but it must have been many times shifted in the course of the retreat of the ice. As a result of this alternate shifting, together with the changing of the level of the lake, there are to be found the markings of numerous shore lines, some of which pass under the present level of the waters.

These different variations must of necessity have had a great effect on the work of Niagara River. When the Niagara began to flow, instead of its terminal being nearly seven miles from the escarpment, it was only between one and two miles away, and the surface of the lake was about seventy-five feet higher than now. While the outlet remained at Rome, the eastern end of the lake was continually rising, which caused the waters at the western end to rise over one hundred feet.

This placed the shore of Ontario almost at the foot of the beautiful cliff at Queenston and Lewiston. After having occupied this position for a long period, the surface of the waters again fell over two hundred feet, carving an old shore line which is now submerged. After this, various changes of level in the land and shiftings of the ice barrier caused numerous old shore lines to be faintly carved. These changes continued until the present outlet was established and the waters began to flow along the present course of the St. Lawrence.

One might think that with these changes all the variable factors of our problem have been discussed; but these same factors also had their effect upon the upper lakes. In a study of the old markings of all the lakes of this region, it seems that the northern shores were continually rising; this, of course, points to an occupation of a more northerly position by the lakes than at present, and also a laying bare of northern parts, and shifting of waters south, or possibly both of these changes at once.

In the most ancient system of which we can obtain an approximately definite knowledge, Lake Huron was not more than half its present size, while Georgian Bay formed the main body, connecting with Huron by a narrow strait. Michigan and Superior occupied about their present limits, but were connected with Huron by rivers rather than short straits; Erie occupied only a fraction of its present position, having no connection with Huron. The waters of the upper lakes were doubtless discharged from the eastern end of Georgian Bay, which then included Lake Nipissing, by way of the Ottawa River, into the St. Lawrence. Thus the Niagara was deprived of about seven-eighths

The Birth of Niagara

of its present drainage area, and consequently was totally unlike its present self. There is some indication that there may have been an outlet from Georgian Bay by a more southerly route, namely, the Trent River. If this were so, the northern route must have been blocked by the ice, since the Trent Pass is much higher than the one leading from Lake Nipissing, by way of the Ottawa. These are some of the possibilities which must be taken into consideration before any sure calculation can be made as to the age of the Falls, for there must have been an epoch in the history of the river, were it short or long, during which it carried only a very small fraction of the waters which it bears at present.

Let us turn again to the gorge of the river itself. We have noted the similarity of structure of its two sides. This similarity is continuous throughout except at about half-way from Queenston to the Falls, where the river makes a turn in its course of almost ninety degrees. On the outside of this angle is the only place in the whole course where the material of the cliff changes. Here there is a break in the solid rock of the bank, which is filled with loose rock and gravel. This rift, to whatever it may be due, is of pre-glacial origin, for it is filled with the same material, the glacial drift, which covers the whole region. The cliff along Lake Ontario also presents very few breaks; but a few miles to the west of Queenston at St. Davids a broad gap is found in the otherwise unbroken wall. This gap is also filled with glacial drift. On its first discovery it was supposed to be a buried valley, and no connection with the Whirlpool was attributed to it. Later it was supposed that the break in the side of the

Gorge, and the one at St. Davids, were parts of one and the same course of some pre-glacial stream. This supposition has been proven by the course having been traced through most of its distance by the wells sunk in the region. Later this interpretation of the facts found was destined to furnish further explanations. The question at once arose: How far and where did the upper course of this ancient valley extend? If it had cut across the course of the modern river, there would have been a break in the continuity of the cliff somewhere on the opposite side of the Gorge; but this can nowhere be found to be the case. The upper course of this ancient channel, therefore, must have coincided with that of the present channel. When, then, the Falls had receded to the side of the present Whirlpool, it reached a point where the greater part of its work had been performed. From here to whatever distance the upper course of the ancient river extended, the only work to do was to remove the loose gravel and boulders with which the glacier had filled its channel. This, of course, was effected much more rapidly than the wearing away of the hard limestone bed. Just what was the depth, and how far this old deserted valley extended, it is almost impossible to estimate. These changes are some of the most potent with which one must reckon in any calculation of the time since the beginning of Niagara's history. However, some work has been done in this line; and a broad field is still open for future investigation.

At a very early date (1790), and when it was supposed by many to be almost sacrilegious to discuss the antiquity of the earth, Andrew Ellicott made an estimate of the age of the Falls by dividing the length

Ice Mountain on Prospect Point.

Cave of the Winds in Winter.

The Birth of Niagara

of the Gorge by the supposed rate of recession. This gave as a result 55,000 years as the age of Niagara River. The next estimates which commanded attention were those of Bakewell and Sir Charles Lyell. Each of these men made separate estimates, but were compelled to take as the basis of their calculation the recession as given by residents of the district. Bakewell's calculations preceded Lyell's by several years, and resulted in ascribing to the Falls an age of 12,000 years. Lyell found the age to be about 36,000 years. The popularity of the latter caused his estimate to be accepted for a long period; many persons undoubtedly placing more faith in his results than he himself did. This method of dividing the distance by the rate of recession would be correct if there were no variables entering into the problem, and if the rate of recession were known; but these first calculations involved errors in the rate of movement of the Falls besides making no allowance for the variations which have been mentioned above.

In order to obtain a sure means for measuring the recession of the Falls, Professor James Hall made a survey of the Horseshoe Falls in 1842, under the authority of the New York Geological Survey. This survey plotted the position of the crest of the Falls, and established monuments at the points at which the angles were taken; thus leaving lasting marks of reference to which any future survey might be referred. In 1886, Professor Woodward of the United States Geological Survey, by reference to the markings left by Hall, found the rate of recession for the period to be about five feet per annum. It would, however, be necessary to extend these observations over a long period of time, since certain periods are marked by large falls of rock. Sometimes the centre of the Falls recedes very rapidly, while at other times the centre is almost stationary and the sides show the greater action. One of the most recent calculations of the age of the Falls was made by J. W. Spencer. Having made a thorough study of the history of the river revealed in its markings, and also of the Lakes, making allowance for all the variable factors, he calculated the duration of each epoch separately; and found the age of the river to be about 32,000 years. This result is about the same as that obtained from those based upon the relative elevations of different parts of the old deserted shore lines; and another based upon the rate of the rising of the land in the Niagara district.

The many variable factors entering into the calculations so far discussed, have led to an earnest search for some means of determining the age of the river, which does not involve so many indeterminate and unknown quantities. This means of calculation, and one which seems to be much more free from unknown factors, seems to have been hit upon by Professor George Frederick Wright, whose calculations are based upon the rate of enlargement of the mouth of the river at the Niagara escarpment, where the Falls first began their existence. The cliffs at the mouth of the Gorge, as is the case with the newer portions of the river and indeed is characteristic of all canyons when first formed, were undoubtedly almost perpendicular when they were first cut by the rushing waters of the Niagara River. The mouth of the Gorge at Lewiston is of course the oldest part of the river; and if it were possible to measure the age of this part, this would surely give the date of the birth of Niagara. Immediately upon the formation of the Falls at Lewiston, the waters began the cutting of the Gorge; and immediately upon the formation of a gorge there was set to work upon its walls the disintegrating agencies of the atmosphere, free from indeterminate variables, tending to pull down the cliffs upon each side of the stream which jealously walled it in.

This work has gone on year after year and century after century, without being affected by either the volume of the river's waters or the shifting in the elevation of the land. The work of the atmospheric agencies in enlarging the mouth of the Gorge has had the effect of changing its shape from that of a rectangle, whose perpendicular sides were 340 feet, to a figure with a level base formed by the river, whose sides slope off at the same angle on each side. Now if it were possible to measure the rate at which this enlargement is taking place, the problem of determining the age of the river would be a more simple one.

The relative thickness of the different layers of material forming the walls of the Gorge is not the same throughout; at the escarpment at Lewiston, the summit is found to consist of a stratum of Niagara limestone, about twenty-five feet thick. Beneath this layer of lime is to be found about seventy feet of Niagara shale. The Niagara shale rests upon a twenty foot layer of hard Clinton limestone, which in turn is supported by a shale seventy feet thick. Forming the base is twenty feet of hard Medina sandstone, beneath which is another sandstone which is much softer and much more susceptible to erosion and the disintegrating forces of the atmosphere. These thick layers of shale form the part upon which the atmospheric powers exert their energies, undermining the strata composed of material which with much more effect resists the attempt of any agency to break it down. As the shale is removed from beneath the harder layers immense masses of the latter fall and form a talus along the lower part of the cliff. This in brief is the manner in which the mouth of the Gorge is growing wider.

The present width of the mouth of the Gorge at the water's level is 770 feet. It is not likely that the river was ever any wider than now at this point, since its narrowest portion is over 600 feet, and this where the hard layer of Niagara limestone is much thicker than at the mouth. The current here is comparatively weak, so that there has been little erosion due to it. On the contrary the falling masses of sandstone and limestone have probably encroached somewhat upon the ancient margin of the stream, its weak current being unable to sweep out these obstructions which have formed an effectual protection to the bank.

The observations necessary to Dr. Wright's calculations were taken along the line of a railroad, which, very opportunely, had been constructed along the eastern cliff. Here for a distance of about two miles the course of the road runs diagonally down the face of the cliff, descending in that distance about two hundred feet, and in its descent laying bare the layers of shale upon which the observations must be made. Along the course of the road at this point, watchmen are continually employed to remove obstructions falling down or to give warning of danger when any large masses fall. The disintegration goes on much more

The Birth of Niagara

rapidly in wet thawing weather than at other times of the year. Often in the spring the whole force of section hands is required for several days to dispose of the material of one single fall. At the rate of one-fourth of an inch a year of waste along this cliff there ought to fall slightly over six hundred cubic yards annually for each mile where the wall is 150 feet high. At this rate the enlargement at the terminal of the Gorge would take place, Dr. Wright estimates, in somewhat less than ten thousand years. No accounts have been kept by the railroad of the amount of fallen material, but some estimate can be made from the cost of removal of the falling stone, together with the observations of the watchmen, one of whom has been in the employ of the railroad in this capacity for twelve years, and also by noticing the distance to which the cliff has receded since the construction of the road.

Only a superficial observer can see at once that the amount of removal has been greatly in excess of the rate mentioned above. The watchman, of whom mention has been made, was in the employ of the company which constructed the road in 1854, and therefore knows where the original face of the cliff was located. At one point, where the road descends to the Clinton limestone, the whole face of the Niagara shale is laid bare. Here the shale has been removed to a distance of twenty feet from its original position, and the rocks forming the roof overhang to about that distance. Now this mass of shale must have been removed since 1854. This would require a rate of disintegration much in excess of the one assumed. Necessarily some allowance must be made for the fact that the atmospheric agencies have here had a fresh section of the shale upon which to work. Yet making all due allowance for the above condition, the rate at the mouth of the Gorge could not have been much less than that assumed above. The actual process of the enlargement has been periodic. As the falling shale undermines more and more the capping hard layers, from time to time these latter fall in immense masses. Any calculation of age based upon a few years of disintegration would be worthless; but one based upon centuries would come very near a true average. The walls of the Gorge were at first perpendicular, but as the undermining process goes on they become sloped more and more, the falling masses forming a protection to the lower parts of the softer strata. One fact, however, to be noticed is that this protecting talus has never as yet reached so high as to stop the work of the disintegrating agencies. The horizontal distance from the water's edge back to the face of the Niagara limestone, which forms the top of the cliff, is 380 feet. On the above assumption of the rate of recession as one-fourth of an inch annually, the rate at the top of the cliff must have been about one-half inch for each year. From the observations made, it is difficult to believe that the retreat of this upper portion has been at a lower rate than a half-inch yearly; if this be true, this new line of evidence places the birth of the Niagara and the beginning of the cutting of the Gorge at Lewiston at about ten thousand years ago.

The history of the Great Lakes and the birth of Niagara have a different interest for us, than alone to form the connecting link between the present and a past age devoid of life. Closely connected with this geologic history is the history of the human race. Unfortunately for us, the men inhabiting these parts in

"Maid of the Mist" under Steel Arch Bridge.

Beacon on Old Breakwater at Buffalo.

The Birth of Niagara

prehistoric ages have not left the traces of their existence upon the rocks and sands as have the waters of Niagara and the Lakes. Meagre, however, as is our knowledge we are still confident that man has been a comrade of the river during its entire history. Much to our disappointment, he was not possessed with the means of recording his knowledge for the satisfaction of future generations. Probably no such thought ever entered his brain. All that we know is, that along the old deserted shores of Lake Ontario in New York, which now form the Ridge Road, he constructed a rude hearth and built a fire thereon. The shifting of elevation or the rising of the surface of the lake buried beneath the waters hearth, ashes, and charred sticks, and thus by a mere accident do we know that human history extends back at least as far as the Ice Age.

In these modern days, when we are prone to believe that all forms of animate existence and inanimate as well have been the result of an evolution, we cannot think of the man who possessed the art of fire as the primeval man. Whatever age may be assigned to the Niagara, whatever may be the antiquity of that great cataract, upon which we are wont to look as everlasting, the age of the human race must be considered greater.

Chapter IV

Niagara Bond and Free

NO one acquainted with the Niagara of to-day can imagine what were the conditions existing here before the days of the New York State Reservation and Queen Victoria Park. That old Niagara of private ownership, with a new fee for every point of vantage, was a barbarous incongruity only matched by the wonder and beauty of the spectacle itself. The admission to Goat Island was fifty cents, and to the Cave of the Winds, one dollar. To gain Prospect Park, the "Art Gallery," the inclined railway, or the ferry, the charge was twenty-five cents. It cost one dollar to go to the "Shadow of the Rock," or go behind the Horseshoe Fall. The admission to the Burning Spring was fifty cents, likewise to Lundy's Lane battle-ground, the Whirlpool Rapids, the Whirlpool. It cost twenty-five cents to go upon either of the suspension bridges. In addition to this a swarm of pedlars were hawking their wares at your elbows, and tents were pitched at every vantage point, containing the tallest man or the fattest woman, or the most astonishing reptile then in a state of captivity in all the world.

Not even the five-legged calves missed their share of plunder at Niagara, according to Mr. Howells, who paid his money out to assure himself, as he affirms, that this marvel was in no wise comparable to the Falls. "I do not say that the picture of the calf on the outside of the tent," he observes, "was not as good as some pictures of Niagara I have seen. It was, at least, as much like." A writer of a decade before this (1850) speaks very strongly of the impositions to which a traveller is subjected at Niagara. How early in the century complaints began to appear cannot be stated; it would be interesting to be able to get information on this point since it would determine a more important matter still —the time when the Falls began to attract visitors in sufficient proportions to bring into existence the evils we find very prevalent at the middle of the century. The latter writer observes:

It would be paying Niagara a poor compliment to say that, practically she does not hurl off this chaffering by-play from her cope; but as you value the integrity of your impression, you are bound to affirm that it hereby suffers appreciable abatement; you wonder, as you stroll about, whether it is altogether an unrighteous dream that with the slow progress of culture, and the possible or impossible growth of some larger comprehension of beauty and fitness, the public conscience may not tend to ensure to such sovereign phases of nature something of the inviolability and privacy which we are slow to bestow, indeed, upon fame, but which we do not grudge, at least, to art. We place a great picture, a great statue, in a museum; we erect a great monument in the centre of our largest square, and if we can suppose ourselves nowadays building a cathedral, we should certainly isolate it as much as possible and subject it to no ignoble contact. We cannot build about Niagara with walls and a roof, nor girdle it with a palisade; but the sentimental tourist may muse upon the chances of its being guarded by the negative homage of empty spaces, and absent barracks, and decent forbearance. The actual abuse of the scene belongs evidently to that immense class of iniquities which are destined to grow very much worse in order to grow a very little better. The good humour engendered by the main spectacle bids you suffer it to run its course.

There was at least no bettering of conditions at Niagara between 1850 and 1881, when more or less active steps began to be taken for the freeing of the beautiful shrine. True, Goat Island was kept ever in its primeval beauty, which by far counterbalanced the Porter mills on Bath Island; as William Dean Howells wrote, while these "were impertinent to the scenery they were picturesque with their low-lying, weather-worn masses in the shelter of the forest trees beside the brawling waters' head. But nearly every other assertion of private rights in the landscape was an outrage to it."

One of the strongest direct appeals to the nation's conscience in behalf of enslaved Niagara appeared in 1881 and is worthy of reproduction, if only for its vivid description of the status of affairs at the Falls at that time:

The homage of the world has thrown a halo round Niagara for those who have not seen it, and Niagara has left its own impress upon every thoughtful person who has seen it, and every unpleasant feature therefore is brought into bold relief. Where the carcass is, there also will the eagles be gathered together. A continuous stream of open-mouthed travellers has offered rare opportunities to the quick-witted money-makers of all kinds; the contrast between the place and its surroundings, perceived at first by the few, has been for years trumpeted throughout the country by the number of correspondents who write periodical accounts of the season, and to-day every sane adult citizen may be said to know two things about Niagara: first, that there is a great waterfall there, and second, that a

Winter Scene in Prospect Park.

Bath Island, American Rapids, in 1879.
From New York Commissioners' Report.

man's pockets will be emptied more quickly there than anywhere else in the Union. . . . Niagara is being destroyed as a summer resort. It has long since ceased to be a place where people stay for a week or more, and it is now given up to second-class tourists, and excursionists who are brought by the car-load. The constant fees, the solicitation of the hackmen, the impertinences of the store-keepers, have actually been so potent that it is a rare thing to find any of the best people here. The hotels are not to blame; the Cataract House for instance, is a quiet, comfortable hotel, excellently managed, and in the hands of gentlemanly proprietors, and it is probably by no means alone in this respect. The hotel-keepers are aware of the state of things; they do not encourage the excursion traffic. Some even seek to avoid the patronage of the excursionists. From all over the country— from places as far as Louisville—the railway company bring the people by thousands: they pour out of the station in a stream half a mile long. Of course, like locusts, they sweep everything before them. Several places—Prospect Park, for instance— cater to the tastes of this class alone. Several evenings in the week Prospect Park is filled with a crowd of free-and-easy men and women, fetching their own tea and coffee and provisions and enjoying a rollicking dance in the Pavilion. And all this within fifty yards of the American fall! For their entertainment there is an illuminated spray-fountain, and their appreciation knows no bounds when various coloured lights are thrown upon the Falls. Then a crowd of fifty swoops down upon one of the hotels—men, women, and children—all in brown linen dusters; all hot, hungry, and careless. These people must not be deprived of their recreation. Heaven forbid! None have a greater right than they to the influence of Niagara. But this way of visiting the place is all wrong; they derive little benefit, and they do infinite harm.

In this second sense the destruction of Niagara is making rapid strides in a far more dangerous direction. The natural attractions of the place are being undermined. On the American side the bank of the river above the Falls is covered for a quarter of a mile with structures of all kinds, from the extensive parlors and piazzas of the Cataract House to the little shanty where the Indian goods of Irish manufacture are sold.

For the purpose of securing bathrooms and water-power, dams of all kinds have been built; these are wooden trenches filled with rough paving-stones. Some of the structures project over the Rapids, being supported by piles. The spaces between the various buildings are used to store lumber, and as dust heaps. One of them contains a great heap of saw-dust, another a pile of scrap-iron. The banks and fences bear invitations to purchase Parker's hair-balsam and ginger tonic. The proprietor of Prospect Park has made a laudable attempt to plant trees upon his land; these extend for a few yards above the Falls. In return, however, he has erected coloured arbours, and a station for his electric light, which are almost as unpleasant as the other buildings.

Just below the Suspension Bridge the gas-works discharge their tar down the bank into the river; a few yards further on there are five or six large manufactories, whose tail-races empty themselves over the cliff. The spectator on Goat Island, on the Suspension Bridge, or on the Canadian side cannot help seeing this mass of incongruous and ugly structures extending along the whole course of the Rapids and to the brink of the Falls. Of course, under these circumstances the Rapids are degraded into a mill-race, and the Fall itself seems to be lacking a water-wheel.

One half of Bath Island—which lies between Goat Island and the shore—is filled with the ruins of a large paper-mill which was burnt in 1880. It is now being rebuilt and greatly enlarged. Masses of charred timbers, old iron, calcined stones and bricks, two or three great rusty boilers, the dirty heaps surmounted by a tall chimney—such are the surroundings of a spot, which, for grandeur and romantic beauty, is not equalled in the world. A short distance below Bath Island lies Bird Island, a mere clump of trees in the midst of the rushing water, a mass of dark-green foliage overhanging its banks and trailing its branches carelessly in the foam. This little spot has been untrodden by man—the most fearless savage would not risk his birch-bark boat in these waters. But what those who profit by it call the rapid strides of commercial industry, or possibly the development of our national resources, will soon destroy this little piece of Nature; already the owners of the paper-mill have built their dam within twenty yards of it, extending through the waters like

Niagara Bond and Free

the limb of some horrid spider, slowly but surely reaching its prey. Let the connection be made, and a couple of men with axes turned loose in this little green island, and before long the rattle of a donkey-engine or the howl of a saw-mill swells the chorus of this *soi-disant* civilisation. The following does not sound very encouraging for the preservation of Niagara's scenery. It is taken from a paper, *Niagara as a Water Power:*

" . . . Hence it is that we are soon to see a development of this peculiar power of Niagara which will stand unrivalled among motors of its class in the world.

" Already people talk of the storage of electricity and quote the opinions of scientists about the possibilities of the future. Sir William Thompson—it is said—gave as his opinion that it would be perfectly feasible to light London with electricity generated at Niagara.

" There is no assurance that Goat Island may not be sold at any moment for the erection of a mill or factory. Indeed if a rapid development of the mechanical application of electricity should take place—thus enabling speculators to offer very high prices for the immense power that could be controlled from Goat Island, it is almost certain that such a sale would result. And with its accomplishment would disappear the last chance of saving Niagara ! "

The honour of first suggesting the preservation of Niagara Falls has been claimed by many persons. But the first real suggestion dates back as early as 1835, though made without details. It came from two Scotchmen, Andrew Reed and James Matheson, who, in a volume describing their visits to Congregational churches of this country, first broached the idea that Niagara should "be deemed the property of civilised mankind."

In 1885, by the labours of several distinguished men, principally Mr. Frederick Law Olmsted, a bill was passed in the Legislature of New York instructing the commissioners of the State Survey to prepare a report on the conditions and prospects of Niagara. This report was prepared by Mr. James T. Gardner, the director of the New York State Survey, and Mr. Olmsted. It strongly protested against such waste and degradation of the scenery as have been described in this chapter; it set forth the dangers of ultimate destruction, and made an eloquent appeal in favour of State action to preserve this natural treasure. The report strongly urged the establishment of an "International Park," and gave details of its construction with maps and views. It proposed that a strip of land a mile long and varying from one hundred feet to eight hundred feet broad, together with the buildings on it, should be condemned by the State, appraised by a commission, and purchased. The erections on Bath Island and in the Rapids were to be swept away. Trees and shrubberies were to be planted, roads and foot-paths appropriately laid out. The cost was estimated at one million dollars.[1]

Why the bill should have met with so much opposition before it was finally passed, is to-day a question hard to answer; at any rate the political history of the bill is interesting.

As in the case of most modern propositions the question was generally asked:

"Is the game worth the candle? Is it worth while to spend a million dollars—to take twenty-five cents out of the pocket of each tax-payer in the State of New York—in order to destroy a lot of good buildings and plant trees in place of them, and, moreover, to do this for the sake of a few persons whose nerves are so deli-

[1] *The Nation*, No. 84 (September 1, 1881).

Niagara Bond and Free 79

cate that the sight of a tremendous body of water rushing over a precipice is spoiled for them by a pulp-mill standing on the banks?"

Indeed, it is said on good authority, that Governor Cornell, after listening to a description of the shameful condition at the Falls and the surroundings at the time when he sat in the gubernatorial chair remarked: "Well, the water goes over just the same does n't it?"

Mr. Cleveland, being elected Governor of New York in 1882 seemed always in favour of the preservation of the scenery at Niagara Falls. Governor Robinson, in 1879, likewise an advocate of the idea, even caused some preliminary steps to be taken but the following gentlemen especially deserve to be entered in the *Golden Book of Niagara:* Thomas K. Beecher, James J. Belden, R. Lenox Belknap, Prof. E. Chadwick, Erastus Corning, Geo. W. Curtis, Hon. James Daly, Benjamin Doolittle, Edgar van Etter, R. E. Fenton, H. H. Frost, General James W. Husted, Thomas L. James, Thomas Kingsford, Benson J. Lossing, Seth Low, Luther R. Marsh, Randolph B. Martine, Rufus H. Peckham, Howard Potter, D. W. Powers, Pascal P. Pratt, Ripley Ropes, Horatio Seymour, Geo. B. Sloan, Samuel J. Tilden, Senator Titus, Theodore Vorhees, Francis H. Weeks, Wm. A. Wheeler. They all made strenuous efforts to advance the bill introduced into the Legislature by Jacob F. Miller of New York City. One of its foremost promoters also was Mr. Thomas V. Welch, Superintendent of the New York State Reservation at Niagara, whose valuable pamphlet *How Niagara was Made Free* affords much of our material for this chapter. A bill entitled "Niagara Reservation Act" passed the New York Assembly and the

Senate, and was signed by Grover Cleveland on April 30, 1883. Commissioners were appointed consisting of William Dorsheimer, Sherman S. Rogers, Andrew H. Green, J. Hampden Robb, and Martin B. Anderson. But the final bill had to undergo many vicissitudes ere it was lastly amended and passed. The appraisals alone amounted to $1,433,429.50, and the then existing financial depression had to be dispelled before anything definite could be done. Between 1883 and 1885 there arose a most unjustifiable raid against the measure. I have already alluded to it above. John J. Platt of the *Poughkeepsie Eagle* wrote for instance: "We regard this Niagara scheme as one of the most unnecessary and unjustifiable raids upon the State Treasury ever attempted." Mr. Platt became later on a warm advocate of the plan, but the wrong was done. Some denounced the bill as a "job" and a "steal" and berated Niagara Falls and its citizens, particularly the hackmen, hotel-men, and bazaar-keepers as sharks and swindlers, who had robbed the people individually and were now seeking to rob them collectively. They said they would oppose the bill by every means, hoped it would be defeated—bursts of temper mildly suggestive of strangers who had visited Niagara and had suffered at the hands of her showmen in the golden days of Niagara's army of fakirs and extortionists.

Thus the matter dragged and great fears were entertained that the case would be lost. Meanwhile the above-named prominent citizens had not been idle. They had sent to their friends and constituents a kind of a circular and obtained about four thousand signatures in favour of the measure. Clergymen, educators, editors, and attorneys were well represented;

medical men without exception signed the petition, which was finally submitted to Governor Hill. For a time it almost seemed that the Governor shared the views of Governor Cornell. He was "pestered to death" in behalf of the bill until the matter actually created a stir, as though the very welfare of the State depended on it. Great pressure was brought on Mr. Hill to sign the bill; he visited the Falls himself, went over the ground, but he was non-committal and even his intimates had no idea whether he would affix his signature. Yet he seemed apparently more favourably disposed than heretofore.

There was left a feeling of uneasiness and uncertainty [writes Mr. Welch], concerning the fate of the bill. Another week passed. Rumours were rife concerning the intention of the Governor to let the bill die, in lack of his signature, and thus arrived the 30th of April, 1885, the last day for the scheme allowed by law.

The forenoon was spent in a state of feverish anxiety—not lessened by frequent rumours of a veto in the Senate or Assembly; some of them started in a spirit of mischief by the newspaper reporters. When noon came, it seemed as if the bill would surely fail for lack of executive approval. But the darkest hour is just before daybreak. Shortly after noon a newspaper man hurriedly came to the writer [1] in the Assembly chamber and said that the Governor had just signed the Niagara Bill. A hurried passage was made to the office of the Secretary of State to see if the bill had been received from the Governor. It had not been received. At that moment the door was opened by the Governor's messenger who placed the bill in the hands of the writer saying " Here is your little joker." A glance at the bill showed it to be the "Niagara Reservation Bill," and on the last page was the much coveted signature of David B. Hill, rivalling that of Mr. Grover Cleveland in diminutive handwriting.

It is reported that the " King of the Lobby," a man notorious for years in Albany, expressed his satisfaction at the approval

[1] Mr. Thomas V. Welch, *loc. cit.*

of the bill, saying "The 'boys' wanted to 'strike' that bill, but I told them that they must not do it; that it was a bill which ought to pass without the expenditure of a dollar—and it did."

The Report of the Commissioners of the State Reservation at Niagara lies before me. It is dated February 17, 1885.[1] The commissioners were appointed in 1883 to consider and report what, if any, measures it might be expedient for the State to adopt carrying out the project to place Niagara under the control of Canada and New York according to the suggestions contained in the annual message of Governor Cleveland with respect to Niagara Falls. The report states that the attractions of the scenery and climate in the neighbourhood of the Falls are such that with their ready accessibility by several favourite routes of travel it might reasonably be expected that Niagara would be a popular summer resort; that there was nevertheless, no desirable summer population, attributed chiefly to the constant annoyances to which the traveller is subjected: pestering demands and solicitations, and petty exactions and impositions by which he is everywhere met. While it is true that such annoyances are felt wherever travellers are drawn in large numbers, at Niagara the inconvenience becomes greater because the distinctive interest of Niagara as compared with other attractive scenery is remarkably circumscribed and concentrated. That the value of Niagara lies in its appeal to the higher emotion and imaginative faculties and should not be disturbed and irritated; that tolls and fees had to be removed; traffic was to be excluded from the limits from whence

[1] Senate Document, No. 35, Albany, N. Y.

the chief splendour of the scenery was visible. That the only prospect of relief was to be found in State control; that the forest was rapidly destroyed which once formed the perfect setting of one of Nature's most gorgeous panoramas, and that the erection of mills and factories upon the margin of the river had a most injurious effect upon the character of the scene.

It was therefore resolved on June 9, 1883, that

in the judgment of this board it is desirable to select as proper and necessary to be reserved for the purpose of preserving the scenery of the falls of Niagara and of restoring the said scenery to its natural condition, the following lands situate in the village of Niagara and the County of Niagara to-wit: Goat Island, Bath Island, the Three Sisters, Bird Island, Luna Island, Chapin Island, and the small islands adjacent to said islands in the Niagara River, and the bed of said river between said islands and the main land of the State of New York; and, also, the bed of said river between Goat Island and the Canadian boundary; also a strip of land beginning near "Port Day" in said village, running along the shore of said river, to and including "Prospect Park" and the cliff and debris slope, under the same, substantially as shown by that part coloured green on the map accompanying the fourth report of the Board of Commissioners of the State Survey, dated March 22, 1880; and including also at the east end of said strip sufficient land not exceeding one acre for purposes convenient for said reservation, and also all lands at the foot of said falls, and all lands in said river adjoining said islands and the other lands hereinbefore described.

By the adoption of the foregoing resolution, the area of a reservation was preliminarily defined. A commission of appraisement was installed. As was to be expected the claims for the condemned land were about four million dollars. The awards, however, amounted to $1,433,429.50 only. Some interesting and important questions were raised as to the rights of the riparian owners to use the power afforded by the Niagara River for hydraulic purposes and to receive compensation therefor. Upon this basis the owners were prepared to present claims aggregating twenty or thirty millions of dollars. After full argument and careful consideration, the commissioners of appraisement rejected all such claims, except where the water power had been actually reduced to use and used for a period long enough to create a prescriptive right. They held:

(1) that Niagara is a public stream, and its bed and waters belong to the State; (2) that as against the State private riparian owners have no right to encroach on its bed to divert its waters or to subject them to the burden of manufacturing uses, unless they have acquired such right by grant from the State or by prescription.

The preamble of the Preservation Act[1] which was to make Niagara free read:

Whereas, the State Engineer and Surveyor has completed and submitted to this board a map of the lands selected and located by it in the village of Niagara Falls and the County of Niagara and State of New York, which, in the judgment of this board are proper and necessary to be reserved for the purpose of preserving the scenery of the falls of Niagara, and restoring the said scenery to its natural condition; now, therefore, it is Resolved, etc.

[1] *Resolved,* That this board hereby selects and locates the lands hereafter described, situate in the village of Niagara Falls, and the County of Niagara and State of New York, as in the opinion of this board proper and necessary to be reserved for the purpose of preserving the scenery of the falls of Niagara, and restoring the said scenery to its natural condition, and does hereby determine to take such land for the purposes aforesaid, and which said land is bounded and described as follows, to-wit: All that certain piece or parcel of land situate in the village of Niagara Falls, town and County of Niagara, State of New York, distinguished in part as part of lots numbers forty-two (42), forty-three (43), and forty-four (44)

Niagara Bond and Free

On the morning of July 15th the Seventh Battery unlimbered its howitzers to salute the rising sun with a hundred salvos. The day unfortunately proved dark and foreboding. A storm burst in the morning and drove the crowds to shelter, and the last drops had hardly ceased pattering, when the hour of noon, the time fixed for the ceremony, arrived. The grounds of

of the mile strip, as the same was surveyed and conveyed by the State of New York, in part as islands known as Goat island, Bath island, the Three Sisters, Bird island, Luna island, Chapin island, Ship island, Brig island, Robinson's island, and other small islands lying in Niagara river adjacent and near to the islands above-named, and in part as lands lying under the Niagara river, bounded and described as follows, to-wit:

Beginning at a point on the easterly bank of the Niagara river, where the same is met and intersected by the division line between lands now or formerly occupied by Albert H. Porter, and lands now or formerly owned or occupied by the Niagara Falls Hydraulic and Manufacturing Canal Company; running thence on a course north three degrees forty-nine and one-fourth minutes west; along said last mentioned division line, one (1) chain and ninety-five (95) links to a stone monument standing in the southerly line of Buffalo street, in the village of Niagara Falls; thence on a course south eighty-six degrees forty-five and one-fourth minutes west along said southerly line of Buffalo street ninety and nine-tenths (90.9) links to a point in the division line between lands now or formerly owned or occupied by Albert H. Porter, and lands now or formerly owned or occupied by the estate of Augustus S. Porter; thence on a course south eighty-six degrees forty-five and one-fourth minutes west along said southerly line of Buffalo street ninety and nine-tenths (90.9) links to a point in the division line between lands now or formerly owned or occupied by the estate of Augustus S. Porter and lands owned or occupied by Jane S. Townsend; thence on a course south eighty-six degrees forty-five and one-fourth minutes west, along said southerly line of Buffalo street, two (2) chains and seventy (70) links to the intersection of the same with the easterly line of Seventh street; thence on the same course south eighty-six degrees forty-five and one-fourth minutes west, across said Seventh street, one (1) chain and three-tenths (.3) of a link to the westerly boundary thereof; thence along said westerly boundary of Seventh street and on a course south three degrees forty-nine and one-half minutes east, one (1) chain and fifty-four and seventy-seven one-hundredths (54.77) links to a point in said westerly line of Seventh street, distant seventy-six(76) links northerly, measuring on said westerly line of Seventh street, from the intersection of the same with the northerly

Prospect Park were wet and the trees shook their water freely in the light breeze, but some thousands collected on the grass around the pavilion, notwithstanding these disheartening circumstances. When President Dorsheimer, however, began his speech the sun smiled through the clouds, and the day thereafter was perfect overhead.

line of River street; thence on a course south fifty-seven degrees forty-seven and one-fourth minutes, west one (1) chain and sixteen (16) links to a point in the division line between lands now or formerly owned or occupied by Albert H. Porter and lands now or formerly owned or occupied by Mrs. George W. Holley, which said point is distant northerly measuring along said division line seventy (70) links from the northerly line of River street; thence on a course south fifty-six degrees fifty-five and one-half minutes west, one (1) chain and sixteen (16) links to a point; thence south fifty-eight degrees forty minutes west, one (1) chain and fifteen (15) links to a point; thence south sixty-three degrees forty-three and one-fourth minutes west one (1) chain and eleven (11) links to a point; thence south sixty-seven degrees nineteen and one-fourth minutes west, one (1) chain and sixty (60) links to a point in the division line between lands owned or occupied by Mrs. George W. Holley and lands owned or occupied by Jane S. Townsend distant sixty (60) links northerly measured on said division line from the northerly boundary of River street; thence on a course south seventy-two degrees nineteen minutes west, two (2) chains and ten (10) links to a point in the division line between lands owned or occupied by Jane S. Townsend, and lands owned or occupied by Josephine M. Porter, distant, measuring on said division line sixty-four (64) links northerly from the northerly boundary of River street; thence on a course south seventy-three degrees thirty-four and one-half minutes west, one (1) chain and four (4) links to a point; thence south seventy-six degrees twenty-eight and one-half minutes west, one (1) chain and two (2) links to a point; thence south eighty-two degrees four and three-fourths minutes west, one (1) link to a point, thence south eighty-six degrees forty-three and one-fourth minutes west, one (1) chain to a point; thence south eighty-nine degrees fifty-six minutes west, one (1) chain to a point; thence north eighty-eight degrees forty-three minutes west one (1) chain and one (1) link to a point in the easterly boundary of Fourth street, distant ninety (90) links northerly, measuring on said easterly boundary of Fourth street, from the intersection of the same with the northerly boundary of River street; thence across said Fourth street and on a course north eighty-two degrees thirty-two and one-half minutes west, one (1) chain and one (1) link to

Path to Luna Island.

Green Island Bridge.

Niagara Bond and Free 87

The excursion trains began to pour their passengers into the village early. They came from the counties bordering on the Pennsylvania line and from the northern and western ends of the State and from the towns in the Canadian dominion. It is estimated that at least thirty thousand strangers were unloaded in the village. The visitors included country folk and residents

---

a point in the westerly boundary of Fourth street, distant eighty-six (86) links northerly measuring on said westerly boundary of Fourth street; from the intersection of the same with the northerly line of River street; thence on a course north seventy-eight degrees fifty-three minutes west, two (2) chains and six (6) links to a point in the division line between lands owned or occupied by Peter A. Porter, and land owned or occupied by S. M. Whitney, which point is distant seventy (70) links northerly, measuring on said division line, from the northerly line of River street; thence on a course north seventy-nine degrees seventeen and three-fourths minutes west, one (1) chain and three (3) links to a point; thence north seventy-six degrees eight minutes west, one (1) chain and four (4) links to a point; thence north seventy-three degrees seven and one-fourth minutes west, ninety-five (95) links to a point; thence north seventy-one degrees twenty-five and one-fourth minutes west, fifty (50) links to a point in the division line between lands owned or occupied by S. M. Whitney, and lands owned or occupied by Albert H. Porter which point is distant northerly, measuring on said division line, seventy (70) links from the northerly line of River street; thence on a course north sixty-eight degrees thirty-five and one-fourth minutes west, sixty-eight (68) links to a point; thence north sixty-three degrees thirty-eight and one-fourth minutes west, ninety-eight (98) links to a point; thence north fifty-three degrees fifteen and one-fourth minutes west, one (1) chain and thirteen (13) links to a point in the division line between lands owned or occupied by Albert H. Porter and lands owned or occupied by Jane S. Townsend, which point is distant northerly, measuring on said division line, ninety-two (92) links from the northerly line of River street; running thence on a course north forty-eight degrees fifty-six and one-fourth minutes west, eighty-nine (89) links to a point; thence north fifty degrees one and one-half minutes west, one (1) chain and two (2) links to a point; thence north fifty-five degrees two and one-half minutes west, one (1) chain and one (1) link to a point; thence north sixty degrees ten minutes west, fifty (50) links to a point in the division line between lands owned or occupied by Jane S. Townsend and lands owned or occupied by the heirs of Augustus S. Porter, which point is distant northerly, measuring on said division-line, one (1) chain and fifty-six (56) links from the northerly

of the city, and about two thousand militiamen, principally from the Fourth Division, although there were several organisations among them representing Cleveland, Detroit, Utica, Buffalo, and Rochester. There was a sprinkling of British redcoats among the gold-laced officers who dotted the village streets. One of the Canadian battalions desired to come over and join

line of River street; thence on a course north sixty degrees fifteen and one-half minutes west, fifty (50) links to a point; thence north sixty-seven degrees ten and one-half minutes west, ninety-nine (99) links to a point; thence north sixty-eight degrees nineteen and three-fourths minutes west, one (1) chain to a point; thence north seventy-one degrees forty-five and one-fourth minutes west, one (1) chain to a point distant one (1) chain and twenty-eight (28) links, measuring on a course north twenty-seven degrees east from the northerly line of River street; thence on a course north sixty-three degrees fifty-five and one-half minutes west, one (1) chain and eleven (11) links to a point; thence north fifty-five degrees one and one-fourth minutes west, one (1) chain to a point; thence north fifty-one degrees forty-one and one-half minutes west, eighty-nine (89) links to a point; thence north forty-seven degrees fifty minutes west eighty-three (83) links to a point; thence north forty-five degrees forty-two minutes west, one (1) chain and two (2) links to a point; thence north forty-two degrees twenty-five minutes west, two (2) chains and two (2) links to a point; thence north forty-three degrees seventeen and three-fourths minutes west, one (1) chain and nine (9) links to a point in the easterly boundary of Mill street, distant northerly, measuring along said easterly boundary of Mill street, twenty (20) links from the intersection of the same with the northerly boundary of River street; thence on a course north twenty-eight degrees nineteen and one-fourth minutes east, and along said easterly boundary of Mill street, two (2) chains and thirty (30) links to the intersection of said easterly line of Mill street with the southerly line of Buffalo street; thence on a course north sixty-two degrees forty-five minutes west, across said Mill street, one (1) chain to the westerly boundary line thereof, and to the point of intersection of the westerly line of Mill street with the southerly line of Buffalo street; thence on a course north sixty-one degrees thirty-two minutes west, along the southerly boundary of Buffalo street, five (5) chains and thirty-two (32) links to the point of intersection of the southerly line of Buffalo street with the easterly boundary line of the Mill slip (so called), which point is distant northerly measuring on said easterly line of the Mill slip, seventy-one (71) links from the intersection of the same with the northerly line of River street; thence on a course north sixty-one degrees thirty-two

Niagara Bond and Free

in the celebration. The United States authorities extended a welcome but the Canadian authorities declined to allow their soldiers to cross the river. A few of the officers got permit to come. Governor Hill and his staff were met by a committee appointed to receive them, consisting of Thomas V. Welch and O. W. Cutter. There were also Senators

minutes west, across said Mill slip, fifty-one and forty-two one-hundredths (51.42) links to a point in the westerly boundary line thereof, distant northerly, measuring along said westerly line of said Mill slip, seventy-five and twenty-three one-hundredths (75.23) links from the intersection of the same with the northerly line of River street; thence along said westerly boundary line of said Mill slip and on a course south fifty-four degrees four and three-fourths minutes west, seventy-five and twenty-three one-hundredths (75.23) links to the intersection of said westerly boundary line of said Mill slip with the northeasterly boundary line of River street; thence on a course north thirty-three degrees ten minutes west, along said north-easterly boundary line of River street, five (5) chains and seventy-four and two-tenths (74.2) links to a point in said northeasterly line of River street, where the same is intersected by the southerly line of Bridge street, which point is marked by a stone monument erected at the intersection of said lines of said streets; thence on a course north six degrees thirty-six and one-fourth minutes east, across said Bridge street, one (1) chain and three (3) links to the northerly boundary line thereof, and to the point of intersection of the northerly boundary line of Bridge street with the northeasterly line of Canal street; thence on a course north thirty-seven degrees thirty-three and one-half minutes west, and along said northeasterly boundary line of Canal street four (4) chains and eighty-seven (87) links to the intersection of said northeasterly line of Canal street with the southerly line of Falls street; thence on a course north thirty-seven degrees thirty-six and three-fourths minutes west, one (1) chain and eighty-two (82) links across Falls street to the northerly boundary thereof; thence on a course north thirty-seven degrees thirty-six and three-fourths minutes west, and along said north-easterly line of Canal street, one (1) chain and twenty-two (22) links to an angle in said north-easterly line of Canal street; thence on a course north two degrees thirty-eight and one-fourth minutes west, and along the easterly line of Canal street, ten (10) chains and one and eighty-five one-hundredths (1.85) links to the intersection of the easterly line of Canal street with the southerly line of Niagara street; thence on a course south eighty-seven degrees fourteen minutes west, across said Canal street, one (1) chain and fifty and thirty-four one-hundredths (50.34) links to the

Bowen, Low, Lansing, Ellsworth, Baker, Van Schaick, Titus and "Tim" Campbell. Of Assemblymen there were present Mr. Hubbell of Rochester, who fathered the bill in the last Legislature which led to the day's ceremonies; Hon. Jacob L. Miller, who, in 1883, introduced the bill creating the Niagara Park Commission; Hendricks, Kruse, McEwen, Bailey, Scott, Raines, Haskell, Dibble, Connelly, Major Haggerty, General Barnum, Whitmore, Storm, Ely, Secretary of the Senate John W. Vrooman, and Ex-Senators MacArthur and Loomis.

westerly boundary line thereof; thence on a course south two degrees fifty-one minutes east, along said westerly boundary line of Canal street, two (2) chains and sixty-seven and twelve one-hundredths (67.12) links to a point in the westerly line of Canal street, supposed to be the northeasterly corner of Prospect Park (so called); thence on a course south eighty-six degrees nineteen and one-half minutes west, along the north boundary of said Prospect Park, one (1) chain and three (3) links to an angle in said boundary line; thence on a course north fifty-two degrees eighteen minutes west, along said northerly boundary of said Prospect Park, six (6) chains and eighty-five (85) links to the water's edge of the Niagara river; thence along said line prolonged into said river, and on a course north fifty-two degrees eighteen minutes west, more or less, to the boundary line between the United States of America and the Dominion of Canada; thence along said boundary line up the middle of said river to the Great Falls; thence up the falls through the point of the Horse Shoe, keeping to the west of Iris or Goat island and the group of small islands at its head, and following the bends of the river, and along said boundary line to a point at which said boundary line meets, and is intersected by the prolongation of the line running north three degrees forty-nine and one-fourth minutes west, first above mentioned; thence following said line, and on a course north three degrees forty-nine and one-fourth minutes west, more or less, to the point or place of beginning.

Together with all the right, title, and interest of all persons or corporations of, in, and to the premises embraced within said boundary lines, including all water-rights, made-land (so called), débris, titles, or claims (if any) to lands lying under the Niagara river, rights of riparian owners, easements, and appurtenances of every name and nature whatsoever, including all the rights of, in, and to all streets, or portions of streets, embraced and included within said boundary lines.

Of editors and other public men well known "up in the State" there were Carroll E. Smith and W. H. Northrup of Syracuse; S. Callicott and John A. Sleicher of Albany; Willard S. Cobb of Lockport; William Purcell of Rochester; Congressman Wadsworth; Ex-Congressmen Brewer and Van Abram and Solomon Scheu. Of State officials were mentioned Civil Service Commissioner Henry A. Richmond; Professor Gardner of the old State survey; Secretary Carr; Attorney-General O'Brien; Treasurer Maxwell; Engineer Sweet; Insurance Superintendent John A. McCall; and Superintendent of Public Instruction William H. Ruggles. Letters of regret were received from Governor-General Lansdowne of Canada, Samuel J. Tilden, and President Cleveland.

The last admission fee to Prospect Park was collected in the night of July 15, 1885, and a till full of quarters was taken before the gates were thrown open at midnight. The owners of Goat Island left their gates open all night. Everything was free, however, on the 15th and such a company as swarmed over the islands in consequence was never seen before. They crowded the walks and fringed the cliffs and shores at every available point. They recklessly clambered down to the bottom of the Falls and clustered on the ledge of rocks overlooking the Horseshoe and American Falls. Persons who had lived all their lives within twenty miles of the Falls now beheld them for the first time. They brought their luncheons, and when the sun came out they picnicked on the greensward.

The hurdy-gurdy shows which had sprung up like mushrooms within twenty-four hours all over the village were doing a brisk business. The Indian shops also were all open but the other stores and places of business in the village were closed for the day. The air was filled from morning till night with the blare of military bands, the monotonous sound of numberless organs, and the shouts and cries of venders and showmen. Every building in the village was decorated with bunting.

The pavilion in the park was reserved for invited guests and for those who participated in the ceremonies. Near the Governor and his staff sat the Commissioners of the Niagara Park Reservation. Among the distinguished guests were prominent Canadians who took a warm interest in the project of an International Park at Niagara. They were Lieutenant-Governor Robinson, Captain Geddes, and Lieutenant-Colonel Gowski, members of the Niagara Park Association; the Hon. O. S. Hardy, Secretary of Ontario, and the Attorney-General of that Province, the Hon. O. Mowat.

The opening-prayer was offered by the Right-Reverend A. Cleveland Coxe. He was followed by Erastus Brooks, who, in a brief speech, introduced the subject of the day's celebration, and concluded by saying that no better investment had ever been made by any State, corporation, or people, and added that Lord Dufferin had promised that Canada would join in establishing a free park on their own side of the Falls. Great enthusiasm followed, and the whole audience of five thousand people then joined in singing *America*. President Dorsheimer, in behalf of the Commission, then formally presented the Park to the State of New York. After briefly reciting what the Commission had done he said: "From this hour

Niagara Bond and Free

Niagara is free. But not free alone; it shall be clothed with beauty again, and the blemishes which have been planted among these scenes will presently be removed. As soon as the forces of Nature, nowhere more powerful than at this favoured place, can do the work, these banks will be covered with trees, these slopes made verdant, and the Cataract once more clothed with the charms which Nature gave it."

As he concluded the firing of guns signalled to the crowds on the islands and on the Canadian side that Niagara was the possession of the State of New York, and that Governor Hill was about to accept the gift in the name of the people of the State. The Governor was warmly cheered when he stepped forward to speak. He gave a brief sketch of the history of the Falls, and likewise alluded to the opening of the Erie Canal, the laying of the corner-stone of the State's magnificent Capitol at Albany and the opening of the East River bridge. Then he accepted the Park with some appropriate words, concluding as follows: "The preservation of Niagara Park, the greatest of wonders is, indeed, a noble work. Its conception is worthy the advanced thought, the grand liberality, and the true spirit of the nineteenth century."

After this followed the singing of the *Star Spangled Banner*, the audience joining earnestly in the chorus. The oration was delivered by that polished member of the New York Bar, Mr. James C. Carter, giving a full history of the region. The two Canadian officials, Lieutenant-Governor Robinson and Attorney-General Mowat were then introduced, and congratulated the State of New York for the enterprise and public spirit shown by the people and the public officers. The exercise concluded with the Doxology and a benediction. In the afternoon Governor Hill with Generals Jewett and Rogers reviewed the militia. In the evening fireworks were set off from Prospect Park, Goat Island, and the brink of the Falls from the Canadian side. Earlier in the day the Comptroller's check for five hundred thousand dollars was received by the Porter family, the Goat Island property had been transferred to the commissioners, and Niagara was free.

There had been, of course, strong objection on the part of the army of landholders and monopolists who were to be thrown out of their "easy money" livelihoods. Of this the excellent "leader" in the New York *Times* of July 15th deals as follows:

It would be alike idle and unjust to blame the people of Niagara Falls for this state of mind. They have done what the members of any other community would have done in making the most of their neighbourhood as a wonder of nature. Even the obstinate . . . who declines to be bought out, and insists upon his right to make merchandise out of the river, is entitled to respect for the tenacity with which he proposes to resist the acquisition of his property by the State upon the ground that the law authorising the acquisition is unconstitutional.

He would very possibly be willing to acknowledge the right of eminent domain if it were proposed to take his land for a railroad, but the idea that it shall be taken in order that a river . . . shall be kept for dudes to look at undoubtedly strikes him as unmixed foolishness. However excusable this state of mind may have been, nobody who does not own a point of view or at least a hack at Niagara will dispute that its consequences have been deplorable. Though Niagara has continued to be a frequential resort it has by no means been as popular as it would have become with the increasing facilities of travel and the increasing advantages taken of them, if the fame of the gross and petty extortions had not been almost as widely spread as the fame of Niagara itself. While the local monopolies have deterred people from visiting the Falls, they have nevertheless been so lucrative that the most important of them is reported upon the authority of one of its managers to have returned a net annual profit, of thirty thousand dollars, and the report is not incredible, prodigious as the figure seems as a profit upon the mere command of a point of view. This hedging about and looking up of a boon of nature was perhaps the most objectionable incident of the private shore of Niagara. To a tourist who goes to Niagara from any other motive than that of saying that he had been there the importunity to which he had been subjected at every turn was absolutely destructive of the object of his visit. The prosaic and incongruous surroundings of the cataract completed the disillusion which importunity and extortion were calculated to produce. Many tourists would have been glad to pay down, once for all, as much as their persecutors could have reasonably hoped to extract from them for the privilege of being allowed to look without molestation upon the work of nature undisfigured by the handiwork of man. "For many years this has been impossible, and for several years it has been evident that it could be made possible only by the resumption on the part of the State, as a trustee of its citizens and for all mankind, of the ownership and control of the shore. This resumption will be formally made to day. But it was really brought about in the Legislature in the winter of 1884, when the full force of the opposition to the project was brought out and fairly defeated. The State of New York has in effect decided that the preservation of a sublime work of nature under conditions which will enable it to affect men's minds most strongly is an object for which it is worth while to pay the money of the State. It is this emphatic decision which marks a real advance in civilisation over the state of mind of the Gradgrinds of the last generation and of the contemporaneous wood-pulp grinder that the proper function of the greatest waterfall in the world is to turn mill-wheels and produce pennies by being turned into a peep show."

The Reservation forms a beautiful State Park within the growing city of Niagara Falls, N. Y., which lies just back of it numbering now a population of nearly twenty-five thousand people. The city is well laid out, and its promoters "point with pride" to the advances made during the last decade and bespeak for "Industrial Niagara" a future of great distinction in the commercial world.

The first town worthy of the name here on the American side of the Falls was named Manchester by Judge Porter when he settled here in 1806, 102 years ago, believing that the site could eventually be occupied by the "Manchester of America." Judge Porter's many inducements to promoters were not accepted until about the middle of last century (1853) when the present canal was begun. For many years even this improvement lay unused; it was not until 1878 that the present company was organised and any real advance was made. Of the recent wonderful development along power lines at Niagara we treat in another chapter under the title of "Harnessing Niagara Falls." But the supreme interest in these lines of activity must not let us lose sight of the important element of local environment.

It is of almost national interest that Niagara is so centrally located, that within seven hundred miles of this great cataract live two-thirds of the population of the United States and Canada. This of itself, were there no Niagara Falls, would guarantee the growth of the town of Niagara Falls. Add to this strategic location the exceptional advantages to be found here by industrial plants looking for a home, and also the evident fact that Niagara Falls is a delightful spot in which to reside, it is clear that if a great and beautiful city does not develop here in the next century human prophecy will have missed its guess and tons of advertising will have been wasted. Twenty-five million dollars are, it is said, invested in capital now in the present town, and the value of imports and exports in 1906 was over two millions and over twelve millions, respectively. Fourteen railways here find terminals and the town has over one hundred mails daily. With splendid educational advantages, with twenty miles and more of pavement already laid, with a beautiful and efficiently conducted public library, with a city water pumping plant capable of handling twenty million gallons daily, and nearly forty miles of drains, with a citizenship active, patriotic, and capable, is it any wonder that Niagara Falls' real estate agents and suburban resident promoters are thriving like the old cabmen and side-show operators thrived in the "good old days" of private ownership along the Niagara's bank?

There is no discounting the advances this interesting little city has made in the past ten years and more, and there is very little possibility, on the face of things of a tremendously accelerated growth in the coming century. Big problems are here being worked out; big schemes are afoot, big things will happen—an advance will come because of the plain merit of the bare facts of the case without unnecessary inducement or overcapitalisation of the advertising agencies. The world needs power to do its work, and until we sit down calmly and figure out a way for the ocean tides to do our work, as ought in all conscience to be the case to-day, Niagara Falls will hold out extraordinary inducement to all industrial promoters which cannot be rivalled in many ways at any other point. If only the ends of industry can be achieved without destroying this great continental scenic wonder! There are those who are unwilling to take a single rainbow from that ocean of rainbows amidst the Falls to drive another wheel. But there is surely a sane middle ground to be found here, and it is certain that brave, thinking men are on the sure track to find it.

Similar in geographic position, quite as much could be said for Niagara Falls, Ont., as has been said of her twin city on the American shore. In point of beauty nothing can excel the magnificent Queen Victoria Park, opened in 1888, which lies opposite the New York State Reservation; the view of the two falls from it, or from the airy piazzas of the superb Clifton Hotel which flanks it, is unmatched. At present writing the guardians of the New York State Reservation, and other sensitive persons, are justly exercised over a genuine "Yankee trick," more or less connived in, they darkly hint, by the authorities, who have permitted a series of hideous signboards to be erected on the Canadian shore to serve the purpose of bringing out more vividly by contrast the unrivalled beauties of Queen Victoria Park.

Chapter V

Harnessing Niagara Falls

LORD KELVIN, when visiting Niagara Falls, was not moved by that which appeals to the ordinary tourist, the roaring of the cataract, the waters in their mad rush from the Falls to the whirlpool and thence to Lake Ontario, nor the mists rising night and day from the waters churned into foam. For him, Niagara was a monster piece of machinery, accomplishing nothing but the pounding out of its own life on the rocks which formed its bed. In his mind's eye there appeared vast factories, deriving their power from the Falls, furnishing hundreds of men employment and distributing millions of dollars' worth of products to be placed nearer the hands of the poorer classes because of having been created by the cheap power furnished here by nature.

Various estimates have been made regarding the volume of water flowing over the Falls; but the calculations by United States engineers extending over a number of years places the amount at about 224,000 gallons a foot per second. These are the figures taken as the basis of many calculations; upon this basis the Falls would furnish 3,800,000 horse-power exclusive of the rapids. If the fall of about fifty feet which is produced by the rapids in their descent from the Dufferin Islands be added to this amount, the sum total of power would be greatly increased. To make some use of this almost inconceivable amount of power which has been wasting itself for ages has been the problem which has caused much investigation and to-day it seems to be nearing a practical solution.

Niagara Falls were first used as a source of power in 1725, when a primitive saw-mill was built just opposite Goat Island to saw lumber for the construction of Fort Niagara. For years men have made many attempts to use some of the power to be had here for the taking, and in a very small way have been successful. A number of establishments for several decades have been making use of power developed by the Falls by means of the Hydraulic Canal on the American side. This canal was begun in 1853 and passes through the city of Niagara Falls, terminating on the cliff half a mile below the cataract; here are to be found a number of mills, which however utilise only a small fraction of the fall available, probably because at the time of their construction, the high grade water-wheels of to-day were not in existence. Some of the waste water from the tail races of these mills is now being collected into large iron-tubes and is used again by mills situated at the base of the cliff.

In 1885, the late Thomas Evershed, of Rochester, New York, devised a plan for wheel-pits a mile and a half above the Falls. The water was to be conducted to these pits by lateral canals, from which it was to be taken to the river below the Falls by means of a tunnel cut through the solid rock. This plan seemed more practicable than any proposed heretofore, and commanded the attention of many leading engineers of the country. The present great developments at the Falls had their

Bird's-eye View of the Canadian Rapids and Fall.
From a photograph by Notman, Montreal.

American Falls from Below.

Harnessing Niagara Falls

inception in the organisation of the Niagara Falls Power Company. This company obtained a charter from the State of New York in 1886, giving them permission to use water sufficient to generate two hundred thousand horse-power. This company could accomplish very little on account of its limited capital. In a short time, however, New York capitalists and bankers, perceiving the practicability of the company's plans, became interested in the project, and furnished the necessary funds. The first earth was turned for this great work in October 1890 and the tunnel was completed in the autumn of 1893. The first main wheel-pit was ready for its machinery by the following March.

The device for applying Niagara's power to the turbines is on the same principle of construction, in each of the recently erected plants as in this first one. In the case of the Niagara Falls Power Company, a broad deep inlet leads from the river at a point a mile and a half above the American Falls, two thousand feet back in a north-easterly direction. The canal is protected by a lining of heavy masonry, which is pierced at its upper end by a number of gateways; through these water is admitted by short canals to pits emptying into huge steel pipes or penstocks, as they are called. These penstocks terminate at the bottom in wheel boxes, in which are placed the bronze turbine wheels, connected with the surface by means of steel shafts parallel to the penstocks. From the turbine wheels the water whirls and rushes on through a subterranean passage to the main tunnel. Here it starts on its long journey of over a mile under-ground, beneath the heart of the city, until it emerges again at an opening in the cliff just below what is known as the new suspension bridge. A very ingenious plan was adopted for the application of the power to the turbines. The penstocks are brought down under the wheels and are made to discharge their waters upward into the boxes. This contrivance causes the water to bear up the great weight of the wheels, from the bearings beneath for their support, besides that of the hundred and forty feet of shafting connected with the turbines for transmitting power to the surface.

The tunnel which receives these waters after leaving the turbines is no less than six thousand seven hundred feet long, and discharges below the Falls just past the suspension bridge. Its cross-section somewhat resembles a horseshoe in shape, and this sectional area is three hundred and eighty-six square feet throughout, the average height and width being twenty-one and sixteen feet respectively. The company owning the mills connected with this tunnel, together with the Niagara Falls Hydraulic Power and Manufacturing Company, of which mention has been made, are the only ones using water to any great extent on the American side.

On the Canadian side, three great canals are drawing water from the river. It is the construction of these mammoth Canadian power plants, and the devising of means for leading water to the turbines together with the development of a plan for the disposal of the waste water by means of some form of tail race, which must necessarily consist of a monster tunnel broken through the solid rock, which has developed some of the greatest and most unique engineering problems ever before dreamed of, and which has presented a work hazardous and spectacular in the extreme.

Harnessing Niagara Falls

To meet the engineering problems concerned in locating the three Canadian plants along the shore of the river, involving the taking of water by some form of canal, and the disposal of waste water through tunnel or by other means to the lower river, each without interfering with any of the other plants, taxed even Yankee engineering ingenuity. One company had to unwater a considerable area of Niagara River at Tempest Point where the waters have a great depth and the current is of high velocity. From here then a tunnel, the largest in the world, must be broken through solid rock, under the bed of the river, to a point directly behind the great sheet of water plunging over the apex of the V formed by Horseshoe Falls. A second company takes its water through a short canal to its wheel-pits, which are sunk about half a mile above Horseshoe Falls in Queen Victoria Park, discharging it through a tunnel two thousand feet long into the lower river. To find room for the third of these companies was a puzzling problem for some time. Finally the difficulty was solved by a departure from the plan of the other companies, both in the manner of taking water from the river and in the location of the power-house. Instead of locating the wheel-pits above the Falls as in the case of the others, this company has it power-house located in the Gorge below the Falls along the lower level. It takes its water from farther up the river than any of the companies, thus being further removed from any difficulties arising from recession of the Falls besides obtaining the additional power to be given by the descent of the rapids to the crest of the cliff, which amounts to about fifty feet. The water is taken from near the Dufferin Islands through the largest steel conduit in the world, which runs not far from the shore of the river, skirting the other plants, and terminates at the power-house situated in the canyon below the Falls.

It is interesting to visit and survey these hydro-electric power-generating stations, to note the different methods for taking the water from the river and for carrying it to the lower river after having passed through turbine wheels. It is well here to take a brief résumé of the main features connected with the obtaining of this water supply and its disposal. The first American company, that of the Niagara Falls Hydraulic Power and Manufacturing Company, takes its water through a canal from the upper river. This canal passes through the centre of the city of Niagara Falls to the cliff just below the first steel cantilever bridge, the power plant and industries making use of its waters are located here at the top of the cliff. The other American company known as the Niagara Falls Power Company takes its water by a short canal, about a mile above the Falls and discharges the dead water through a tunnel that runs under the city of Niagara Falls to a point near the water's edge in the lower river directly below the first steel bridge. The Canadian Niagara Falls Power Company, allied with the American company, takes its water from Queen Victoria Park and discharges it below the Falls through a two thousand foot tunnel. The Toronto and Niagara Power Company, with its power plant built in the bed of the river near Tempest Point takes water through massive stone forebays in the river and sends it to the lower level through a tunnel beneath the river's bed opening directly behind the V in the Horseshoe Falls. The Ontario Power

Harnessing Niagara Falls

Company takes its water into large steel conduits near Dufferin Islands. These underground pipes conduct the water along the shore of the river to the power house situated on the lower level. The waste water is discharged through draft tubes directly into the river.

With this general picture of these great power companies in mind, it is proper to survey some of the more interesting details of construction which may appeal to individual taste and curiosity. Space forbids entering into the minutia either of construction or machinery used. Only the main principles of interest to the general reader can be touched upon.

Let us descend first into the tunnel under the bed of the river, which discharges the tail water from the power-house of the Toronto Company, hurling it with almost inconceivable fury against the mass of foaming water plunging over the Horseshoe precipice. Here is a sight to thrill even the most jaded traveller hunting for new wonders. A trip through this underground passage which American genius has shot through a mass of solid shale and limestone, beneath the bed of the river, will in itself more than compensate for a trip to Niagara Falls. Some idea of the size of this tunnel is indicated by the fact that two lines of railways were maintained in it to dispose of the rock and shale excavated by the workmen. Clad in rubber coat and boots the visitor to the Falls may wend his way down along the visitors' gallery which is suspended from the roof of the tunnel, one hundred and fifty-eight feet below the river bed, to where the outrushing waters join the great volume of the river in its headlong plunge over Horseshoe Falls. Here standing behind that mighty veil of rushing water, with the spray swept into the opening by furious storms of howling winds, one beholds a spectacle, almost terrifying in its grandeur, the equal of which perhaps can not be found in any of the numerous attractions of the Falls. Before work on the main tunnel was begun, a shaft was sunk on the river bank just opposite the crest of Horseshoe Falls. From this shaft a tunnel was dug to the point where the lower end of the main tunnel would terminate. No difficulties were experienced in the driving of this opening until near the face of the cliff behind Horseshoe Falls. Here, with only fifteen feet to go, water began to rush into the cavern through a fissure in the rocks. The engineers fought against the water for several days but could not stop its flow. Finally eighteen holes were drilled into the cliff between the end of the tunnel and where the final opening was to be made; these holes were loaded with dynamite, which, together with a large charge placed against the end of the passage, was exploded, after the tunnel had been flooded. This only accomplished a part of what was desired. An opening was made in the cliff but too near the roof of the tunnel to allow of any work. What to do now was a difficult problem, but American daring accomplished the work. Volunteers were called for to crawl along the ledge of rock running along the cliff behind the Falls to where the opening had been made. Several men offered to make this almost impossible trip. Lashed together with cords, with the thunder of the Falls in their ears, blinded by spray which was driven into their faces with cyclonic fury, the men at last reached the opening and placed a heavy charge of dynamite against the opposing wall. This was discharged, making a suffi-

Harnessing Niagara Falls

ciently large opening for the water to run out, and the work was continued.

In the design of the main tunnel, ingenious provision was made for recession of the Falls. From the opening in the cliff for three hundred feet the lining will be put in in rings six feet long; this arrangement will allow a joint to drop out whenever the Falls recede so that it is exposed, thus leaving a smooth section always at the end of the tunnel. Through this main tunnel and through the branch races, the water, after having left the turbines, will whirl along at the rate of twenty-six feet per second, having generated a total of 125,000 electric horse-power. In engineering problems connected with the tunnel and the construction of the plant, the work of this company far surpasses that of any of the others. In order to secure a place for the wheel-pit and gathering dam, an area of about twelve acres in the bed of the river was converted into dry land. To do this a coffer dam was constructed 2153 feet in length and from twenty feet to forty-six feet wide in water varying in depth from seven feet to twenty-four feet, besides being very swift in most places. About two thousand feet above the Falls, in the space thus deprived of its water, an immense wheel-pit was sunk into the solid rock. On the bottom of this pit, 150 feet below the surface rest the monster turbines, from which two tail-races conduct the water to the main tunnel. A large gathering dam sufficient to supply the maximum capacity of this plant runs obliquely across the river for a distance of 750 feet. The height of this dam varies from ten to twenty-three feet; it is constructed of concrete, the top being protected by a course of cut granite. The power plant is located on the original shore line and parallel to it in Queen Victoria Park. In the power room are to be found eleven monster generators capable of developing 12,500 horse-power each.

A short distance farther up the river at the Dufferin Islands is the beginning of the mammoth steel conduits of the Ontario Power Company. These pass about a hundred yards from the shore and conduct the water to the power-house situated in the canyon below the Falls. This contrivance for water transmission consists of three steel pipes, the largest in the world, eighteen feet in diameter, and a little over six thousand feet long. This plant has the advantage of the others in several respects. While it draws its water from farther up the river, it preserves it for a longer time from the recession of the Falls, besides securing to it the greater amount of power per volume by obtaining the additional advantage of the descent of the rapids which amounts to about fifty-five feet. The power plant located as it is in the Gorge discharges its waste waters directly into the lower river without the necessity of an intervening tunnel. Lastly, the plan of applying the power to the turbines is slightly different in this case from the others, being made possible by its different plan. Here the turbines are placed vertical instead of horizontal, and are directly connected with the main generators, which are the only machines located on the floor of the station.

A departure from the ordinary construction of the dynamo is noticed in those for use at Niagara. The ordinary one is built with the field-magnets so placed that the armature revolves between them, the field-magnets being stationary. In these monster dynamos,

Harnessing Niagara Falls

developing thousands of horse-power, and weighing many tons, the field-magnets revolve around the armature which remains stationary. With such an enormous weight of swiftly revolving parts, it became necessary to lessen the immense centrifugal force tending to tear the machine to pieces. Engineering skill surmounted this problem as it did all others in what might be called this mighty scientific drama, and, by reversing the parts of the dynamo, secured the desired result. The field-magnets, being placed on the outside and being made the revolving part, by their mutual attraction for its armature within their ring are pulled, as it were, toward the centre, thus lessening the great strain produced by the centrifugal force upon the large steel ring upon whose inner circumference they are mounted.

The currents furnished by the power-houses at Niagara are all alternating. This kind of current being decided upon for various reasons. It can be used for driving dynamos as well as any, and as nearly all the power developed at the Falls is used in this way no provision is made for a direct current. Where a direct current is desired the electricity is made to drive a dynamo of the alternating type which in turn is made to drive another of the kind of current desired. Establishments on or near the grounds use the power furnished them direct from the power-house. When the power must be transmitted to a distance, it becomes necessary to use a step-up transformer for the purpose of losing as little power as necessary in the transmission, this to produce a higher voltage. When the current reaches those places where it is to be used a low voltage is again obtained by the step-down transformer.

Almost, if not quite as interesting as the development of all this power, together with its transmission, are the manufacturing establishments springing up here to take advantage of the great opportunities offered by the harnessing of this mighty cataract. Among those which stretch along the river for several miles are to be found those interested in the manufacture of carborundum, aluminum, carbide, graphite, caustic potash, muriatic acid, emery wheels, railway supplies, hook-and-eye fastenings, and shredded wheat, which are of special interest to the visitor.

Industrialism has seized upon the immense power of Niagara and is now shaping it into commodities for the use of man. Now what is the real menace to the Falls? Many lament the erection of the power plants and manufacturing establishments in the vicinity; but those, at least already in existence, have come to stay. So we may turn our attention from the marring of the surrounding beauty to the Falls themselves.

Geological changes are taking place so slowly that they need not be reckoned with as a probable destroyer of the Falls for ages yet to come. Moreover, their effect is treated in another chapter. The history of the Niagara Falls Hydraulic Power and Manufacturing Company, as a user of power from the Falls, antedates even its legislative recognition. Between the years of 1888 and 1894 nine companies were recognised or chartered in the State of New York. These charters were granted very freely, no revenue was required for the use of the waters, and in some cases no limitation was placed upon the amount to be used. Of these charters, all were granted in good faith; but it is very doubtful if all were received in that spirit. Some of the companies failed to effect an organisation, others offered to sell their rights as soon as obtained. Various limitations were put upon the time in which work must be begun. At least three of the charters have lapsed by their own time limitations, one franchise was sold by its original owners; one other shows at times faint signs of life; another is leading a questionable existence, while two, the Hydraulic Power and Manufacturing Company and the Niagara Falls Power Company, are producing and selling power. To these two organisations are to be credited the great industrial development on the American side and they are not yet using the amount of water allowed them by their charters.

As a result, of course, the flow of water is of smaller volume; but this cannot be perceived by the casual observer. However, citizens of Niagara Falls insist that the decreased flow is manifested in other ways; such as the annual gorging of ice at the head of the American channel almost laying this channel bare and sending its water to the Canadian side. This happens very rarely with a normal depth. Besides this it became necessary not long ago to move the dock at which the *Maid of the Mist* lands, the water line having retreated as a result of decreased volume.

The two American companies are not expecting to diminish their consumption of water in any way. The growing demands for power have caused each continually to enlarge its plants. The Niagara Falls Power Company, realising the great growing demand for cheap power, has obtained a large interest in one of the Canadian companies. The amount of water which may be used by these companies according to charter limits is as follows:

Niagara Falls Hydraulic Power and Manufacturing Co.................... 7,700 cu. ft. per sec.
Niagara Falls Power Company........... 8,600 " " " "

Total.......................16,300 " " " "

The power produced by these companies at present is no fair estimate of the amount of water taken from the river. On the American side, below the steel arch bridge, may be seen what is called the "back yard view of Niagara." Here a number of small cascades are seen spouting from the side of the cliff, only a small part of the fall being utilised by the factories situated there. Some of this water is now being collected into penstocks, to be utilised again at the base of the cliff.

On turning to the three Canadian companies, those of the American side pale beside their gigantic proportions. In contrast with the companies chartered, it may be said that none of these is inactive; on the contrary they are giving the strongest manifestations of energy. Following are the limits to which they may make use of Niagara's waters:

Canadian Niagara Power Co............ 8,900 cu. ft. per sec.
Ontario Power Co..................... 12,000 " " " "
Toronto and Niagara Power Co........ 11,200 " " " "

Total.........................32,100

Adding to this total the charter limits of the two American companies now operating, the grand total is raised to 48,400 cubic feet per second. This of itself is a dry fact and does not form much of a percentage of the

Harnessing Niagara Falls

whole volume going over the Falls. Such a loss would not mean so much if it would manifest itself the same along the whole crest of the line of the cliff; but here must be taken into consideration the configuration of the bed of the river.

The bed of Niagara is composed of rock which dips gradually and uniformly westward. The ledge is ten feet higher on the American side than on the Canadian. The water of the American fall is therefore ten feet shallower. The amount of water going over the Falls has been variously estimated, engineers differing in their conclusions as much as sixty thousand cubic feet per second. Averages based upon the estimates of United States engineers for forty years, of the amount of mean flow of water passing Buffalo from Lake Erie, shows 222,400 cubic feet per second. This of course does not make allowance for that taken by the Welland and the Erie canals. This is probably about equalised by the amount entering the lake and river between this city and the Falls, so that the figures forming the basis of most computations are 224,000 cubic feet per second. The amount of power capable of development by the Falls is about 3,800,000 horse-power, which would be greatly increased by adding the fall from the beginning of the rapids to the crest of the cataract. Goat Island, situated just off the American shore, divides the waters very unevenly, sending more than three-fourths the volume toward the Canadian shore. Now, as has been seen, less than one-fourth the whole volume pours down the American channel; and as this is much shallower than the main body of water, it is here that any diminished flow will be first felt. At the head of the island the great body of the current turns toward the west, by far the larger amount converging into the funnel of the magnificent Horseshoe Falls. The American channel in contrast contains a very feeble flow, and therefore would be the first to exhibit any dearth of water. Calculations based upon the preceding figures, taking into consideration the length of the Falls, and the difference in elevation of the river's bed at the crest, show that when the flow has been reduced by 184,000 cubic feet per second, or by 40,000 cubic feet, the water in the American channel will be brought down to the rock bottom of the shore's edge. Then, although the Horseshoe Falls will continue to be an object of admiration to the traveller, and although the current will continue to sweep through the American channel and over the American Falls, the beauty and grandeur of the latter will fade away. Let the amount of water abstracted from the river be doubled, and, though the Canadian Falls would still continue an object of admiration, the American channel would be entirely dry.

Returning to the present and immediately contemplated draft upon the river's waters, we find that the two American and the three Canadian companies, when using their charter limits, will take 48,000 cubic feet per second. This will bring the level at the crest of the Falls down to the bottom of the river at the American shore. This, then, is the immediate prospect. Many things may intervene before this point is reached. We are not permitted to stop, however, with the consideration of these five companies alone. One of the last organisations chartered by the State of New York to obtain water from Niagara is the Niagara Lockport and Ontario Power Company. In 1894, this company obtained a franchise placing no restriction upon the amount of water to be used, and limited to ten years in which to begin work. In 1904, they came again to the Legislature, asking for an improved charter in several respects, especially a lengthening of time in which to begin operations. This company proposed to take water from near La Salle and not to return it to the river at all, but to take it overland by canal to Lockport and then empty it directly into Lake Ontario. The bill providing for this charter passed both houses, but it was vetoed by Governor Odell. The veto took place on May 15, 1904. The original charter was granted on May 21, 1894. Six days of grace yet remained of the ten years allowed the company. There is said to be a slender, shallow ditch south of Lockport, which represents the work done in the six days left. It has been rumoured that the most of this company's stock has passed into the hands of a great corporation. Undoubtedly, under some form of reorganisation, there will, in the near future, be an attempt on the part of its members to gain a share of the great free power of Niagara. Under the old charter, which does not limit the amount of water to be consumed, it will probably not consume less than the other large companies, say 10,000 cubic feet per second.

But the only danger to the life of the Falls is not to be found alone in the Niagara power companies. Six hundred miles to the west is the Chicago Main Drainage Canal, which at first took from the Lakes about three thousand cubic feet per minute. Many propositions have been made to enlarge this canal. These are fraught with taxing engineering problems; but it is difficult to say just what the future has in store in this line. This, however, is not all; Canada, in the hope of gaining part of the commerce of the Great Lakes for the St. Lawrence, has proposed a canal by way of Georgian Bay and the Ottawa River, thus shortening the lake route by five hundred miles. To these may be added propositions for a deep-water connection between the Lakes and the Hudson, between Lake Winnipeg and Lake Superior, between Toronto and Lake Huron, the demands of Cincinnati and Pittsburg for canals, Wisconsin's desire for a canal connecting the Lakes through her territory with the Mississippi, the plan for a canal from Duluth to the Mississippi; and one may see with what danger this great natural wonder is threatened. Many of these proposed plans, doubtless, will never be realised; some on account of engineering difficulties, others on account of the failure of their projectors to count upon the true relation between cost of construction and what would likely be the revenue obtained. All these subjects, however, must be given due consideration by one who desires to know what is considered to be the immediate danger to the Falls, or that which may effect them at no very distant future date.

On January 18, 1907, Secretary of War Taft rendered a decision under the Burton Act for the preservation of Niagara Falls on the applications of American companies for the use of water and of Canadian companies wishing to send electric power into the United States, and at the same time announced the appointment of a commission to beautify the vicinity of the Falls. The amount of water allowed to companies in New York is practically that now used, and substantially as limited by the Act of Congress as a

Harnessing Niagara Falls

maximum. The Secretary found no evidence that the flow over the American Falls has been injuriously affected in recent years. The claims of the Canadian companies, acting in conjunction with electric companies on this side of the river, had to be materially cut down to come within the law limiting the total current to 160,000 horse-power. The allotments in electric horse-power to be transmitted to the United States are as follows:

The International Railway Company, 1500. (8000 asked).

The Ontario Power Company, 60,000 (90,000 asked).

The Canadian Niagara Falls Power Company, 52,500 (121,500 asked).

The Electrical Development Company, 46,000 (62,000 asked).

All these permits are revocable at pleasure, and, in the absence of further legislation in Congress, will expire on June 29, 1909.

In the course of his decision, after discussing the intent of the law, Mr. Taft says:

> Acting upon the same evidence which Congress had, and upon the additional statement made to me at the hearing by Dr. John M. Clark, state geologist of New York, who seems to have been one of those engaged from the beginning in the whole movement for the preservation of Niagara Falls, and who has given close scientific attention to the matter, I have reached the conclusion that with the diversion of 15,600 cubic feet on the American side and the transmission of 160,000 horse-power from the Canadian side the scenic grandeur of the Falls will not be affected substantially or perceptibly to the eye.
> With respect to the American Falls, this is an increase of only 2500 cubic feet a second over what is now being diverted

and has been diverted for many years, and has not affected the Falls as a scenic wonder.

With respect to the Canadian side, the water is drawn from the river in such a way as not to affect the American Falls at all, because the point from which it is drawn is considerably below the level of the water at the point where the waters separate above Goat Island, and the Waterways Commission and Dr. Clark agree that the taking of 13,000 cubic feet from the Canadian side will not in any way affect or reduce the water going over the American Falls. The water going over the Falls on the Canadian side of Goat Island is about five times the volume of that which goes over the American Falls, or, counting the total as 220,000 cubic feet a second, the volume of the Horseshoe Falls would be about 180,000 cubic feet. If the amount withdrawn on the Canadian side for Canadian use were 5000 cubic feet a second, which it is not likely to be during the three years' life of these permits, the total to be withdrawn would not exceed ten per cent. of the volume of the stream, and, considering the immense quantity which goes over the Horseshoe Falls, the diminution would not be perceptible to the eye.

Taking up first the application for permits for diversion on the American side, there is not room for discussion or difference. The Niagara Falls Power Company is now using about 8600 cubic feet of water a second and producing about 76,630 horse-power. There is some question as to the necessity of using some water for sluicing. This must be obtained from the 8600 cubic feet permitted, and the use of the water for other purposes when sluicing is being done must be diminished. The Niagara Falls Hydraulic Power and Manufacturing Company is now using 4000 cubic feet a second and has had under construction for a period long antedating the Burton Act a plant arranged to divert 2500 cubic feet a second and furnish 36,000 horse-power to the Pittsburg Reduction and Mining Company. A permit will therefore issue to the Niagara Falls Hydraulic Power and Manufacturing Company for the diversion of 6500 cubic feet a second, and the same rule must obtain as to sluicing, as already stated.

As the object of the act is to preserve the scenic beauty

The Riverside at Willow Island.

Goat Island Bridge, Showing Niagara's Famous Cataract and International Hotels.

of Niagara Falls, I conceive it to be within my power to impose conditions upon the granting of these permits, compliance with which will remedy the unsightly appearance that is given the American side of the canyon just below the falls on the American side, where the tunnel of the Niagara Falls Power Company discharges and where the works of the hydraulic company are placed.

The representative of the American Civic Association has properly described the effect upon the sightseer of the view toward the side of the canyon to be that of looking into the back yard of a house negligently kept. For the purpose of aiding me in determining what ought to be done to remove this eyesore, including the appearance of the buildings at the top, I shall appoint a committee consisting of Charles F. McKim, Frank D. Millet, and F. L. Olmsted to advise me what changes, at an expense not out of proportion to the extent of the investment, can be made which will put the side of the canyon at this point from bottom to top in natural harmony with the Falls and the other surroundings, and will conceal, as far as possible, the raw commercial aspect that now offends the eye. This consideration has been in view in the construction of works on the Canadian side and in the buildings of the Niagara Falls Power Company, above the Falls. There is no reason why similar care should not be enforced here.

Water is being withdrawn from the Erie Canal at the lake level for water-power purposes, and applications have been made for permits authorising this. Not more than four hundred cubic feet are thus used in the original draft of water that is not returned to the canal in such a way as not to lower the level of the lake. The water is used over and over again. It seems to me that the permit might very well be granted to the first user. As the water is taken from the canal, which is state property, and the interest and jurisdiction of the federal government grow out of the direct effect upon the level of the lake, the permit should recite that this does not confer any right upon a consumer of the water to take the water from the canal without authority and subject to the conditions imposed by the canal authorities, but that it is intended to operate and its operation is limited to confer, so far as the federal government is concerned and the Secretary of War is authorised, the right to take the water and to claim immunity from any prosecution or legal objection under the fifth section of the Burton Act.

When Sir Hiram S. Maxim, the distinguished inventor and scientist, made his recent announcement to Peter Cooper Hewitt that the next great achievement of science would be the harnessing of the whole energy of Niagara and the sending of a message to Mars, he hit the nail, in the opinion of Nikola Tesla, squarely on the head.

Mr. Tesla announces that with the co-operation of power-producing companies at Niagara Falls he is preparing to hail Mars with Niagara's voice. A way has been found at last for transmitting a wireless message across the gulf, varying from 40,000,000 to 100,000,000 miles, which separates this earth from Mars. Once that has been accomplished and Mars, which is considerably older and supposedly more advanced in science than we, has acknowledged the receipt of our signal and sent back flash for flash, it will remain to devise an interplanetary code through the medium of which the scientists of this world and of Mars will be able to understand what each is saying to the other.

Mr. Tesla has been quietly working for several years on a wireless power plant capable of transmitting 10,000 horse-power to any part of the world, or to any of our neighbouring planets, for that matter. The mere matter of distance between despatching and receiving points is absolutely no object whatever. Wireless power, Mr. Tesla says may be sent one million or more miles just as easily as one mile.

Harnessing Niagara Falls

Several of the electric power companies with immense generating plants at Niagara Falls, it is reported, have agreed to co-operate with Mr. Tesla in an effort to reach Mars by wireless.

The development of the hydraulic power of Niagara on the Canadian side is leading to some interesting sequences.

A tribunal called the hydro-electric power commission has been created [says a writer in a recent issue of *Cassier's Magazine*], and in the hands of this body has been placed the entire domestic regulation of the power product of stations coming within government control.

In addition there has been given to the various municipalities the right to undertake the distribution of electrical energy within their respective limits.

In order that the commission may be in a position to dictate terms to the existing private companies it is important that the co-operation of the municipalities be obtained, and this appears to be partially accomplished.

The city of Toronto has already arranged for 15,000 horse-power of electric energy from Niagara, the price being $14 to $16 per horse-power for a supply for a 24-hour day, including transmission to Toronto, the local distribution to be in the hands of the municipality, and it is believed that a number of other cities and towns will make similar arrangements.

These arrangements are made with the hydro-electric power commission, and it in turn must either secure the power supply from the existing private companies or else proceed to develop its own stations.

It is hardly probable that the latter alternative will be found necessary, since the result would be to leave the private corporations with the greater part of their prospective custom permanently taken away, so that the real consequence of the recent legislation is to compel the companies to supply the municipalities through the commission at prices determined by the engineers of the new body.

It is possible that such measures will prove advantageous to the public, but much will depend upon the manner in which the law is carried out. It has been intimated that this legislation will render it exceedingly difficult for promoters to induce outside capital to engage in the development of natural resources in Canada hereafter.

Chapter VI

A Century of Niagara Cranks

THE swirling waters of Niagara have ever been a challenge to a vast army of adventurers who found in their own daring heedlessness a means here of gaining money and a mushroom glory. Of all these "Niagara Cranks," as they are known locally, the tight-rope walkers undoubtedly have the strongest claim to our admiration for the utter daring of their feats, however mercenary may have been the motives. "Tut, tut! my friends," would reply one of these brave, popular heroes if you had mentioned fear, "'t is nothing at all"; then, confidentially, he would have whispered in your ear: "You can't help getting across. You get out to the middle of the rope, and there you are. If you turn back you lose your money, and if you go on you get it. That's all."

It was the great Blondin who stands king of the tight-rope walkers of Niagara, leaving behind him a reputation as the greatest tight-rope walker of the century.

Charles Emile Gravelet was born at Hesdin, near Calais, on the twenty-eighth of February, 1824, and died in Ealing, near London, February 22, 1897. His father, whose nickname, "Blondin," from the colour of his hair, descended to his son, was a soldier of the First Empire who had seen service under Napoleon at

Austerlitz, Wagram, and Moscow, but died when his son was in his ninth year. The pluck and strength that young Blondin had was displayed as early as his fourth year; when only a few years older he was trained by the principal of *l'École de Gymnase* at Lyons in many gymnastic feats, and after six months there, was brought out as "The Little Wonder." He excelled especially at tight-rope dancing, jumping, and somersault-throwing. One of his notable jumps was over a double rank of soldiers with bayonets fixed. The agent of an American Company—the Ravels—aware of his success in the French provinces finally gave him a two years' engagement for the United States, which afterwards was extended to eight years. He came to America in 1855; and it was not long after, when looking across the Niagara Falls, that he remarked to Mr. Ravel:

"What a splendid place for a tight-rope performance."

The idea was impressive and as a result, after laborious preparations, Blondin was ready to cross a wire, June 30, 1859. Despite the unanimous howl of derision at the idea, people could not resist the temptation to see the rash performer throw his life away; and the crowd that gathered was the largest ever seen at the Falls. It is interesting, from more than one standpoint, to quote the New York *Herald* of July 1, 1859, on the exploit:

Monsieur Blondin has just successfully accomplished the feat of walking across the Niagara on a tight rope, in the presence of a crowd variously estimated at from five thousand to ten thousand persons. He first crossed from the American side, stopping midway to refresh himself with water raised in a bottle

A Century of Niagara Cranks

with a rope from the deck of the steamer *Maid of the Mist*. The time occupied in the first crossing was seventeen minutes and a half. The return from the British to the American side was accomplished in twelve minutes.

According to other sources, the crowd was estimated at fifty thousand. Blondin did considerably more than merely pass over, for he carried a pole weighing forty pounds, and did some extraordinary feats of balancing and came ashore amid the huzzas of the crowd, with the whole country ringing with the news of the daring exploit.

Some little difficulty was always encountered by tight-rope walkers from proprietors of the river banks where the rope was to be attached on their theory that nothing could be allowed to occur at Niagara of a money-making nature unless they were a party to the plunder. One Hamblin stood surety for the payment for Blondin's rope, which was over fifteen hundred feet long and cost thirteen hundred dollars.

A few months later Blondin carried his manager, Harry Colcourt or Colcord, across on his back. It is said (and also has been denied) that on this occasion Blondin had a quarrel with Colcord. The latter had previously been trained to balance himself in order that he might be let down on the rope in the middle of the river, to permit Blondin to take breath. The wind was strong, and the manager showed visible signs of nervousness, while the rope swayed in a sickly manner. Then, according to the story, Blondin threatened to leave his manager on the rope at the mercy of the waters underneath, unless he kept himself under control. Needless to say, the threat was successful, and the trip across was safely made. For this special feat Blondin received a gold medal from the inhabitants of the village, as a tribute of admiration, with the following inscription:

> Presented to Mons. T. F. Blondin by the citizens of Niagara Falls in appreciation of a feat never before attempted by man, but by him successfully performed on the 19th of August, 1859, that of carrying a man upon his back over the Falls of Niagara on a tight rope.

Of the ordinary run of mortals few would care to attempt Blondin's feat, but it is not impossible that many an actor envied the daring athlete's position of utter mastery over his manager.

A few days later the fearless Blondin again crossed the river chained hand and foot. On his return he carried a cooking stove and made an omelet which he lowered to the passengers on the deck of the *Maid of the Mist* below. At another time he crossed with a bushel basket on each foot, and once carried a woman on his back. On September 8, 1860, Blondin performed before the Prince of Wales, now Edward VII., the rope being stretched 230 feet above the rapids, between two of the steepest cliffs on the river. The cool actor turned somersaults before His Royal Highness, and successfully managed to cross on a pair of stilts. The Prince watched every movement through a telescope and was highly interested, but it is reported that he exclaimed, when Blondin safely reached the end of the rope, "Thank God, he is over!" and hurried him a check for the perilous feat.

Apparently Blondin did not know what nervousness meant; his secret has been described as confidence in himself, obtained by long practice in rope-walking.

There is no doubt some of the victims he has carried across his rope have suffered; it is said that Blondin would talk to his companions on the most indifferent subjects; he would urge them to sit perfectly still, avoid catching him around the neck or looking downward. What he considered as one of his greatest feats was in walking on a rope from the mainmast to the mizzen on board the Peninsular and Oriental steamer *Poonah*, while on her way to Australia, between Aden and Galle, in 1874. He had to sit down five times while heavy waves were approaching the ship. Blondin's last performance was in Agricultural Hall, London, on Christmas, 1894, where he appeared as active and nimble as ever. The fact is certainly wonderful that for nearly seventy years he walked the tight rope without accident.

Mr. W. D. Howells was an eye-witness to three crossings of Blondin's in 1860, which he has graphically described:

> The man himself looked cool and fresh enough but I, who was not used to such violent fatigues as he must have undergone in these three transits, was bathed in a cold perspiration, and so weak and worn with making them in sympathy that I could scarcely walk away.
>
> Long afterwards I was telling about this experience of mine—it was really more mine than Blondin's—in the neat shop of a Venetian pharmacist, to a select circle of the physicians who wait in such places in Venice for the call of their patients. One of these civilised men, asked: "Where was the government?" And I answered in my barbarous pride of our individualism: "The government had nothing to do with it. In America the government has nothing to do with such things." But now I think that this Venetian was right, and that such a show as I have tried to describe ought no more to have been permitted than the fight of a man with a wild beast. It was an offence

to morality, and it thinned the frail barrier which the aspiration of centuries has slowly erected between humanity and savagery.

Enough savage criticism met Blondin in England; his rope-walking in Crystal Palace, Sydenham, upon a rope 240 feet long and at a height of 170 feet, in imitation of the Niagara feat, was considered a sickening spectacle. Said *Once a Week:*

> We wish Mr. Blondin no sort of harm, but if his audiences were to dwindle down to nothing, so as to cause him to retire upon his savings, we should congratulate him upon having escaped a great danger, and the country upon getting rid of a disgrace to the intelligence of the age.

Blondin ended his career as an English country gentleman at Niagara House, South Haling. He was wont to display a profusion of diamond rings and studs, all gifts of admirers, and the cherished gold medal from the citizens of Niagara Falls; he, too, was the proud possessor of one of the two gold medals struck in commemoration of the Crystal Palace in 1854, Queen Victoria having the other. He had also the cross from ex-Queen Isabel of Spain, entitling him to the title of Chevalier. The athlete's baggage, when on a tour, consisted of a main rope of eight hundred feet, six and a half inches in circumference, and weighing eight hundredweight; twenty-eight straining ropes, eighty tying-bars, the average weight, not including poles, being five and a half tons. The freight of his outfit, including a huge travelling-tent, which could encompass fourteen thousand people, amounted to five thousand dollars between Southampton and Melbourne. About three days were consumed in making his preparations by the aid of a dozen assistants. The due adjustment of the rope was his principal care, and he superintended every detail.

Like many a Frenchman, Blondin never mastered the intricacies of the English language. In a rather queer and rambling fragment of autobiography written some years ago, he tells us that the rope he generally used was formed with a flexible core of steel-wire covered with the best manila-hemp, about an inch or three quarters in diameter, several hundred yards in length, and costing about fifteen hundred dollars. A large windlass at either end of the rope served to make it taut, while it was supported by two high poles. His balancing poles of ash wood varied in length and were of three sections, and weighed from thirty-seven to forty-seven pounds. He was indifferent as to the height at which he was to perform. Blondin has never confessed to any nervousness on the rope, and, while walking, he generally looked eighteen or twenty feet ahead, and whistled or hummed some snatch of a song. The time kept by a band frequently aided him in preserving his balance. He was something of both carpenter and blacksmith, and was able to make his own models and fit up his own apparatus.

While Blondin yet performed at the Falls there appeared Signor Farini in 1860, and stretched a cable across the Gorge near the hydraulic canal basin. On August 8, 1864, Farini reappeared walking about the Rapids above the American fall on stilts. He was certainly an expert on the rope and commanded much attention, but he was not able to snatch the laurel from the Frenchman's brow—he has been forgotten, while Blondin's fame has lived. We must, however, chronicle a thrilling incident attached to his performance in 1864. Between Robinson's Island and the precipice Farini was suddenly delayed. He claimed his stilts caught in a crevice. His brother succeeded in reaching a log between the old paper-mill and Robinson's Island, from which he threw a line, with a weight attached, to the adventurer, and by this line a pail of provisions was sent to Farini. A larger line was thrown and both reached shore by way of Goat Island.

There has hardly been a year in which some tight-rope exhibition has not taken place at Niagara Falls.

Harry Leslie crossed the Gorge on a rope-cable in July and August, 1865. He achieved the title of "The American Blondin."

In 1873, when Signor Balleni (Ballini?) stretched a cable from a point opposite the old Clifton House to Prospect Park, he leaped three times into the river as an extra inducement, aided in his descent by a rubber cord. In 1886 he reappeared, climbed to the iron railing on the upper suspension bridge, knocked the ice from under his feet to secure a footing, and at the signal of a pistol shot jumped into the air. He struck the water in four seconds, broke a rib, lost his senses, and came to the surface some sixty feet from where he entered. This was the same man who jumped from Hungerford Bridge, London, in 1888, and was drowned. In July, 1876, Signorina Maria Spelterini crossed the Gorge on a tight-rope with baskets on her feet. The performance brought out a tremendous crowd, probably because she was the first woman daring to try conclusions with Blondin and his many imitators. She got across safely with her baskets and her name. She won great favour and forever established the fact that

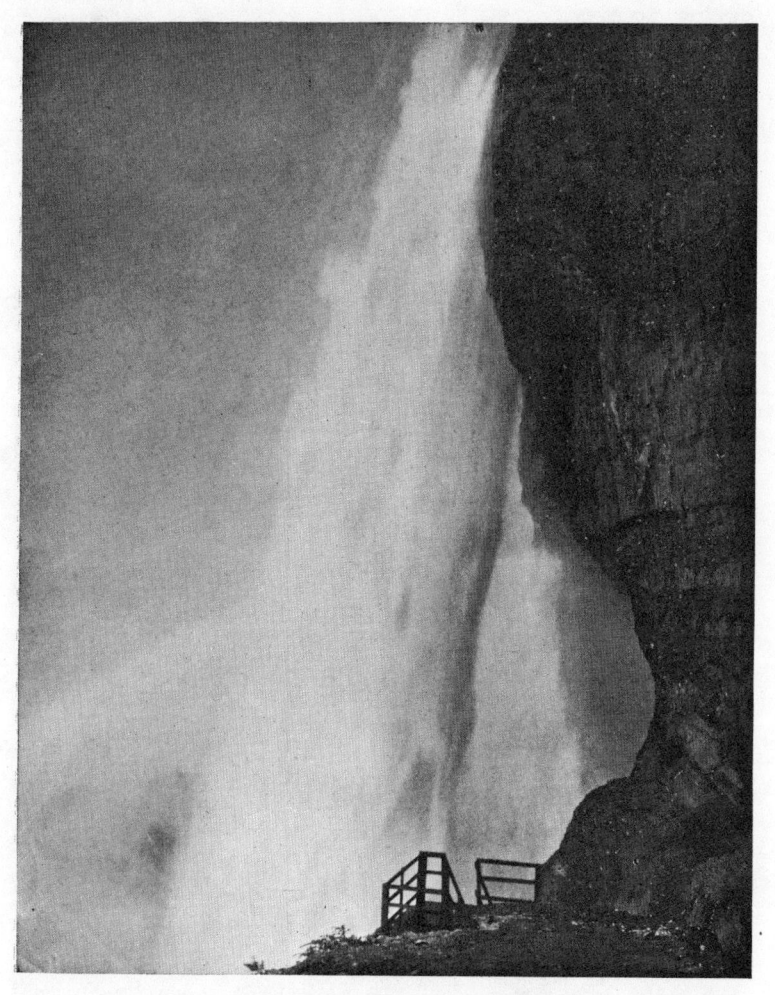

The Path to the Cave of the Winds.
From a photograph by Notman, Montreal.

American Falls from Goat Island.

A Century of Niagara Cranks 131

a woman is as level-headed as a man. In the seventies of the last century, a young fellow, Stephen Peere, a painter by trade, stretched a cable across the Falls. In 1878 he gave variety to his career by jumping from one of the bridges, and in 1887 he finished it by jumping to his death. He had previously, on June 22, 1887, walked across the Gorge on a wire cable six-eighths of an inch in diameter. This was a wonderful performance, considering the fact that all the others had used a rope two inches in diameter. Only three days later he was found dead on a bank beneath his rope, stretched between the old suspension and the cantilever bridges. It is supposed he attempted to practise in night time, but as nobody saw him he met his fate; this is only supposition. A man, "Professor" De Leon, aspiring to become Peere's successor, started out on August 15, 1887, to cross the latter's cable. After going a short distance he became frightened, slid down a rope, and disappeared in the bushes. He was later seen ascending the bank by a ladder, and thus came back to the bosom of his family. MacDonald made several very creditable attempts, and proved himself an excellent walker. He also went across with baskets on his feet, and frightened the gaping crowd by hanging with his legs from the wire, head downwards.

Another freak, I. F. Jenkins, stretched his cable across the Gorge over the Rapids. With a keen eye for effect and sensation he selected as one of his principal feats, crossing by velocipede. The machine, however, was specially constructed for this purpose; it was a turned-down contrivance, only resembling a bicycle, and had an ingeniously devised balancing apparatus in lieu of a pole attached by a metal framework to the wheels. Thus this *pièce de résistance* was not so remarkable after all. Samuel John Dixon, a Toronto photographer, was on his way to a Photographers' Annual Convention when he observed Peere's cable still stretched across the Rapids of Niagara. He remarked that he too could cross on it, but the remark was not taken seriously; to prove that he was in earnest, Dixon, on his return, actually made the dangerous trip on the three-quarter inch cable, measuring 923 feet in length. One of this amateur's crack feats was laying down with his back on the wire. He has made several other passages since,—the first occurring on September 6, 1890—always with great *éclat*. Dixon has always been vigorously applauded. James E. Hardy has also successful crossings at the Gorge to his credit. He also holds the "record" of being the youngest man that ever performed the feat. Another Toronto man, Clifford M. Calverley, has been styled "The World's Champion," and "The American Blondin," but although very clever, many of his feats are just those which made the Frenchman famous over forty years ago. His wheelbarrow feat is certainly middle-aged although it still remains as difficult to perform as it was in Blondin's days. People never tire of it and Calverley was, indeed, a remarkable gymnast. He erected a wire cable at about the same point between the bridges at which Peere and Dixon had crossed, and gave public exhibitions on October 12, 1892, and July 1, 1893. He performed numerous stunning feats as high-kicking, walking with baskets on his feet, cooking meals on the rope, and chair-balancing; he also gave night exhibitions, which was original.

One man at least took the tight-rope route across

Niagara who had not practised the feat. This was a criminal who escaped his captors near this locality in 1883; the sheriff was behind him, the river in front, and only the wires of the old bridge at Lewiston to help him across. Hand over hand he began the passage. His hands quickly blistered, and then they bled. Again and again he rested his arms by hanging by his legs, and at last reached the opposite bank where he lay panting fully an hour before he continued his flight.

We have seen that all the tight-rope walkers at Niagara met with extraordinary luck while crossing the Gorge; in fact, we have no record that anybody ever lost his life while performing on the wire. Peere met with an accident, and was killed in night-time; it is said he was intoxicated and tried to cross with his boots on. Ballini met his death in the Thames River. Many lives, however, have been lost in attempting to brave the waters of the canyon at Niagara.

Attracted by the sensational setting adrift of the condemned brig *Michigan* over the Falls in 1829, Sam Patch, a man who had won fame at Pawtucket Falls and other Eastern points as a high-jumper, erected a ladder on the foot-path under Goat Island, and announced to the world that he would jump into Niagara River. The hotel keepers patted him on the back, and left no stone unturned to enable him to draw the biggest crowd of the season. Patch rested the bottom of his ladder on the edge, just north of the Biddle Stairs, with the top inclining over the river, staying it with ropes to the trees on the bank. At the top was a small platform, and from this Patch dived ninety-seven feet; he jumped a second time to prove that the first feat was not a fluke. Shortly afterwards he leaped to his death from the Genesee Fall in Rochester, N. Y.

Captain Matthew Webb, of Niagara fame, was born in Shropshire, England, in 1840. He went to sea at an early age and became captain of a merchantman, and first attracted notice by jumping from a Cunard steamer to save a man who had fallen overboard, for which he was awarded a gold medal by the Royal Humane Society. In 1875 he accomplished the feat of swimming the English Channel from Dover to Calais, a distance of twenty-five miles.

The disastrous attempt to swim the rapids at Niagara took place on July 2, 1883. Webb wore no life preserver and scorned a barrel, depending solely on his own strength to put him through. Leaving his hotel, the old Clifton House, since destroyed by fire, at 4 P.M., before an immense crowd on the cliffs and bridges (for the event had been well heralded), he entered a small boat with Jack McCloy at the oars, and was carried to a point on the lower river several hundred feet above the lower bridges. It was 4.25 when, clad in a pair of red trunks, he leaped from the boat into the water, and boldly swam towards the Rapids. It was 4.32 when he passed under the bridges. He then stroked out gracefully and beautifully. In three minutes more he had reached the fiercest part of the Rapids when a great wave struck him—and he disappeared from the sight of the thousands of eyes that watched the boiling waters, praying that his life might be spared. He came once again into view but then disappeared forever in the raging waters.

The *Saturday Review* of July 28, 1883,[1] voiced the British feeling when it said:

> It was unquestionably very appropriate that Mr. Webb should have met his death in America, and in sight of the United States. That country has a passion for big shows, and has now been indulged in the biggest thing of its kind which has been seen in this generation. Nothing was to be gained by success—if success had been possible—beyond a temporary notoriety and the applause of a mob. . . .
> As long as there is a popular demand for these essentially barbarous amusements, men and women will be found who are desperate, or greedy, or vain enough to risk their lives and ruin their health for money or applause. . . . The death of Mr. Webb is shocking in the last degree; but it will not be wholly useless if it at least awakens the sight-seeing world to some sense of what it is they have been encouraging.

It is interesting to compare this just criticism with that passed on Blondin's exhibition at Crystal Palace previously quoted.

When Webb swam across the channel, the feat was a remarkable instance of strength and endurance. It showed that a powerful man who was a good swimmer could continue to make progress through the water on a very fine day for over twenty hours. Indeed, shipwrecked sailors have done nearly as much under far less favorable circumstances; but as far as it went, Webb's was a very creditable performance. But in the Channel many vessels were following him and would have picked him up the moment he became exhausted. Yet it was nowise to his credit to throw his life away at Niagara, and render his children orphans, for the ignoble object of pleasing a mob.

It was not long before another swimmer appeared

[1] Vol. lvi., p. 106, seq.

who wore a harness over his shoulders to which was attached a wire running loosely over a cylinder on the bridge, which kept his feet straight towards Davy Jones's locker; he survived the leap to his considerable personal profit. From bridge to water he went in four seconds—the only time on record. Another foolhardy feat was performed by some of the reckless men who decorate almost inaccessible landscapes with possibly truthful but most annoying, puffs of ague-pills, liver-pads, tooth-powder, and such. A log once lodged forty rods above Goat Island, where for four years it lay seemingly beyond human reach. It touched the pride of certain shameless and professional advertisers, who were famous for their ingenious vandalism, that such a chance should be wasted. So, when the Rapids were thinly frozen over, they made their cautious way to the log, and soon there was a gorgeous sign fixed, twelve feet by four, on the very fore-front of one of the world's grandest spots, to-wit:

GO EAST VIA LAKE WINIPISEOGEE R. R.'

Nothing daunted by the sad fate of Captain Webb, a burly Boston policeman, W. I. Kendall, went through the Rapids on August 22, 1886, protected by only a cork life-preserver. All previous trips had been publicly announced, but Kendall slipped through with only a few spectators, accidentally on the cliffs or bridges, to bear witness. For this reason some have felt that the trip was never made, but men of integrity are known who witnessed the performance. On Sunday, August 14, 1887, "Professor" Alphonse King crossed the river below the Falls and bridge on a water bicycle. The wheel with paddles was erected between two water-tight cylinders, eight inches in diameter and ten feet long.

"Steve" Brodie, who had achieved great notoriety by jumping from Brooklyn Bridge, created a greater sensation by going over the Falls. This occurred on September 7, 1889. Brodie wore an india-rubber suit, surrounded by thick steel bands. The suit was very thickly padded, yet Brodie was brought ashore bruised and insensible. His victories won, he became the proprietor of a Bowery bar-room, and the pride of the neighbourhood.

The cranks that were trying to get through the Whirlpool did not arrive at Niagara until about 1886, but from that on we find an *embarras de richesse* of them for a decade or so until the peculiar mania for notoriety died out.

The fate that befell Webb could not discourage others to venture the perilous trip, and, probably, the pioneer of them was C. D. Graham, an English cooper of Philadelphia, who conceived the idea that, though no regular boat could live in the rush of the waters below the Falls of Niagara, it would perhaps be possible for a novel kind of boat, a cask shaped like a buoy, with a man in it, to get down to Lewiston in safety. He therefore made a series of such casks at an expenditure of a great deal of time and labour; and, at last finding a shape to his mind, filled two or three in succession with bags of sand equal to his own weight, and set them afloat at Niagara. They arrived safely in smooth water, threading the Rapids and the Whirlpool after a journey of some five miles; the inventor thereupon resolved to keep one side uppermost, in which was left an air-hole, and fastened in the cask a long canvas bag, made like a suit of clothes, and waterproof. Getting into this bag on July 11, 1886, he grasped two iron handles fixed to the staves on the inner side of the cask; a movable cover being fastened on, the odd craft was shoved into the rushing waters. The cask, of course, turned over and over; and though water got into the air-hole, it did not get into the canvas bag; the surging waters handled the cask so roughly that Graham straightway fell sick, but clung to his iron staples, and in a space of time exceeding thirty minutes—accounts differ here—reached smooth water at Lewiston, five miles away, and was safely taken out, able to boast that he had performed a feat hitherto deemed impossible.

His record trip in a cask was made on August 19, 1886. On this occasion he announced that he would make the trip with his head protruding from the top of the barrel. This was actually done; he went as far as the Whirlpool, but it left him very little hearing, for a big wave gave him a furious slap on the side of the head. Graham made other trips in 1887 and 1889, and his last, probably, in 1901. This nearly ended his life, as he was caught in an eddy where he was held for over twenty minutes; when he finally reached the Whirlpool and was taken out he was nearly suffocated.

Graham's performances, possibly, were also of some practical value. It was proven to the observant that a particular shape of cask might, under certain conditions, be used to draw feeble or sickly passengers from a wrecked ship in bad weather, for a woman or a child could have lived in Graham's machine as well as the cooper himself; however, the circumstances are few under which it would be useful, and Graham, by his own account, had no idea of applying his contrivance in any such way.

It is a question whether the barrel-cranks made any money by their foolhardy feats. That nothing interests callous men like the risk of a human life is undoubtedly true and has been proved by the whole history of amusement. The interest must depend on sight. Nobody would pay merely to know that at a specified hour Blondin was risking his life a hundred miles off. The man in the cask would not be seen, and to see a closed cask go bobbing about down five miles of rapids would not be an exciting amusement, more especially as, after two or three successful trials, the notion of any imminency or inevitableness of actual danger would disappear from the spectator's mind. Captain Webb, of course, expected his speculation to pay him; but then, it was in a somewhat different way. He did not expect any money from those who gazed from the shore, but believed,—as did also the speculators who paid him— that if he swam Niagara, he would revive the waning interest in his really splendid feats of customary swimming.

Copying somewhat the idea that Graham had developed so successfully, George Hazlett and William Potts, also coopers of Buffalo, made a trip through the Rapids in a barrel of their own construction on August 8, 1886. The barrel they used more closely resembled the familiar type of barrel, having no unusual features of form. In this same barrel used by the two coopers, Miss Sadie Allen and George Hazlett made a trip through the Niagara Gorge on November 28, 1886. There was then, I believe, a cessation of the barrel-fiends, who, nevertheless, re-appeared in the twentieth century.

At the end of the summer of 1901, Martha E. Wagenfuhrer, the wife of a professional wrestler, announced that she would go through the river in a barrel, the date of September 6th being selected, possibly because the woman believed that she might have a President of the United States in her audience, for on that day President McKinley visited Niagara. Quite a crowd collected, for she was the first woman to try the feat alone. She was rescued after being in the water over an hour.

It was nearly six o'clock in the afternoon [to quote the New York *Times* of September 7, 1901,] when the barrel containing Martha E. Wagenfuhrer was set adrift on the lower Niagara River, to be carried by the currents into the rapids and vortex of the Whirlpool. The trip through the rapids was quickly made, but the rescue from the Whirlpool was delayed. Night fell before the barrel was recovered, and the woman's friends had availed themselves of the help of a powerful searchlight to illuminate the rushing tossing waters of the pool. She started at 5.56 o'clock, and it was 7 o'clock when the barrel was landed. The head of the cask had to be broken in in order to get the woman out. She was in a semi-conscious condition. Before entering the barrel she had indulged freely in liquor, but when she got out her first call was for water.

Female barrel-fiends now followed in rapid succession. Maud Willard of Canton, Ohio, lost her life on the 7th of September, 1901, in navigating the Whirlpool Rapids in Graham's barrel. Graham, as we have seen, had made five successful trips, and Miss Willard desired to attain fame by doing the same. She and Graham were good friends, and to please her he was to swim from the Whirlpool to Lewiston following her trip through the Rapids. The barrel was taken to the river in the morning. It was an enormous affair, made of oak, and at 4 o'clock Miss Willard got into it, accompanied by her pet dog. The cover was put over the manhole, and she was taken out into the stream in tow of a small boat, and left to the mercy of the currents.

Miss Willard passed safely through the Rapids, but the mighty maelstrom then held her far out from shore, where her friends and would-be rescuers could not reach her. From 4.40 o'clock until after 10 o'clock at night she was whirled about in the peculiar formation of the Niagara here. Messengers were sent to Niagara Falls to have the searchlight car of the electric line sent down the Gorge; huge bonfires were built to warm the spectators, and likewise to illuminate the river. Soon a beam of white light shot across the waters from the American to the Canadian side; now and then the tossing barrel could be seen tumbling and bobbing, and rolling in the currents. The latter were then suddenly changing— first a piece of wood came in drifting toward shore— within a short time the barrel hove in sight within the light of the beacons, and men swam out to catch it.

When the manhole cover was removed, Miss Willard was limp and lifeless. Death probably came gradually, and possibly without much suffering. The little dog came out alive, and none the worse for the perilous trip.

While she was tossing in the Whirlpool, Graham made his trip to Lewiston, the only person who ever swam from the pool to Lewiston. When he returned up the Gorge he found the barrel and Miss Willard still in the terrible pool.

A widow, Mrs. Anna Edson Taylor, safely passed over Niagara Falls in a barrel on Friday, October 24, 1901, the trip from end to end being witnessed by several thousand people. The fact that Mrs. Taylor failed to appear, as advertised, on the Sunday before, and again on Wednesday, did not lessen the confidence of the public. It was beyond belief that she would live to tell the story, but she came out alive and well so soon as she recovered from the shock.

This initial voyage over Niagara's cataract began at Port Day, nearly a mile from the brink of the Falls. At this point the daring woman and her barrel were taken out to Grass Island, where she entered; at 3.50 she was in tow of a boat speeding well out into the Canadian current. Soon after the barrel was cast adrift on the current that never before was known to spare a human life once fallen in its grasp. From the spot where the rowboat left the barrel the current runs frightfully swift, soon boiling on the teeth of the upper rifts; the barrel was weighted with a two hundred pound anvil, and it floated nicely in the water, Mrs. Taylor apparently retaining an upright position for the greater part of the trip down the river and through the rapids. Fortunately the cask kept well within the deep water, and except for passing out of sight several times, in the white-crested waves, it was in view for the greater part of a mile. In passing over the Horseshoe Fall the barrel kept toward the Canadian side at a point three hundred feet from the centre.

It dropped over the Fall at 4.23 o'clock, the bottom well down. In less than a minute it appeared at the base of the Fall, and was swept down stream. The current cast it aside in an eddy, and, floating back up-stream, it was held between two eddies until captured at 4.40 o'clock. As it was grounded on a rock, out in the river, it was difficult to handle, but several men soon had the hatch off. Mrs. Taylor was alive

Horseshoe Falls from Goat Island.

Ice Bridge and American Falls.

and conscious but before she could be taken out of the barrel it was necessary to saw a portion of the top away. Her condition was a surprise to all. She walked along the shore to a boat, and was taken down the river to the *Maid of the Mist* dock, where she entered a carriage and was brought to Niagara Falls. The woman was suffering greatly from the shock, and had a three-inch cut in her scalp, back of the right ear, but how or when she got it she did not know. She complained of pains between the shoulders, but it is thought that this was due to the fact that her shoulders were thrown back during the plunge, as she had her arms in straps, and these undoubtedly saved her neck from breaking.

She admitted having lost consciousness in passing over the Falls. While thanking God for sparing her life, she warned every one not to repeat her foolhardy trip. So severe was the shock that she wandered in her talk, with three doctors attending her; she, however, soon recovered.

Mrs. Taylor was forty-three years old when she made this marvellous trip. She was born in Auburn, N. Y., and was a school teacher in Bay City, Mich., before she came East. She had crossed the American continent from ocean to ocean eight times, and during her stay East impressed everybody with her wonderful nerve.

The barrel in which Mrs. Taylor made the journey was four and one-half feet high, and about three feet in diameter. A leather harness and cushions inside protected her body. Air was secured through a rubber tube connecting with a small opening near the top of the barrel. Her warning evidently has been heeded.

To our knowledge no barrel-fiend has reappeared at the shores of Niagara within the last five years.

In the year 1846, a small steamer was built in the eddy just above the suspension bridge to run up to the Falls, and very appropriately named the *Maid of the Mist*. Her engine was rather weak, but she safely accomplished the trip. Since she took passengers aboard only from the Canada side, however, she did little more than pay expenses, and in 1854, a larger, better boat, with a more powerful engine, a new *Maid of the Mist*, was put on the route and many persons since have made this most exciting and impressive voyage along the foot of the Falls.

Owing to some change in the appointments of the *Maid of the Mist* which confined her landings to the Canadian shore she too became unprofitable and her owner having decided to leave the place wished to sell her as she lay on her dock. This he could not do, but having received an offer of more than half of her cost, if he would deliver her at Niagara-on-the-Lake, he determined a consultation with Joel Robinson, who had acted as her captain and pilot on her trips under the Falls to make the attempt to take her down the river. Mr. Robinson agreed to act as pilot on the fearful voyage; the engineer, Mr. Jones, consented to go with him and a courageous machinist by the name of McIntyre volunteered to share the risk with them. The boat was in complete trim, removing from deck and hold all superfluous articles and as notice was given of the time of starting, a large number of people assembled to watch the spectacular plunge, few expecting to see either boat or crew again. About three o'clock in the afternoon of June 15, 1861, the engineer took his place in the hold, and, knowing that their drifting would be short at the longest, and might be only the preface to a swift destruction, set his steam valve at the proper gauge and awaited —not without anxiety—the tinkling signal that should start them on their flying voyage. McIntyre joined Robinson at the wheel on the upper deck. Self-possessed, and with the calmness which results from undoubted courage and confidence, yet with the humility which recognises all possibilities, Robinson took his place at the wheel and pulled the starting bell. With a shriek from her whistle and a white puff from the escape-pipe to take leave, as it were, of the multitude gathered at the shores, she soon swung around to the right, cleared the smooth water and shot like an arrow into the rapid under the bridge. She took the outside course of the rapid and when a third of the way down it, a jet of water struck against her rudder, a column dashed up under her starboard side, hurled her over, carried away her smoke-stack, threw Robinson flat on his back, and thrust McIntyre against her starboard wheel-house with such a force as to break it through. The little boat emerged from the fearful baptism, shook her wounded sides, and slid into the Whirlpool riding for the moment again on an even keel. Robinson rose at once, seized the helm, set her to the right of the large pot in the pool, then turned her directly through the neck of it. Thence, after receiving another drenching from its combing waves, the craft dashed on without further accident to the quiet of the river at Lewiston.

Thus was accomplished one of the most remarkable and perilous voyages ever made by man; the boat was seventy-two feet long with seventeen feet breadth of beam and eight feet depth of hold, and carried an engine of one hundred horse-power.

Robinson stated after the voyage that the greater part of it was like what he had always imagined must be the swift sailing of a large bird in a downward flight; that when the accident occurred the boat seemed to be struck from all directions at once, that she trembled like a fiddlestring and felt as if she would crumble away and drop into atoms; that both he and McIntyre were holding to the wheel with all their strength, but this produced no more effect than if they had been two flies;

that he had no fear of striking the rocks, for he knew that the strongest suction must be in the deepest channels, and that the boat must remain in that. Finding that McIntyre was somewhat bruised and bewildered by excitement on account of his fall, and did not rise, Robinson quickly put his foot on him to keep him from rolling round the deck, and thus finished the voyage.

The effect of this trip upon Robinson was decidedly marked. To it, as he lived but few years afterward, his death was commonly attributed. "He was," said Mrs. Robinson in an interview, "twenty years older when he came home that day, than when he went out. He sank into his chair like a person overcome with weariness. He decided to abandon the water, and advised his sons to venture no more about the Rapids. Both his manner and appearance were changed." Calm and deliberate before, he became thoughtful and serious afterwards. He had been borne, as it were, in the arms of a power so mighty, that its impress was stamped on his features and on his mind. Through a slightly opened door he had seen a vision which awed and subdued him. He became reverent in a moment. He grew venerable in an hour.

As an illustration of the lengths unscrupulous sensationalists will go at Niagara to satisfy the curious throngs, in September, 1883, several enterprising citizens of Niagara Falls purchased a small boat which they fitted up to represent the *Maid of the Mist*, and sent it through the Rapids. Men were stationed about the boat in effigy, but no human beings were allowed on board, although, indeed there were many applications for passage. The boat passed through the Gorge in good shape.

On August 28, 1887, Charles Alexander Percy, a waggon-maker of Suspension Bridge, went over the

Rapids to win fame. He had conceived the idea of constructing a boat, and, having been previously a sailor he knew how to build a staunch craft. The vessel was of hickory, seventeen feet long and four feet ten and one-quarter inches wide. It had sixty-four oak ribs, and an iron plate weighing three hundred pounds was fastened to the bottom. The boat as completed weighed nine hundred pounds, and was covered with white canvas. At 3.30 o'clock in the afternoon on the day mentioned, Percy, having with great difficulty transported his craft to the old *Maid of the Mist* landing above the cantilever bridge, took off his coat and waistcoat, put them in a valise and stowed it away in one of the compartments. Then he sat in the middle part of the boat, which had no deck, rowed out into the Niagara, just above the cantilever, unshipped his oars and fastened them to the boat and then crawled into one of his air-tight compartments. Many people watched his white craft from the bridges and banks, but the excursion had not been advertised and many visitors to the Falls knew nothing of it. The boat shot down toward the Whirlpool. On the theory that there was an undercurrent which ran stronger than the surface current, Percy had attached a thirty-pound weight to a ten-foot line, which he threw overboard to act as a drag; this had no apparent effect; the two-mile trip to the Whirlpool occupied less than five minutes, and while the boat was submerged repeatedly, it did not turn over. When near the Whirlpool it drifted close to the American shore, Percy, thinking he was in the quiet water on the further side of the Whirlpool, stuck out his head, but closed the aperture just in time to escape a tremendous wave. The boat passed straight across the Whirlpool, and on the other side Percy crawled out of the compartment, took his oars, and rowed leisurely around to the foot of the inclined railway on the Canadian side, where he landed, his voyage having lasted twenty-five minutes. He gave much the same account of the adventure as was given by Graham of barrel fame, and Kendall, the Boston policeman, who swam into the Whirlpool in 1886. He thought he struck rocks in the passage down, but the boat showed no marks.

Percy and a friend, William Dittrick, repeated the trip on September 25, 1887, through the lower half of the Gorge from the Whirlpool to Lewiston, having a thrilling experience. Dittrick occupied one of the air compartments, while Percy sat in the cockpit.

Finally, on September 16, 1888, Percy again risked his life in making a voyage through the waters of the Gorge near Lewiston. In this trip he narrowly escaped death and the boat was lost.

Elated by his success, Percy now made a wager with Robert William Flack of Syracuse, "for a race through the Whirlpools in life-boats for five hundred dollars a side." The race was set for August 1, 1888, but on July 4th, Flack was first to show that his craft was seaworthy. The boat was of the clinker pattern, had no air-cushions, and was partly constructed of cork. In the presence of an immense concourse of spectators it went first along gaily, but in three minutes the boat was upset and carried into the Whirlpool bottom upwards. It was a frightful spectacle, witnessed by thousands of people. The boat capsized three times; the last time it tossed high in the air. It stood on end for an instant and then it toppled over on poor Flack, who was strapped to the boat helpless and floated about the pool upside down for about an hour, until captured on the Canadian side. Flack's body was only a mass of bruised flesh. Percy meantime, having witnessed the tragedy from the American side, jumped into a trap, and drove to the Whirlpool on the Canadian side where, throwing off his clothes, he leaped into the river and swam for the boat which was now approaching the shore. But he was too late. His courageous feat could not help Flack, who was found dead, hanging on the straps he had placed there to aid him to save his life.

In 1889 Walter G. Campbell tried to make the perilous trip in an open, flat-bottomed boat, which he launched above the Rapids. His only companion was a black dog. Campbell, with a life-preserver about his body, stood up, using his oar as a paddle, and boldly drifted with increasing speed toward the seething pool. The trip took about twenty minutes, but, fortunately, the boat capsized before the worst water was reached, and Campbell just managed to struggle to the shore. The poor black dog paid the penalty of his master's folly.

Peter Nissen, of Chicago, made a successful trip through the Whirlpool Rapids of Niagara on July 9, 1900, being the first man to go through in an open boat and come out unharmed. He entered the Rapids at 5 P.M., the boat gliding down easily bow first, entering the first wave end on, and going partly over and partly under the water, drenched its occupant completely. The second wave struck him with terrific force almost broadside, the boat being partly turned by the first wave, smashing Nissen against the cockpit, knocking off his hat and nearly smothering him. A moment later he entered the frightful mass of warring waters opposite the Whirlpool Rapids station, and for a few moments it looked as though his end had come, the boat being tossed with terrific force out of the water, broadside up, the iron keel, weighing 1250 pounds, being plainly seen. Boat and occupant then disappeared altogether, not being again seen for several seconds until the worst was feared. Suddenly both man and boat reappeared farther down the stream, and the hundreds of onlookers gave vent to their feelings in cheers. The hardy navigator now went under the waters again receiving a crushing blow as he entered every succeeding wave when the staunch craft and its master raced into the Whirlpool. But Nissen was not yet safe. Having no means of guiding or propelling the boat, Nissen was compelled to sit in the water in the cockpit for fifty minutes, being carried around the Whirlpool four times. Once the boat approached the vortex and was sucked down about half its length, the other half standing out of the water in an almost vertical position. It was immediately thrown out, however, and resumed its course around the pool. When at the farther end, where the current has the least strength the boat then being about fifty feet from shore, three young men swam out with a rope and fastened it to the boat, which was then drawn in by very willing hands. Nissen, when questioned, said he was not injured in the least, only feeling cold and weak. He was stripped and given dry clothing, and he then declared he felt all right. In making the trip he wore his usual clothing, pulling on an ordinary life-preserver to aid him if he should be thrown out. He did not intend to fasten himself in the boat, but at the last moment passed a rope over his shoulder, which probably saved his life.

A Century of Niagara Cranks 151

The boat, which he had named the *Fool-Killer*, was twenty feet long, four feet wide, and four feet deep. The deck was slightly raised in the centre, gently sloping to the gunwales. In the centre of the deck a cockpit four feet long and twenty inches wide extended down to the keel, a distance of four feet. The side-planking of the cockpit was carried above the deck, forming a combing six inches in height; six water-tight compartments were built in the boat, two at each end and one on each side of the cockpit; three hundred pounds of cork were also used, so that the boat was unsinkable. The main feature of the boat was the keel. This was a shaft of round iron, four inches in diameter and twenty feet long, hanging two feet below the bottom of the boat, and held in position by five one-inch iron bars.

Our record of sensationalism at Niagara would be lacking in fulness, at least, if mention were not made of the many gruesome suicides that have occurred here, but we forbear. A story of what a dog endured, however, is quite in place:

A large dog lately survived the passage over Niagara Falls and through the rapids to the whirlpool. He was first noticed while he was within the influence of the upper rapids. As he was whirled rapidly down over the Falls, every one imagined that that was the last of him. Shortly afterwards, however, he was discovered in the gorge below the Falls vainly endeavouring to clamber up upon some of the debris from the remains of the great ice bridge which recently covered the water at this point, but which had nearly all gone down the river. The news spread rapidly through the, village, and a large crowd gathered at the shore. Strenuous efforts were made to get the struggling animal on shore, for an animal which had gone safely over the Falls would be a prize worth having, but without success. Finally the dog succeeded in getting upon a large cake of ice, and floated off upon it down towards Suspension Bridge and the terrible Whirlpool

Rapids. Information of the dog's coming was telephoned to Suspension Bridge village, and a large crowd collected on the bridge to watch for the coming wonder. In due time the poor fellow appeared upon his ice-cake, howling dismally the while, as if he appreciated the terrors of his situation. An express-train crossing the bridge at the time stopped in order to let the passengers witness the unusual spectacle. Round and round whirled the cake, in a dizzy way, and louder and more prolonged grew the howls of the poor dog. As the influence of the Whirlpool Rapids began to be felt, the cake increased in speed, whirled suddenly into the air, broke in two, and the dog disappeared from view. No one thought that he could possibly survive the wild rush through the rapids. When, therefore, word was received that the dog was in the whirlpool, still living, and once more struggling vainly to swim to land, it was received with marked incredulity. This story was substantiated by several trustworthy witnesses. It seems incredible that an animal could go through the upper rapids, over the Falls, through the Gorge, through the Whirlpool Rapids, and into the whirlpool itself, a distance of several miles, and still be alive. The poor animal perished in the whirlpool.

In various instances dogs have been sent over the Falls and survived the plunge.

As early as November, 1836, a troublesome female bull-terrier was put in a coffee sack by a couple of men who had determined to get rid of her, and thrown off from the middle of Goat Island Bridge. In the following spring she was found alive and well about sixty rods below the Ferry, having lived through the winter on a deceased cow that was thrown over the bank the previous fall. In 1858, another dog, a male of the same breed, was thrown into the Rapids, also near the middle of the bridge. In less than an hour he came up the Ferry stairs, very wet and not at all gay. He was ever after a sadder, if not a better dog.

Chapter VII

The Old Niagara Frontier

WHAT has been loosely called the "Niagara Frontier" embraces all the beautiful stretch of territory south of Lakes Ontario and Erie, extending westward quite to Cleveland, the Forest City on the latter lake. It would be difficult to point to a tract of country in all America the history of which is of more inherent interest than this far-flung old-time frontier of which the Niagara River was the strategic key. The beautiful cities now standing here, Buffalo, Cleveland, and Toronto, as well as the ancient Falls, forever new and wonderful, bring to this fair country, in large volume, the modern note that would drown the memory of the long ago; but here, as elsewhere, and particularly here, the Indian left his names upon the rivers and the shores of the lakes, beautiful names that will neither die nor permit the days of Iroquois, Eries, and Hurons to pass forgotten.

Historically, the Niagara frontier is memorable, firstly, because it embraced in part the homes and hunting-grounds of the Six Nations, the pre-eminent Indian confederacy of the continent. The French name for the confederacy was Iroquois; their own, "Ho-de-no-sote," or the "Long House," which extended from the Hudson to Lake Erie and from the St. Lawrence to the valleys of the Delaware, Susquehanna, and Allegheny. This domain was divided between the several nations by well-defined boundary lines, called "lines of property." The famous Senecas were on the Niagara frontier.

In this pleasant land the Iroquois dwelt in palisaded villages upon the fertile banks of the lakes and streams which watered their country. Their houses were built within a protecting circle of palisades, and, like all the tribes of the Iroquois family, were long and narrow, not more than twelve or fifteen feet in width, but often exceeding one hundred and fifty in length. They were made of two parallel rows of poles stuck upright in the ground, of sufficient widths at the bottom to form the floor, and bent together at the top to form the roof; the whole was entirely covered with strips of peeled bark. At each end of the long house was a strip of bark or a bear skin hung loosely for a door. Within, they built their fires at intervals along the centre of the floor, the smoke rising through the opening in the top, which served, as well, to let in light. In every house were fires and many families, and every family having its own fire within the space allotted to it.

Among all the Indians of the New World, there were none so politic and intelligent, none so fierce and brave, none with so many heroic virtues mingled with savagery, as the people of the Long House. They were a terror to all the surrounding tribes, whether of their own or of Algonquin speech. In 1650 they overran the country of the Huron; in 1651 they destroyed the neutral nation along the Niagara; in 1652 they exterminated the Eries. They knew every war-path and "their war-cry was heard westward to the Mississippi and southward

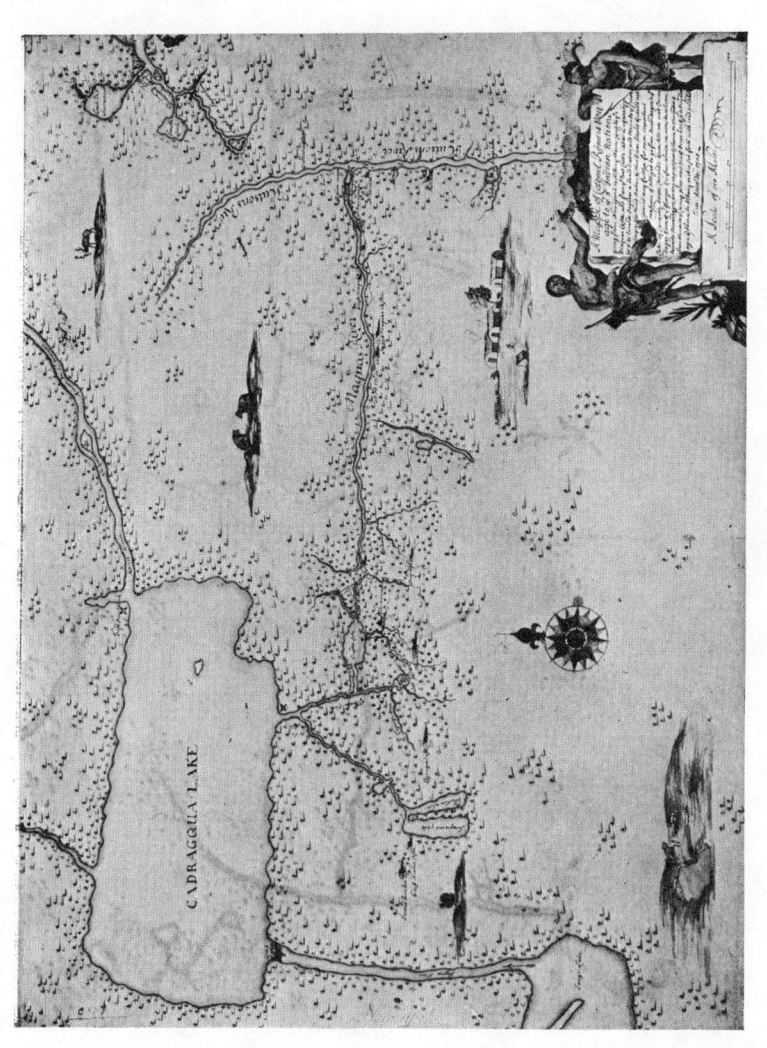

Colonel Römer's Map of the Country of the Iroquois, 1700.

Champlain.

The Old Niagara Frontier

to the great gulf." They were, in fact, the conquerors of the New World, perhaps not unjustly styled the "Romans of the West." Wrote the Jesuit Father Ragueneau, in 1650, "My pen has no ink black enough to describe the fury of the Iroquois." In 1715, the Tuscaroras, a branch of the Iroquois family, in the Carolinas, united with the Five Nations, after which the confederacy was known as the Six Nations, of which the other five tribes were named in order of their rank, Mohawks, Onondagas, Senecas, Oneidas, and Cayugas.

Iroquois government was vested in a general council composed of fifty hereditary sachems, but the order of succession was always in the female and never in the male line. Each nation was divided into eight clans or tribes. The spirit of the animal or bird after which the clan was named, called its "To-tem," was the guardian spirit of the clan, and every member used its figure in his signature as his device. It was the rule that men and women of the same tribe could intermarry. In this manner relationships were interlocked forever by the closest of ties. The name of each sachemship was permanent. When a sachem died the people of the league selected the most competent from among those of his family, who by right inherited the title, and the one so chosen was raised in solemn council to the high honour, and dropping his own received the name of the sachemship. Two sachemships, however, after the death of the original sachems ever remained vacant, those of the Onondagas and "Ha-yo-went-ha" (Hi-a-wat-ha) immortalised by Longfellow, of the Mohawks. Daganoweda was the founder of the league, whose head was represented as covered with tangled serpents; Hi-a-wat-ha (meaning "he who combs") put the head in order and this aided the formation of the league. In honour of these great services this sachemship was afterward held vacant.

The entire body of sachems formed the council league; their authority was civil, confined to affairs of peace, and was advisory rather than otherwise. Every member of the confederacy followed, to a great extent, the dictates of his own will, controlled very much by the customs of his people and "a sentiment that ran through their whole system of affairs which was as inflexible as iron."

The character of the Iroquois confederacy has a bearing on the history of the Niagara country of prime importance; while their immediate seats were somewhat south of Niagara River itself, they were the red masters of the eastern Great Lake region when white men came to know it, conquering, as we have noted, the earlier red races, the Eries and Neutrals, who lived beside Lake Erie and the Niagara River. Of these very little is known; placed between the Iroquois on the South and the Hurons on the North both are accounted to have been fierce and brave peoples, for a long time able to withstand the savage inroads of the people of the Long House. The Eries occupied the territory just south of Lake Erie, while the Neuter or Neutral towns lay on the north side of the lake—stretching up perhaps near to Niagara Falls. They claimed the territory lying west of the Genesee River, and extending northward to the Huron land about Georgian Bay as their hunting-ground, and could, it was affirmed by Jesuits, number twelve thousand souls or four thousand fighting men in 1641, only a decade before annihilation by the southern foe.

The Old Niagara Frontier

Although the French applied to them the name of "neuter" [writes Marshall, the historian of the Niagara frontier], it was always an allusion to their neutrality between the Hurons and the Iroquois. These contending nations traversed the territories of the Neutral Nation in their wars against each other, and if, by chance, they met in the wigwams or villages of this people, they were forced to restrain their animosity and to separate in peace.

Notwithstanding this neutrality, they waged cruel wars with other nations, toward whom they exercised cruelties even more inhuman than those charged upon their savage neighbours. The early missionaries describe their customs as similar to those of the Hurons, their land as producing Indian corn, beans, and squashes in abundance, their rivers as abounding in fish of endless variety, and their forests as filled with animals yielding the richest furs.

They exceeded the Hurons in stature, strength, and symmetry of form, and wore their dress with a superior grace, and regarded their dead with peculiar affection; hence arose a custom which is worthy of notice, and explains the origin of the numerous burial mounds which are scattered over this vicinity. Instead of burying the bodies of their deceased friends, they deposited them in houses or on scaffolds erected for the purpose. They collected the skeletons from time to time and arranged them in their dwellings, in anticipation of the feast of the dead, which occurred once in ten or twelve years. On this occasion the whole nation repaired to an appointed place, each family, with the greatest apparent affection, bringing the bones of their deceased relatives enveloped in the choicest furs.

The final disruption between Neuters and Senecas

came, it would seem, in 1648, in the shape of a challenge sent by the latter and accepted; the war raged until 1651, when two whole villages of Neuters were destroyed, the largest containing more than sixteen hundred men. Father Fremin in 1669 found Neuters still living in captivity in Gannogarae, a Seneca town east of the Genesee. Some two years later, seemingly by accident, a rupture between Senecas and Eries, farther to the westward, took place, resulting in a similar Seneca victory; thus the Iroquois came to be the masters of the Niagara country.

What this meant becomes very evident with the advance of France to this old-time key of the continent; here lay the strongest, most civilised Indian nations, conquerors of half a continent; what the friendship of the Iroquois meant to these would-be white conquerors of the self-same empire no words could express; as we have noted, the Niagara River was the direct passageway to the Mississippi basin. It is one of the most interesting caprices of Fate that France should have been given the great waterway—key of the continent; now, with a friendly alliance with the Six Nations the progress of French arms could hardly be challenged. But France, in the early hours of her progress, and by the hand of her best friend and wisest champion, Champlain, incurred the inveterate hatred of these powerful New York confederates. This he did in 1609 by joining a war-party of Algonquins of the lower St. Lawrence region on one of their memorable raids into the Iroquois country by way of the Richelieu River and Lake Champlain. Dr. Bourinot,[1] perhaps most clearly of all, has explained Champlain's own

[1] *Canada*, p. 72, Story of the Nations Series.

comprehension of the matter by saying that the dominating purpose of his life in New France was the exploration of the vast region from which came the sweeping tides of the St. Lawrence; supposing, naturally, that the Canadian red men were to be eventually the victors in the ancient war, especially if aided by the government of New France, it was politic for Champlain to espouse their cause since no general scheme of exploration "could have been attempted had he by any cold or unsympathetic conduct alienated the Indians who guarded the waterways over which he had to pass before he could unveil the mysteries of the Western wilderness."

In June this eventful invasion of the Iroquois country was undertaken, and on the last day of July but one, near what was to become the historic site of Fort Ticonderoga, a pitched battle was fought. Champlain's own account of this the first decisive battle of America cannot be excelled in its quaint and picturesque simplicity:

At night [he wrote] we embarked in our canoes, and, as we were advancing noiselessly onward, we encountered a party of Iroquois at the point of a cape which juts into the lake on the west side. It was on the twenty-ninth of the month and about ten o'clock at night. They, as well as we, began to shout, seizing our arms. We withdrew to the water, and the Iroquois paddled to the shore, arranged their canoes, and began to hew down trees with villainous-looking axes and fortified themselves very securely. Our party kept their canoes alongside of the other, tied to poles, so as not to run adrift, in order to fight all together if need be. When everything was arranged they sent two canoes to know if their enemies wished to fight. They answered that they desired nothing else but that there was not then light enough to distinguish each other and that they would fight at sunrise. This was agreed to. On both sides the night was spent in dancing, singing, mingled with insults and taunts. Thus they sang, danced, and insulted each other until daybreak. My companions and I were concealed in separate canoes belonging to the savage Montagnoes. After being equipped with light armour, each of us took an arquebus and went ashore. I saw the enemy leaving their barricade. They were about two hundred men, strong and robust, who were coming toward us with a gravity and assurance that greatly pleased me, led on by three chiefs. Ours were marching in similar order, and told me that those who bore the three lofty plumes were chiefs and that I must do all I could. The moment we landed they began to run toward the enemy, who stood firm and had not yet perceived my companions who went into the bush with some savages. Ours commenced calling me with a loud voice, opening the way for me and placing me at their head, about twenty paces in advance, until I was about thirty paces from the enemy. The moment they saw me they halted, gazing at me and I at them. When I saw them preparing to shoot at us, I raised my arquebus, and aiming directly at one of the chiefs, two of them fell to the ground by this shot, and one of their companions received a wound of which he died afterwards. I had put four balls into my arquebus. Ours, on witnessing a shot so favourable to them, set up such tremendous shouts that thunder could not have been heard, and yet there was no lack of arrows on the one side or the other. The Iroquois were greatly astonished at seeing two men killed so instantaneously, notwithstanding that they were provided with arrow-proof armour woven of cotton thread and wood. This frightened them very much.

Whilst I was unloading; one of my companions fired a shot which so astonished them anew, seeing their chiefs slain, that they lost courage, took to flight, and abandoned the field and their fort, hiding in the depths of the forest, whither pursuing them I killed some others. Our savages also killed several of them and took ten or twelve of them prisoners. The rest carried off the wounded. These were promptly treated.

After having gained this victory, our party amused themselves plundering Indian corn and meal from the enemy, and also their arms which they had thrown away the better to run. And having feasted, danced, and sung, we returned three hours afterwards with the prisoners.[1]

No victory could have been so costly as this; indeed, one is led to wonder whether any battle in America ever cost more lives than this; for one hundred and fifty years and forty-five days, or until the fall of Quebec and New France, this strongest of Indian nations remembered Champlain, and was the implacable enemy of the French; and, what was of singular ill-fortune, these very Iroquois, in addition to holding the key of the West in their grasp, lay exactly between the French and their English rivals at the point of nearest and most vital contact. After the Ticonderoga victory an Iroquois prisoner, previous to being burned at the stake, chanted a song; wrote the humane Champlain, "the song was sad to hear." For a century and a half sad songs were sung by descendants of those Algonquin and French victors who listened in the wavering light of that cruel fire to the song of the captive from the land of Long Houses below the Lakes! True, the Iroquois and the French were not continually at war through this long series of years; and French blandishments had their effect, sometimes, even on their immemorial foe, especially at the Seneca end of the Long House, nearest Niagara.

Six years later, in 1615, Champlain set out on his most important tour of western discovery, largely for the purpose of fulfilling a promise made to one of his lieutenants on the upper Ottawa to assist him in the continual quarrel between the Hurons to the northward

[1] A very excellent account of the battle of Lake Champlain is found in *The St. Lawrence River*, Ch. vi., by George Waldo Browne.

and the Iroquois. Here again is forced upon our attention one of the most important sequences of the battle of Lake Champlain. The two routes to the Great Lakes of Montreal were by the St. Lawrence River and by the Ottawa River. Either route the voyage was long and difficult, but by the Ottawa the voyageur came into the "back door" of the Lakes, Georgian Bay, by a taxing portage route; while, once stemming the St. Lawrence, Lake Ontario was gained and, with the Niagara portage accomplished the traveller was afloat on Lake Erie beyond which the waterway lay fair and clear to the remotest corner of Superior. But the St. Lawrence led into the Iroquois frontier, and the Ottawa to the country of the French allies, the Hurons. The result was that, to a great extent, French movement followed the northerly course; no one could bring this out more clearly than Hinsdale and those whom he quotes:

[The Iroquois] turned the Frenchmen aside from the St. Lawrence and the Lower Lakes to the Ottawa and Nipissing; they ruined the fur trade "which was the life-blood of New France"; they "made all her early years a misery and a terror"; they retarded the growth of Absolutism until Liberty was equal to the final struggle; and they influence our national history to this day, since "populations formed in the ideas and habits of a feudal monarchy, and controlled by a hierarchy profoundly hostile to freedom of thought, would have remained a hindrance and a stumbling-block in the way of that majestic experiment of which America is the field."[1]

Two insignificant historical facts illustrate this power exerted on westward movement from Canada: Lake Erie was not discovered until half a century after

[1] *The Old Northwest*, p. 25. A novel, *The Road to Frontenac*, presents a clear picture of French-Iroquois hostility on the St. Lawrence.

The Old Niagara Frontier

Lake Superior, in fact was practically unknown even for fifty years after Detroit was founded in 1701.

From the rendezvous in the Huron country this second army of invasion, at the head of which rode Champlain, set out for the Iroquois land, to carry fire and sword to the homes of the enemy and forge so much the more firmly the chains of prejudice and hatred. Crossing Lake Ontario at its western extremity the march was taken up from a point near Sacketts Harbour for the Onondaga fort, which was located, probably, a few miles south of Lake Oneida.

The importance of the campaign on the Niagara frontier history is sufficient for us to include again Champlain's account of it:

> We made about fourteen leagues in crossing to the other side of the Lake, in a southerly direction, towards the territories of the enemy. The Indians concealed all their canoes in the woods near the shore. We made by land about four leagues over a sandy beach, where I noticed a very agreeable and beautiful country, traversed by many small streams, and two small rivers which empty into the said Lake. Also many ponds and meadows, abounding in an infinite variety of game, numerous vines, and fine woods, a great number of chestnut trees, the fruit of which was yet in its covering. Although very small, it was of good flavour. All the canoes being thus concealed, we left the shore of the Lake, which is about eighty leagues long and twenty-five wide, the greater part of it being inhabited by Indians along its banks, and continued our way by land about twenty-five or thirty leagues. During four days we crossed numerous streams and a river issuing from a lake which empties into that of the *Entouhonorons*. This Lake, which is about twenty-five or thirty leagues in circumference, contains several beautiful islands, and is the place where our Iroquois enemies catch their fish, which are there in great abundance. On the 9th of October, our people being on a scout, encountered eleven Indians whom they took

prisoners, namely, four women, three boys, a girl, and three men, who were going to the fishery, distant four leagues from the enemies' fort. . . . The next day, about three o'clock in the afternoon, we arrived before the fort. . . . Their village was enclosed with four strong rows of interlaced palisades, composed of large pieces of wood, thirty feet high, not more than half a foot apart and near an unfailing body of water. . . . We were encamped until the 16th of the month, . . . As the five hundred men did not arrive, the Indians decided to leave by an immediate retreat and began to make baskets in which to carry the wounded, who were placed in them doubled in a heap, and so bent and tied as to render it impossible for them to stir, any more than an infant in its swaddling clothes, and not without great suffering, as I can testify, having been carried several days on the back of one of our Indians, thus tied and imprisoned, which made me lose all patience. As soon as I had strength to sustain myself I escaped from this prison, or to speak plainly, from this hell.

The enemy pursued us about half a league, in order to capture some of our rear guard, but their efforts were useless and they withdrew. . . . The retreat was very tedious, being from twenty-five to thirty leagues, and greatly fatigued the wounded, and those who carried them, though they relieved each other from time to time. On the 18th considerable snow fell which lasted but a short time. It was accompanied with a violent wind, which greatly incommoded us. Nevertheless we made such progress, that we reached the banks of the lake of the *Entouhonorons*, at the place where we had concealed our canoes, and which were found all whole. We were apprehensive that the enemy had broken them up.

As the roar of Niagara greets from afar the listening ears of the innumerable host of pilgrims who come to it to-day, so the fame of the cataract reached the first explorers of the continent long before they came to it, indeed almost as soon as their feet touched the shore of the New World. Four centuries ago Niagara was the

Map of French Forts in America, 1750-60.

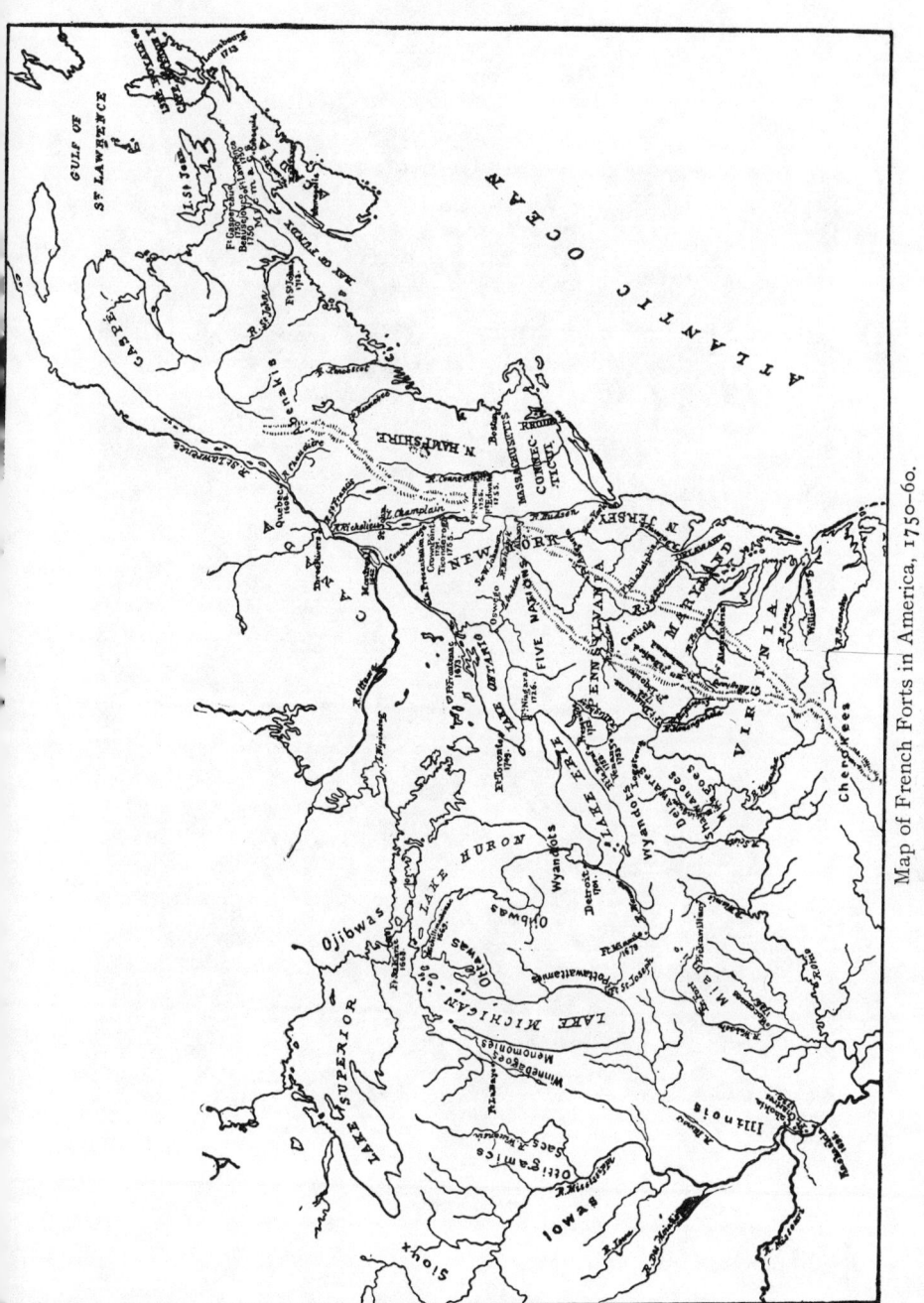

Niagara Falls by Father Hennepin.
The first known picture of Niagara, dated 1697.

The Old Niagara Frontier

wonder of the world as it must be four centuries hence and four times four.

In May, 1535, Jacques Cartier left France on his second voyage to America in three ships; reaching the St. Lawrence, which he so named from the Saint, he asked concerning its sources and

was told that, after ascending many leagues among rapids and waterfalls, he would reach a lake 140 or 150 leagues broad, at the western extremity of which the waters were wholesome and the winters mild; that a river emptied into it from the south, which had its source in the country of the Iroquois; that beyond the lake he would find a cataract and portage, then another lake about equal to the former, which they had never explored.

This is the first known mention of Niagara Falls. Champlain mapped the Niagara frontier, and his map of 1613 shows the position of the great Falls; he refers to it only as a "waterfall," which was "so very high that many kinds of fish are stunned in its descent." He probably never saw Niagara but wrote his description from hearsay. During the half century between Champlain's Lake Ontario tour and the coming of La Salle and Hennepin the Niagara must have been often visited by the Catholic missionaries, but few of them left mention of it.

In 1615, Champlain's interpreter, Etienne Brule, was sent southward to seek aid from the Andastes and is lost to sight in the western forests for three years; it is possible that Brule even reached the copper region of Lake Superior at this time, and it is fairly probable that this intrepid wanderer, first of all Frenchmen, followed the Niagara River and gazed upon its mighty cataract. The first knowledge we have, however, of a Frenchman's presence on Niagara River is of Father Joseph de la Roche Dallion, who crossed it near Lewiston eleven years later, 1626. Nicolet was in the Straits of Mackinac and at Sault Ste. Marie in 1634, at the time that Champlain (now in the last year of his eventful life) founded Three Rivers on the St. Lawrence above Quebec for the defence of this endangered capital!

Father L'Allemant, in his *Relation* of 1640–41, refers to the Niagara River as the *Onaguiaahra*, and calls it the "celebrated" river of the Neutral Nation.

Montreal was founded in 1642, simultaneously with the memorable capture of Father Jogues, who now, first of Europeans, passed through Lake George en route to the homes of the merciless Iroquois. In fact it was Father Jogues who first named this beautiful sheet of water, when he entered it on the eve of Corpus Christi, "Lake Saint Sacrament"; Sir William Johnson, at a later date rechristened it Lake George. Jogues may have heard the Niagara cataract.

Ragueneau, writing to France in 1648, affirmed that "North of the Eries is a great lake, about two hundred leagues in circumference, called Erie, formed by the discharge of the *mer-douce*, or Lake Huron, and which falls into a third lake called Ontario, over a cataract of frightful height." The description by La Salle's Sulpician companion, Galinee, in 1669, is the most accurate of all early accounts. After La Salle's visit to the Senecas the party struck westward toward Niagara.

We found [wrote Galinee] a river, one-eighth of a league broad and extremely rapid, forming the outlet of communication from Lake Erie to Lake Ontario. The depth of the river (for it is properly the St. Lawrence), is, at this place extraordinary, for, on sounding close by the shore, we found 15 or 16 fathoms of water. The outlet is 40 leagues long, and has, from 10 to 12 leagues above its embouchure into Lake Ontario, one of the finest cataracts, or falls of water, in the world, for all the Indians of whom I have enquired about it, say, that the river falls at that place from a rock higher than the tallest pines, that is about 200 feet. In fact we heard it from the place where we were, although from 10 to 12 leagues distant, but the fall gives such a momentum to the water, that its velocity prevented our ascending the current by rowing, except with great difficulty. At a quarter of a league from the outlet where we were, it grows narrower, and its channel is confined between two very high, steep, rocky banks, inducing the belief that the navigation would be very difficult quite up to the cataract. As to the river above the falls, the current very often sucks into this gulf, from a great distance, deer and stags, elk and roebucks, that suffer themselves to be drawn from such a point in crossing the river, that they are compelled to descend the falls, and to be overwhelmed in its frightful abyss.

Our desire to reach the little village called Ganastogue Sononotoua O-tin-a-oua prevented our going to view the wonder, which I consider as so much the greater in proportion as the river St. Lawrence is one of the largest in the world. I will leave you to judge if that is not a fine cataract in which all the water of that large river, having its mouth three leagues broad, falls from a height of 200 feet, with a noise that is heard not only at the place where we were, 10 or 12 leagues distant, but also from the other side of Lake Ontario, opposite its mouth, where M. Trouve told me he had heard it.

We passed the river, and finally, at the end of five days' travel arrived at the extremity of Lake Ontario, where there is a fine large sandy bay, at the end of which is an outlet of another small lake which is there discharged. Into this our guide conducted us about half a league, to a point nearest the village, but distant from it some 5 or 6 leagues, and where we unloaded our canoes.

The first eye-witness to describe Niagara Falls was Father Hennepin who visited them in the winter of

1678-79, and made the first pictorial representation of them.

Betwixt the Lake *Ontario* and *Erie*, there is a vast and prodigious Cadence of Water which falls down after a surprizing and astonishing manner, insomuch that the Universe does not afford its Parallel. 'T is true, *Italy* and *Suedeland* boast of some such Things; but we may well say they are but sorry Patterns, when compared to this of which we now speak. At the foot of this horrible Precipice we meet with the River *Niagara*, which is not above half a quarter of a League broad, but is wonderfully deep in some places. It is so rapid above this Descent, that it violently hurries down the Wild Beasts while endeavouring to pass it, to feed on the other side; they not being able to withstand the force of its Current, which inevitably casts them down head-long above Six hundred foot.[1]

This wonderful Downfall is compounded of two great Cross-streams of Water, and two Falls, with an Isle slopeing along the middle of it. The Waters which fall from this vast height do foam and boil after the most hideous manner imaginable, making an outrageous Noise, more terrible than that of Thunder; for when the Wind blows from off the South, their dismal roaring may be heard above fifteen Leagues off.

The River *Niagara* having thrown itself down this incredible Precipice continues its impetuous course for two Leagues together, to the great Rock above-mentioned, with an inexpressible Rapidity: But having pass'd that, its Impetuosity relents, gliding along more gently for two Leagues, till it arrives at the Lake *Ontario* or *Frontenac*.

Any Barque or greater Vessel may pass from the Fort to the foot of this huge Rock above-mention'd. This Rock lies to the Westward, and is cut off from the Land by the River *Niagara*, about two Leagues farther down than the great Fall; for which

[1] Hennepin's exaggerations add a spice to his marvellous stories as is true of Arabella B. Buckley's *The Fairyland of Science* (p. 122) wherein we read: "The river Niagara first wanders through a flat country and then reaches the Great Lake Erie in a hollow plain. After that it flows gently down for about fifteen miles and then the slope becomes greater and it rushes on to the Falls of Niagara." Every age has its Hennepins!

two Leagues the People are oblig'd to carry their Goods overland; but the way is very good, and the Trees are but few, and they chiefly Firrs and Oaks.

From the great Fall unto this Rock, which is to the West of the River, the two Brinks of it are so prodigious high, that it would make one tremble to look steadily upon the Water, rolling along with a Rapidity not to be imagin'd. Were it not for this vast Cataract, which interrupts Navigation, they might sail with barques or greater Vessels, above four hundred and fifty Leagues further, cross the Lake of *Hurons*, and up to the farther end of the Lake *Illinois*; which two Lakes, we may well say, are little Seas of fresh Water.

In 1646 Father Jogues was killed in the Long House, and though in 1647 eighteen priests were at work in the eleven missions in the West (most of them in the Huron country), the Iroquois carried the war to their very altars, the mission of St. Joseph being destroyed and the Hurons, blasted as a nation, scattered to the four winds of heaven. In 1656 Mohawks even descended upon fugitive Hurons hovering about Quebec under the very guns of Fort St. Louis; it is interesting to compare these far-eastwardly onslaughts with the simultaneous far-eastern progress of the French explorers, for, as the Mohawks were falling upon Quebec those adventurous pioneers, Raddison and Grossilliers, were (it is now believed) on the point of discovering the Mississippi River, which they probably did in 1659.

The plan of a grand Iroquois campaign against Canada in 1660 probably had its part in the awakening of the monarchy at home to the real state of affairs in America; if New France was to be more than a myth something must now be done or the entire European population of the St. Lawrence—not yet numbering more than two thousand souls—might be swept away as were the Hurons. The energy of Louis's famous minister, Colbert, is now in evidence as Marquis de Tracy, special envoy, appeared on the scene, as the population of Canada doubled in a score of months, the Richilieu was manned with forts and an army of thirteen hundred men invaded the Iroquois country and secured a comparatively lasting peace.

A new era dawned, renewed spirit enthused the explorer, missionary, *coureur-de-bois*, and soldier. In 1669 the boldest man after Champlain, as Frontenac was the most chivalrous, La Salle, crossed Lake Ontario and in the two following years probably discovered and followed the Ohio, if not the Mississippi itself. In 1671 the noblest soldier of the cross in early American annals, Marquette, founded St. Ignace, and, two years later, in company with Joliet, found and descended the "Missipi." Simultaneously, as if to end once for all fear of Iroquois opposition, Frontenac erected the fort named for himself near the present site of Kingston, Canada. But French activity proved a little too successful, for it not only awed the Iroquois but alarmed the English, who had taken New York from the Dutch nine years before.

La Salle was in France during 1677, where he received letters-patent concerning forts to be built south and west, in which direction "it would seem a passage to Mexico can be discovered," while Father Hennepin, soon to be the great discoverer's companion and mouthpiece, was among the Senecas near the Niagara frontier gaining a useful fund of information for the grand campaign of empire founding that La Salle had planned with Fort Frontenac as his base of supplies.

Chapter VIII

From La Salle to De Nonville

RECEIVING authority to explore the Mississippi to its mouth, as well as a grant made in 1675 of Fort Frontenac and surrounding lands as a seigniory, La Salle returned from France in 1678, and began the wonderful career that will hand his name down through countless years as the greatest explorer in the annals of America. He allied with him Tonty and Father Hennepin, the latter already known, as we have seen, along the Niagara frontier.

La Salle at once advanced to Fort Frontenac, which was to be his point of rendezvous and eastern base of supplies. His first act was to fortify this point strongly as though already foreseeing the recall of the sturdy Frontenac and the consequential uprising of the slumbering Iroquois.

The plan of Fort Frontenac published by Faillon shows that Frontenac's hasty palisades were replaced by La Salle with hewed stone on at least two landward sides, and within were to be found a barrack, bakery, and mill; by 1780 fourteen families replaced the four lone *habitans* left at the fort in 1677; his improvements had cost La Salle thirty-five thousand francs. In Parkman's graphic words we see La Salle reigning

the autocrat of his lonely little empire, as feudal lord of the forests around him, commander of a garrison raised and paid by himself, founder of the mission, patron of the church. But he had no thought of resting here. He had gained what he sought, a fulcrum for bolder and broader action. His plans were ripened and his time was come. He was no longer a needy adventurer, disinherited of all but his fertile brain and his intrepid heart. He had won place, influence, credit, and potent friends. Now, at length, he might hope to find the long-sought path to China and Japan, and secure for France those boundless regions of the west.[1]

La Salle now pushed his impetuous campaign, showing as much foresight as daring in this conception. To hold the golden West in fee three important projects at once demanded attention: fitting out two ships, one for Lake Ontario and one for the upper Niagara River and the lakes from which its waters came, and the acquiring at some proper rendezvous of the first invoice of furs. A brigantine of ten tons was building simultaneously with Fort Frontenac, and in the fall of the year (1678) was ready for its cargo of material for a sister-ship to be built above the great falls. A party in canoes, carrying some six thousand francs' worth of goods, had gone forward to the further lakes to engage and secure from the Indian tribes provisions for the expedition and a consignment of furs for the homeward voyage.

On November 18th, the brigantine with its singular freight weighed anchor and sped from sight of La Salle and the watchers at Fort Frontenac; the party was under the temporal command of Sieur la Motte de Lussière and the spiritual guidance of the famous historian Father Hennepin, "who belonged," writes one scholar, "to that class of writers who speak the truth by acci-

[1] *Discovery of the West*, pp. 115-16.

R. Réné Cavelier, Sieur De La Salle.

Frontenac, from Hébert's Statue at Quebec.

dent"; of him La Salle generously said that he wrote more in conformity to his wishes than his knowledge. After a rough voyage this unknown craft entered "the beautiful river Niagara," as Hennepin truthfully stated, on St. Nicholas's Day, December 6th and the *Te Deum Laudamus* was sung feelingly by the crew, which had barely escaped shipwreck near the mouth of Humber River.

Here, near the mouth of the Niagara River, La Salle had planned to build a fort to bear the name Fort Conti in honour of his chief patron, the Prince of Conti; Lake Erie he had already named Lac de Conti. "It is situated," he wrote Conti, before it was built, "near that great cataract, more than a hundred and twenty toises [780 feet] in height, by which the lakes of higher elevation precipitate themselves into Lake Frontenac." A party of Senecas welcomed the little party, listening wonderingly to their anthem, supplying them with no end of white fish which they had come to catch here, living the while in a sort of a village near by, comprising probably a few huts erected for temporary purposes. It is possible these dwellings were of a more permanent character; at any rate Seneca sovereignty was assured, as the Frenchmen discovered just as soon as post-holes for Fort Conti were being dug. Concerning this, as well as the other features of this early Niagara River history, the record of Father Hennepin is about our only source of information; let us, therefore, quote from his *A New Discovery* concerning Frontenac and Niagara days:

That very same Year, on the Eighteenth of **November**, I took leave of our Monks at Fort Frontenac, and after mutual Embraces and Expressions of Brotherly and Christian Charity, I embark'd in a Brigantine of about ten Tuns. The Winds and the Cold of the Autumn were then very violent, insomuch that our Crew was afraid to go into so little a Vessel. This oblig'd us and the Sieur de la Motte our Commander, to keep our course on the North-side of the Lake, to shelter ourselves under the Coast, against the North-west Wind, which otherwise would have forced us upon the Southern Coast of the Lake. This Voyage prov'd very difficult and dangerous, because of the unseasonable time of the Year, Winter being near at hand.

On the 26th, we were in great danger about Two large Leagues off the Land, where we were oblig'd to lie at an Anchor all that Night at sixty Fathom Water and above; but at length the Wind coming to the North-East, we sail'd on, and arriv'd safely at the further end of the Lake Ontario, call'd by the Iroquese, Skannadario. We came pretty near to one of their Villages call'd Tajajagon, lying about Seventy Leagues from Fort Frontenac, or Catarakouy.

We barter'd some Indian Corn with the Iroquese, who could not sufficiently admire us, and came frequently to see us on board our Brigantine, which for our greater security, we had brought to an Anchor into a River, though before we could get in, we run aground three times, which oblig'd us to put Fourteen Men into Canou's, and cast the Balast of our Ship overboard to get her off again. That River falls into the Lake; but for fear of being frozen up therein, we were forced to cut the Ice with Axes and other Instruments.

The Wind turning then contrary, we were oblig'd to tarry there till the 15th of December, 1678, when we sailed from the Northern Coast to the Southern, where the River Niagara runs into the Lake; but could not reach it that Day, though it is but Fifteen or Sixteen Leagues distant, and therefore cast Anchor within Five Leagues of the Shore, where we had very bad Weather all the Night long.

On the 6th, being St. Nicholas's Day, we got into the fine River Niagara, into which never any such Ship as ours entred before. We sung there Te Deum, and other Prayers, to return our Thanks to God Almighty for our prosperous Voyage. The Iroquese Tsonnontouans inhabiting the little Village, situated

From La Salle to De Nonville

at the Mouth of the River, took above Three Hundred Whitings which are bigger than Carps, and the best relish'd, as well as the wholsomest Fish in the World; which they presented all to us, imputing their good luck to our Arrival. They were much surprized at our Ship, which they call'd the Great Woodden Canou.

On the 7th, we went in a Canou two Leagues up the River to look for a convenient Place for Building; but not being able to get the Canou farther up, because the Current was too rapid for us to master, we went over land about three Leagues higher, though we found no Land fit for culture. We lay that Night near a River, which runs from the Westward, within a League above the great Fall of Niagara, which, as we have already said, is the greatest in the World. The Snow was then a Foot deep, and we were oblig'd to dig it up to make room for our Fire.

The next day we return'd the same way we went, and saw great Numbers of Wild Goats, and Wild Turkey-Cocks, and on the 11th we said the first Mass that ever was said in that Country. The Carpenters and the rest of the Crew were set to work; but Monsieur de la Motte, who had the Direction of them, being not able to endure the Fatigues of so laborious a Life, gave over his Design, and return'd to Canada, having about two hundred Leagues to Travel.

The 12th, 13th, and 14th, the Wind was not favourable enough to sail up the River as far as the rapid Current above mention'd where we had resolv'd to build some Houses.

Whosoever considers our Map, will easily see, that this New Enterprise of building a Fort and some Houses on the River Niagara, besides the Fort of Frontenac, was like to give Jealousie to the Iroquese, and even to the English, who live in this Neighbourhood, and have a great Commerce with them. Therefore to prevent the ill Consequences of it, it was thought fit to send an Embassie to the Iroquese, as it will be mention'd in the next Chapter.

The 15th I was desired to sit at the Helm of our Brigantine while three of our Men hall'd the same from the Shore with a Rope; and at last we brought her up, and moor'd her to the Shore with a Halser, near a Rock of a prodigious heighth lying upon the rapid Currents we have already mentioned. The 17th, 18th, and 19th, we were busie in making a Cabin with Pallisado's, to serve for a Magazine; but the Ground was so frozen, that we were forc'd to throw several times boiling Water upon it to facilitate the beating in and driving down the Stakes. The 20th, 21st, 22d, and 23d, our Ship was in great danger to be dash'd in pieces, by the vast pieces of Ice that were hurl'd down the River; to prevent which, our Carpenters made a Capstone to haul her ashore; but our great Cable broke in three pieces; whereupon one of our Carpenters surrounded the Vessel with a Cable, and ty'd it to several Ropes, whereby we got her ashore, tho' with much difficulty, and sav'd her from the danger of being broke to pieces, or carryed away by the Ice, which came down with an extream violence from the great Fall of Niagara.

Returning to Niagara with little or no promise of success, yet La Salle's *avant-couriers* were in no way dissuaded from their purposes of fortifying the important Niagara portage and building a vessel for the upper lakes in which to carry the produce of those regions to Niagara and from thence to Canada. Reaching the Niagara January 14th, the French party was joined six days later by the indomitable La Salle who, he reported, had paused on his way thither from Fort Frontenac and visited the unmoved Iroquois and secured their consent to the plan of fortification. Yet even La Salle was too optimistic as to his success,

for certain Persons [wrote Hennepin], who made it their Business to Cross our Design, inspired the *Iroquese* with many suspicions, about the fort we were building at *Niagara*, which was in great forwardness; and their Suspicions grew so high, that we were obliged to give over our Building for some time, contenting ourselves with an Habitation encompass'd with Pallisado's.

The embassy to the Iroquois mentioned by Hennepin was duly organised and sent forward through the winter snows to seek the good-will of the famous owners of the soil in a fort-building project; in order to allay the suspicions of the Senecas in what Hennepin calls "the little village of Niagara," they were told that their purpose was, not to build a fort, but "a Hangar, or Store-house, to keep the Commodities we had brought to supply their Occasions." Nevertheless it was necessary to supply gifts and make assurances that an embassy would forthwith depart for the Iroquois council house. Anything less than Hennepin's own account would not fairly describe this interesting mission:

We travelled with Shoes made after the Indian way, of a single Skin, but without Soles, because the Earth was still cover'd with Snow, and past through Forests for thirty two Leagues together carrying upon our Backs our Coverings and other Baggage, lying often in open Field, and having with us no other Food but some roasted Indian Corn: 'T is true, we met upon our Road some Iroquese a hunting, who gave us some wild Goats, and Fifteen or Sixteen black Squirrels, which are excellent Meat. However, after five Days' Journey, we came to Tagarondies, a great Village of the Iroquese Tsonnontouans, and were immediately carry'd to the Cabin of their Principal Chief, where Women and Children flock'd to see us, our Men being very well drest and arm'd. An old Man having according to Custom made publick Cries, to give Notice of our arrival to their Village; the younger Savages wash'd our Feet, which afterwards they rubb'd over with the Grease of Deers, wild Goats, and other Beasts, and the Oil of Bears.

The next Day was the First of the Year 1679. After the ordinary Service I preach'd in a little Chapel made of Barks of Trees, in presence of two Jesuites, viz. Father Garnier and Rafeix; and afterwards we had a Conference with 42 old Men, who make up their Council. These Savages are for the most part tall, and very well shap'd, cover'd with a sort of Robe made of Beavers and Wolves-Skins, or of black Squirrels, holding a Pipe or Calumet in their Hands. The Senators of

Venice do not appear with a graver Countenance, and perhaps don't speak with more Majesty and Solidity, than those Ancient Iroquese.

This Nation is the most cruel and barbarous of all America, especially to their Slaves, whom they take above two or three hundred Leagues from their Country, . . . however, I must do them the Justice to observe, that they have many good qualities; and that they love the Europeans, to whom they sell their Commodities at very reasonable Rates. They have a mortal Hatred for those, who being too self-interested and covetous, are always endeavouring to enrich themselves to the Prejudice of others. Their chief Commodities are Beavers-Skins, which they bring from above a hundred and fifty Leagues off their Habitations, to exchange them with the English and Dutch, whom they affect more than the inhabitants of Canada, because they are more affable, and sell them their Commodities cheaper.

One of our own Men nam'd Anthony Brossard, who understood very well the Language of the Iroquese, and therefore was Interpreter to M. de la Motte; told their Assembly:

First, That we were come to pay them a Visit, and smoak with them in their Pipes, a Ceremony which I shall describe anon: And then we deliver'd our Presents, consisting of Axes, Knives, a great Collar of white and blue Porcelain, with some Gowns. We made Presents upon every Point we propos'd to them, of the same nature as the former.

Secondly, We desir'd them, in the next place to give notice to the five Cantons of their Nation, that we were about to build a Ship, or great woodden Canou above the great Fall of the River Niagara, to go and fetch European Commodities by a more convenient passage than the ordinary one, by the River St. Laurence, whose rapid Currents make it dangerous and long; and that by these means we should afford them our Commodities cheaper than the English and Dutch of Boston and New-York. This Pretence was specious enough, and very well contriv'd to engage the barbarous Nation to extirpate the English and Dutch out of America: For they suffer the Europeans among them only for the Fear they have of them, or else

From La Salle to De Nonville

for the Profit they make in Bartering their Commodities with them.

Thirdly, We told them farther, that we should provide them at the River Niagara with a Black-smith and a Gun-smith, to mend their Guns, Axes, &c. having no body among them that understood that Trade, and that for the conveniency of their whole Nation, we would settle those Workmen on the Lake of Ontario, at the Mouth of the River Niagara. We threw again among them seven or eight Gowns, and some Pieces of fine Cloth, which they cover themselves with from the Wast to the Knees. This was in order to engage them on our side, and prevent their giving ear to any who might suggest ill things of us, entreating them first to acquaint us with the Reports that should be made unto them to our Prejudice, before they yielded their Belief to the fame.

We added many other Reasons which we thought proper to persuade them to favour our Design. The Presents we made unto them, either in Cloth or Iron, were worth above 400 Livres besides some other European Commodities, very scarce in that Country: For the best Reasons in the World are not listened to among them, unless they are enforc'd with Presents.

The next Day the Iroquese answered our Discourse and Presents Article by Article, having laid upon the Ground several little pieces of Wood, to put them in mind of what had been said the Day before in the Council; their Speaker, or President held in his Hand one of these Pieces of Wood, and when he had answer'd one Article of our Proposal, he laid it down, with some Presents of black and white Porcelain, which they use to string upon the smallest Sinews of Beasts; and then took up another Piece of Wood; and so of all the rest, till he had fully answer'd our Speech, of which those Pieces of Wood, and our Presents put them in mind. When this Discourse was ended, the oldest Man of their Assembly cry'd aloud three times, Nioua; that is to say, It is well, I thank thee, which was repeated with a full Voice; and in a tuneful manner by all the other Senators.

'T is to be observ'd here, that the Savages, though some are more cunning than others, are generally all addicted to their own Interests; and therefore tho' the Iroquese seem'd to be pleas'd with our Proposals, they were not really so; for the English and Dutch affording them the European Commodities at cheaper Rates than the French of Canada, they had a greater Inclination for them than for us. That People, tho' so barbarous and rude in their Manners, have however a Piece of Civility peculiar to themselves; for a Man would be counted very impertinent if he contradicted anything that is said in their Council, and if he does not approve even the greatest Absurdities therein propos'd; and therefore they always answer Niaoua; that is to say Thou art in the right Brother; that is well.

Notwithstanding that seeming Approbation, they believe what they please and no more; and therefore 't is impossible to know when they are really persuaded of those things you have mention'd unto them, which I take to be one of the greatest Obstructions to their Conversion: For their Civility hindering them from making any Objection, or contradicting what is said unto them, they seem to approve of it, though perhaps they laugh at it in private, or else never bestow a moment to reflect upon it, such being their indifference for a future Life. From these Observations, I conclude that the Conversion of these People is to be despair'd of, 'till they are subdu'd by the Europeans, and that their Children have another sort of Education, unless God be pleas'd to work a Miracle in their Favour.

On the 22nd of the month the party struck out for the upper Niagara for the purpose of carrying out the original design of building a ship for the upper lake trade. Hennepin gives the site of this interesting adventure as "two leagues above the great Fall—this was the most convenient place we could pitch upon, being upon a River which falls into the Streight [Niagara River] between the Lake *Erie*, and the great Fall of Niagara." Even had the common portage around the Falls and Rapids been on the American side Hennepin's account makes it fairly clear that the boat building took place on Cayuga Creek; the only other "river" above the Falls falling into the Niagara is the Chippewa, and Hennepin clearly notes this stream in his first tour of exploration above the Falls as "within a league above the great Fall"; it is clear that the Cayuga, therefore, is the probable site of this first boat building along the Niagara frontier.[1] The little village at this point has been appropriately named La Salle from the famous adventurer who here dreamed that emparadising dream of discovery and empire-founding. Hennepin's account, quaintly worded, again becomes of more interest than any record of those days to be made from it:

> The 26th, the Keel of the Ship and some other Pieces being ready, M. de la Salle sent the Master-Carpenter, to desire me to drive in the first Pin; but my Profession obliging me to decline that Honour, he did it himself, and promis'd Ten Louis d'Or's, to encourage the Carpenter, and further the Work. The Winter being not half so hard in that Country as in Canada, we employ'd one of the two Savages of the Nation call'd the Wolf, whom we kept for Hunting, in building some Cabins made of Rinds of Trees; and I had one made on purpose to perform Divine Service therein on Sundays, and other occasions.
> M. de la Salle having some urgent Business of his own, return'd to Fort Frontenac, leaving for our Commander one Tonti, an Italian by Birth, who had been forc'd to retire into France after the Revolution of Naples, in which his Father was concern'd. I conducted M. de la Salle as far as the Lake Ontario at the Mouth of the River Niagara, where we order'd a House to be built for the Smith he had promis'd to the Iroquese; but this was only to amuze them, and therefore I cannot but own that the Savages are not to be blam'd for having not believ'd

---

[1] The exact spot of building is the subject of a monograph *The Shipyard of the Griffon* by Cyrus Kingsbury Remington (Buffalo, N. Y. 1891), in which the author, while advocating his own theory, presents liberally views held by those in disagreement with himself. We find O. H. Marshall in accord with Mr Remington that what is known as the "Old Ship Yard" or Angevine place, at La Salle, was the site of the building of the *Griffon*.

every thing they were told by M. la Motte in his Embassie already related.

He undertook his Journey a-foot over the Snow, having no other Provisions, but a little Sack of Indian Corn roasted, which fail'd him two Days before he came to the Fort, which is above fourscore Leagues distant from the Place where he left us. However he got home safely with two Men, and a Dog, who dragg'd his Baggage over the Ice or frozen Snow.

When I return'd to our Dock, I understood that most of the Iroquese were gone to wage War with a Nation on the other side of the Lake Erie. In the mean time, our Men continu'd with great Application to build our Ship; for the Iroquese who were left behind, being but a small number, were not so insolent as before, though they come now and then to our Dock, and express'd some Discontent at what we were doing. One of them in particular, feigning himself drunk, attempted to kill our Smith, but was vigorously repuls'd by him with a red-hot Iron-barr, which, together with the Reprimand he receiv'd from me, oblig'd him to be gone. Some few Days after, a Savage Woman gave us notice, that the Tsonnontouans had resolv'd to burn our Ship in the Dock, and had certainly done it, had we not been always upon our Guard.

These frequent Alarms from the Natives, together with the Fears we were in of wanting Provisions, having lost the great Barque from Fort Frontenac, which should have reliev'd us, and the Tsonnontouans at the same time refusing to give us of their Corn for Money, were a great discouragement to our Carpenters, whom on the other hand, a Villain amongst us endeavour'd to reduce: That pitiful Fellow had several times attempted to run away from us into New-York, and would have been likely to pervert our Carpenters, had I not confirm'd them in their good Resolution, by the Exhortations I us'd to make every Holy-day after Divine Service; in which I represented to them, that the Glory of God was concern'd in our Undertaking, besides the Good and Advantage of our Christian Colonies; and therefore exhorted them to redouble their Diligence, in order to free our selves from all those Inconveniences and Apprehensions we then lay under.

The two Savages we had taken into our Service, went all this while a Hunting, and supply'd us with Wild-Goats, and other Beasts for our Subsistence; which encouraged our Workmen to go on with their Work more briskly than before, insomuch that in a short time our Ship was in a readiness to be launched; which we did, after having bless'd the same according to the use of the Romish Church. We made all the haste we could to get it afloat, though not altogether finish'd, to prevent the Designs of the Natives, who had resolv'd to burn it.

The Ship was call'd the Griffon, alluding to the Arms of Count Frontenac, which have two Griffons for Supporters; and besides, M. la Salle us'd to say of the Ship, while yet upon the Stocks, that he would make the Griffon fly above the Ravens. We fir'd three Guns, and sung Te Deum, which was attended with loud Acclamations of Joy; of which those of the Iroquese, who were accidentally present at this Ceremony, were also Partakers; for we gave them some Brandy to drink, as well as our Men, who immediately quitted their Cabins of Rinds of Trees, and hang'd their Hammocks under the Deck of the Ship, there to lie with more security than ashore. We did the like, insomuch that the very same Day we were all on Board, and thereby out of the reach of the Insults of the Savages.

The Iroquese being returned from hunting Beavers, were mightily surprised to see our Ship a-float, and call'd us Otkon, which is in their Language, Most penetrating Wits: For they could not apprehend how in so short a time we had been able to build so great a Ship, though it was but 60 Tuns. It might have been indeed call'd a moving Fortress; for all the Savages inhabiting the Banks of those Lakes and Rivers I have mentioned, for five hundred Leagues together, were filled with fear as well as Admiration when they saw it. . . .

Being thus prepar'd against all Discouragements, I went up in a Canou with one of our Savages to the Mouth of the Lake Erie, notwithstanding the strong Current which I master'd with great difficulty. I sounded the Mouth of the Lake and found, contrary to the Relation that had been made unto me, that a Ship with a brisk Gale might sail up to the Lake, and surmounted the Rapidity of the Current; and that therefore with a strong North, North-East Wind, we might bring our Ship into the Lake Erie. I took also a view of the Banks of the Streight, and found that in case of Need, we might put some of our Men a-shore to hall the Ship, if the Wind was not strong enough.

The *Griffon* being more or less completed Father Hennepin followed La Salle in returning to Fort Frontenac to secure necessaries for the tour of the upper lakes. Returning, La Salle and Hennepin did not reach Niagara again until the 30th of July, but found the *Griffon* riding safely at anchor within a league of Lake Erie.

We were very kindly receiv'd [writes the Father], and likewise very glad to find our Ship well rigg'd, and ready fitted out with all the Necessaries for sailing. She carry'd five small Guns, two whereof were Brass, and three Harquebuze a-crock. The Beak-head was adorn'd with a flying Griffon, and an Eagle above it; and the rest of the Ship had the same Ornaments as Men of War use to have.

The Iroquese were then returning from a Warlike Expedition with several Slaves, and were much surpriz'd to see so big a Ship, which they compar'd to a Fort, beyond their Limits. Several came on board, and seem'd to admire above all things the bigness of our Anchors; for they could not apprehend how we had been able to bring them through the rapid Currents of the River St. Laurence. This oblig'd them to use often the Word Gannorom, which in their Language signifies, That is wonderful. They wonder'd also to find there a Ship, having seen none when they went; and did not know from whence it came, it being about 250 Leagues from Canada.

Having forbid the Pilot to attempt to sail up the Currents of the Streight till farther order, we return'd the 16th and 17th to the Lake Ontario, and brought up our Bark to the great Rock of Niagara, and anchor'd at the foot of the three Mountains Lewiston, where we were oblig'd to make our Portage; that is, to carry over-land our Canou's and Provisions, and other

Luna Island Bridge.

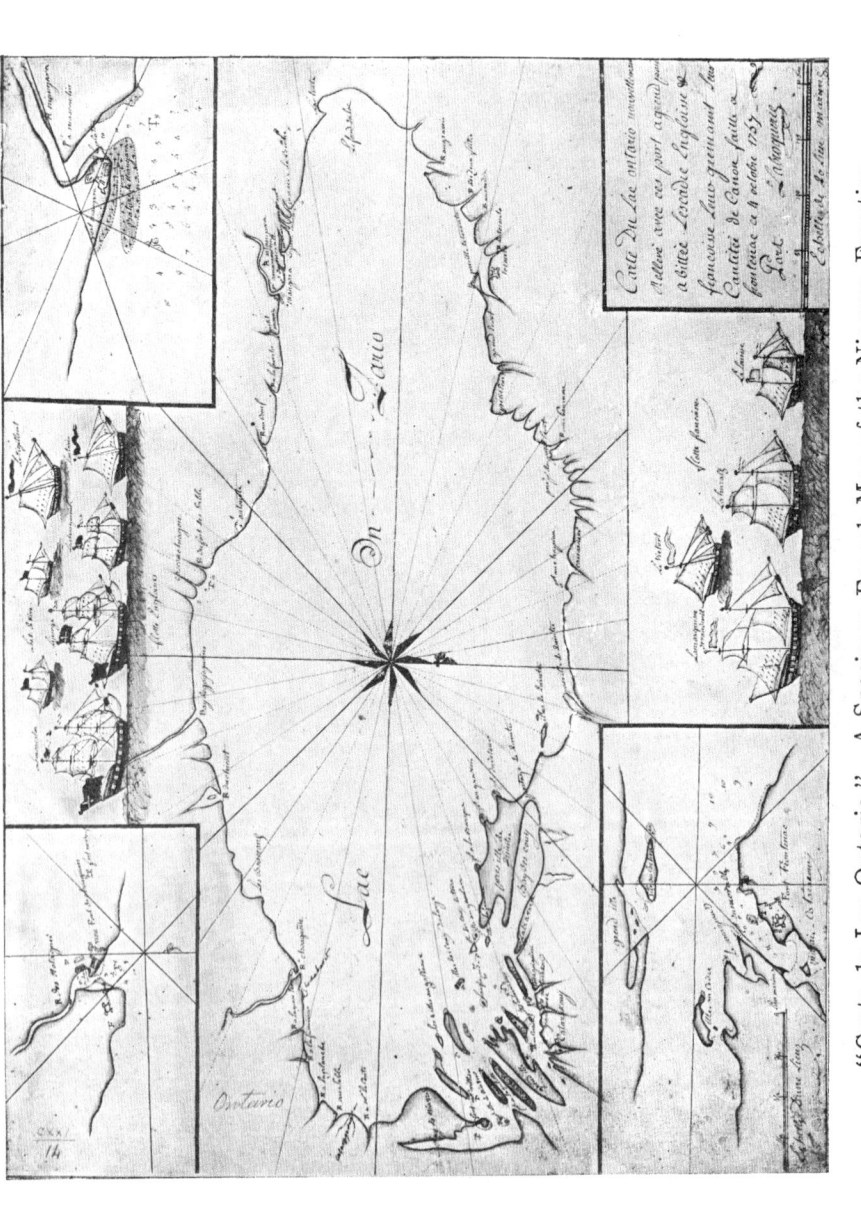

"Carte du Lac Ontario." A Specimen French Map of the Niagara Frontier. Dated October 4, 1757. From the original in the British Museum

Things, above the great Fall of the River, which interrupts the Navigation: and because most of the Rivers of that Country are interrupted with great Rocks, and that therefore those who sail upon the same, are oblig'd to go overland above those Falls, and carry upon their Backs their Canou's and other Things. They express it with this Word, To make our Portage; of which the Reader is desir'd to take notice, for otherwise the following Account, as well as the Map, would be unintelligible to many.

Father Gabriel, though of Sixty five Years of Age, bore with great Vigour the Fatigue of that Voyage, and went thrice up and down those three Mountains, which are pretty high and steep. Our Men had a great deal of trouble; for they were oblig'd to make several Turns to carry the Provisions and Ammunition, and the Portage was two Leagues long. Our Anchors were so big that four Men had much ado to carry one; but the Brandy we gave them was such an Encouragement, that they surmounted cheerfully all the Difficulties of that Journey; and so we got on board our Ship all our Provisions, Ammunitions, and Commodities. . . .

We endeavour'd several times to sail up that Lake; but the Wind being not strong enough, we were forc'd to wait for it. In the mean time, M. la Salle caus'd our Men to grub up some Land, and sow several sorts of Pot-Herbs and Pulse, for the conveniency of those who should settle themselves there, to maintain our Correspondence with Fort Frontenac. We found there a great quantity of wild Cherries and Rocambol, a sort of Garlick, which grow naturally in that Ground. We left Father Melithon, with some Work-men, at our Habitation above the Fall of Niagara; and most of our Men went a-shore to lighten our Ships, the better to sail up the Lake.

The Wind veering to the North-East, and the Ship being well provided, we made all the Sail we could, and with the help of Twelve Men who hall'd from the Shoar, overcame the Rapidity of the Current, and got into the Lake. The Stream is so violent, that our Pilot himself despair'd of Success. When it was done, we sung Te Deum, and discharg'd our Cannon and other Fire-Arms, in presence of a great many Iroquese, who came from a Warlike Expedition against the Savages of Tintonha; that is to say, the Nation of the Meadows, who live above four hundred Leagues from that Place. The Iroquese and their Prisoners were much surpriz'd to see us in the Lake and did not think before that, we should be able to overcome the Rapidity of the Current: They cry'd several times Gannorom, to shew their Admiration. Some of the Iroquese had taken the measure of our Ship, and immediately went for New-York to give notice to the English and Dutch of our Sailing into the Lake: For those Nations affording their Commodities Cheaper than the French, are also more belov'd by the Natives. On the 7th of August, 1679, we went on board being in all four and thirty men, including two Recollets who came to us, and sail'd from the Mouth of the Lake Erie.

The loss of the *Griffon* by shipwreck on its initial voyage and the subsequent misfortunes that seemed to follow the brave La Salle up to the very day that witnessed his brutal murder in a far Texan prairie in 1687, are, in a measure only a part of the story of Niagara. Had that great man lived to realise any fair fraction of his emparadising dream of empire the effect on the history of the Niagara frontier would have been momentous; a mere comparison of what now did transpire at the mouth of the Niagara, in the very year of La Salle's death, illustrates perfectly the lack of enterprise that seems suddenly to have faded from the situation. With La Salle gone, the whole attitude of the regime in power at Quebec seems to change; whereas La Salle was on the very point of establishing at Niagara an important station on the communication to Louisiana. What actually did happen here is pitiful by comparison.

The new Governor, De Nonville, in order to bring the Iroquois into a proper state of submission and compell them to desist from annoying travellers on

From La Salle to De Nonville

the St. Lawrence, determined to repeat Champlain's feat of invading their homeland. The record of this expedition from the mouth of its commanding officer, the Governor himself, is a very interesting document, especially to those interested in the study of that famous Long House that lay south of Lake Ontario.[1] Embarking at Fort Frontenac July 4, 1687, the expedition landed at Irondequoit Bay six days later, where De Nonville was reinforced by a party of French which had rendezvoused at Niagara from the West. Of this party little is known; possibly some of La Salle's crew were here, coming from their cabins at either end of the Niagara portage path, or possibly from the ship yard at the present La Salle. "It clearly appears," writes Marshall, "from De Nonville's narrative, that the party which he met at the mouth of the bay, was composed of French and Indians from the far west, who sailed from . . . Niagara, to join the expedition pursuant to his orders." These Indians, Mr. Browne affirms, were from Michilimackinac. Marching inland to the region Mr. Marshall believed, in the neighbourhood of the village of Victor, ten miles north-west of Canandaigua, a party of Senecas was put to flight and the entire region devastated until the 23rd; it was estimated that in the four Seneca villages the soldiers had destroyed about 1,200,000 bushels of corn—350,000 minots, of which all but 50,000 were green. On the 24th the lake was again reached.

The situation on the Niagara frontier at this moment could not better be described than it has been by Mr. Browne in his *The St. Lawrence River*, as follows:

[1] The Narrative is given in full with careful introduction and explanations in Marshall's *Writings*, 123–186.

Denonville had now a clear way to build his fort at Niagara, which he proceeded to do, and then armed it with one hundred men. If triumphant in his bold plans, he had to learn that the viper crushed might rise to sting. The Senecas had their avengers. Maddened by the cowardly onset of Denonville and his followers, the Iroquois to a man rose against the French. This was not done by any organised raid, but, shod with silence, small, eager war-parties haunted the forests of the St. Lawrence, striking where they were the least expected, and never failing to leave behind them the smoke of burning dwellings and the horrors of desolated lives. From Fort Frontenac to Tadousac there was not a home exempt from this deadly scourge; not a life that was not threatened. Unable to cope with so artful a foe, Denonville was in despair. He sued for peace, but to obtain this he had to betray his allies, the Indians of the Upper Lakes, who had entered his service under the conditions that the war should continue until the Iroquois were exterminated. The latter sent delegates to confer with the French commander at Montreal.

While this conference was under way, a Huron chief showed that he was the equal of even Denonville in the strategies of war where the code of honour was a dead letter. Anticipating the fate in store for his race did the French carry out their scheme of self-defence, this chief, whose name was Kandironk, "the Rat," lay in ambush for the envoys on their way home from their conference with Denonville, when the latter had made so many fair promises. These Kandironk captured, claiming he did it under orders from Denonville, bore them to Michilimackinac, and tortured them as spies. This done, he sent an Iroquois captive to tell his people how fickle the French could be. Scarcely was this accomplished when he gave to the French his exultant declaration, "I have killed the peace!" The words were prophetic. Nothing that Denonville could say or do cleared him of connection with the affair. His previous conduct was enough to condemn him. To avenge this act of deceit, as the Iroquois considered it, they rallied in great numbers, and on the night of August 4, 1689, dealt the most cruel and deadly blow given during all the years of warfare in the St. Lawrence valley. Fifteen hundred strong, under cover of the darkness, they stole down upon the settlement of La Chine situated at the upper end of the island of Montreal, and surprised the inhabitants while they slept in fancied security. More than two hundred men, women, and children were slain in cold blood, or borne away to fates a hundred times more terrible to meet than swift death. The day already breaking upon the terror-stricken colonists was the darkest Canada ever knew.

The result of the expedition, so far as result appears, was effected when the ships bearing his men turned toward the Niagara River and were anchored off the point of land where now stands historic Fort Niagara. Here a fort was to be built forthwith, as much to secure the fur trade and to overawe the Indians as to keep the English from making any advance toward the territory of the Lakes. On the very day of his arrival De Nonville set his men to work. The fortification was constructed partly of earth surmounted by palisades. The building of the structure was no easy matter. There were no trees in the immediate vicinity, so the soldiers had to obtain their timber to the east along the lake or across the river. After the timber had been obtained from these forests, it was a very difficult matter to drag it up the high bank. However, De Nonville was so energetic and his men worked so faithfully that in three days a fort was built with four bastions, where were mounted two large guns. Several cabins were also built. As the work progressed, many of those who had come with De Nonville, both French and Indians, began to leave. Du Luth, Durantaye, and Tonty, together with the Illinois Indians who had allied themselves with the French against the Iroquois, departed for the trading-posts of

Detroit and Michilimackinac. Soon after De Nonville himself left for Montreal, taking with him all but a hundred men. Those whom he left behind were placed under the command of De Troyes, with promises to send provisions as soon as possible, and fresh troops in the spring.[1]

The men left behind were truly in a surly mood. In spite of De Nonville's assurance of provisions, and his assertion that the Senecas had been subdued, these men knew only too well not to depend too much on the first, and as to the second, that the Indians had only been enraged, rather than vanquished.

For a time there was enough work to keep all hands busy. M. de Brissay left on the 3d of August, commanding M. de Vaudreuil to help in the constructing of the cabins and the completion of the fort. There was an immense amount of work to be accomplished in the cutting, dragging, hewing, and sawing of the timbers; but, despite the hot weather, there was soon completed a house with a chimney of sticks and clay for the commandant. Three other cabins were afterward built in the square and in the midst of these a well was dug; but its waters were always roiled from improper curbing.

Vaudreuil left toward the latter part of August after having seen the company well roofed. Many of the number, who were at first fired by the spirit of adventure and a desire to remain at Niagara, now, foreseeing the suffering to be undergone, desired to return with Vaudreuil; but nearly all were compelled to remain at the fort.

[1] A most thrilling account of this fort-building effort at the mouth of the Niagara is to be found in Severance, *Old Trails of the Niagara Frontier*, on which the present writer has based his description he₁ ₂ given.

From La Salle to De Nonville

Although the expedition when it set out against the Senecas was tolerably well supplied with necessaries for an Indian campaign, those who were left at the fort were left in a bad condition indeed. About three thousand bushels of corn had been destroyed which belonged to the Senecas; but scarcely a week's rations had been brought along to their destination. Very few had brought any seeds, and not much gardening could have been done anyway, on account of the lateness of the season. The few attempts that were made brought no returns on account of a drought. No hunting could be undertaken except in large parties so as to be secure from the savages. Almost the only food supply was the fish caught in the lake.

There was unbounded joy at the fort when the sail of the ship with supplies, which had been promised by Denonville, was seen on the horizon. But even then the unlading was delayed two days by calms which prevented the vessel from coming nearer than several miles from the shore. Finally a landing was effected; and the cargo was quickly stowed in the fort. The ship immediately returned to Canada.

From the very first the provisions proved to be bad. Still with these, together with the few herbs of the forest, a small amount of game and fish, the men managed to eke out an existence. There was no labour to perform—nothing to do but complain of the food and hard life which they were compelled to live.

Toward the latter part of September, the Indians made their first appearance. A hunting party in the vicinity of the Falls lost two men. Another party was cut off from the fort. Their dead bodies were found scalped and mutilated by the savages. The commander,

De Troyes, soon fell ill, as did also Jean de Lamberville, the only priest in the colony. Thus at almost the same time was the company deprived of leadership and religious consolation. Christmas season drew on; but it was a sorry time for those at the fort. The weather had become severe, and fierce snow-storms were frequent. No one ventured beyond the palisades except in quest of firewood; and it was almost impossible at times to obtain this. Many were nearly frozen in their cabins. One day the wood-choppers were overwhelmed in the snow in sight of the fort. No one dared to go to their succour for fear of suffering the same fate. Two days after, those within the stockade saw their dead comrades devoured by wolves. Not a charge of powder was left. The food was almost unbearable. The biscuits were full of weevil from the first, and the meat was in such a putrefied condition that no one could eat it. Scurvy broke out. De Troyes could not leave his cabin and was compelled to trust everything to his men.

From a band of gallant soldiers, they had been reduced to a mere handful of disease-infected skeletons. In six weeks there were sixty deaths; and this was only the middle of February. Only a few of the stronger were left able to do the work which was absolutely necessary, such as supplying firewood and burying the dead, and these duties were performed with infinite toil and danger. More than twenty died in the month of March; in this number was the brave commander De Troyes. With their leader seemed to perish all the little spirit left in his followers. Almost no hope was left for the suffering inmates of the fort. It was still many weeks until the promised succour could possibly come from Montreal. The Western savages had promised an alliance and aid to the French against the Iroquois, but little confidence was to be placed in their promises.

Just as the men left in the fort were reduced to the very last extremity, and were wishing for death to relieve them of their miseries, a war-party from the Miamis on an expedition against the Senecas reached the fort and gave that relief so long vainly looked for by the inmates. Several of these who first regained their strength set out for Montreal to carry the news of their sore straits to the government; and on one pleasant, beautiful day in April the long expected sail was seen on the horizon bringing relief to the remnant of those who had been left in the fort the preceding summer.

In command of the expedition was D'esbergeres, and with him Father Milet, besides a large company of companions. As soon as they landed, Father Milet conducted mass and then put all the men who were able to work constructing a large cross. While they were at the work, Father Milet traced upon its arms: "Regnat, Vincit, Imperat Christus."

On Good Friday, the priest again held mass, and erected the cross in the centre of the square of the fort, thus symbolising a victory wrung from the clutches of defeat itself.

With spring, the new companions, and a goodly supply of provisions, was born new hope in the fort. The little company were very busy during the summer, despite the fact that the Iroquois, stirred on by the English, gave them continual trouble. In September Mahent came with the vessel *La Général,* with orders to D'esbergeres to abandon the fort. This was quite a blow to the commander, as having held the post all summer he hoped to continue to do so. The outer barracks were all destroyed, which was not so difficult a task, as the severe storms of the previous winter had done much of this work; but the cabins were all left standing. On the morning of the 15th of September, 1688, the garrison sailed away, once more leaving the shores of the great Niagara untroubled by the contentions of white men, and open to the nation who should seize it or conciliate the savages who held the surrounding regions.

Yet De Nonville had done something for which to be remembered beyond raiding the Long House and fortifying the river of the Neuters; he had left it a name that should live as he had, first of white men, so far as we know, written it. The orthography of the name Niagara seems to have now been established—1687. Champlain did not use any name in 1613, though on his map we find the following words attached to the stream connecting Lakes Erie and Ontario, *chute d'eau*, giving us our first genuine record of Niagara Falls.

We have seen that L'Allemant spelled the name *Onguiaahra* in 1640. In 1657 it appears on Sanson's map as *Ongiara*, and is applied to the Falls; in 1660 Ducreux's map shows us "*Ongiara* Cataractes." In 1687 De Nonville gives us our present Niagara. Of the name Mr. Marshall has left this authoritative opinion:

Onguiaahra and Ongiara are evidently identical, and present the same elements as Niagara. They are undoubtedly compounds of words expressive of some meaning, as is usual with aboriginal terms, but which meaning is now lost. The "o" which occurs in both the French and English orthography is probably a neuter prefix, similar to what is used by the Senecas and Mohawks. One writer contends that Niagara is derived from Nyah'-gaah', or as he writes it, "Ne-ah'-gah," said to be the name of a Seneca village which formerly existed on the Niagara River below Lewiston, and now applied by the Senecas to Lake Ontario. This derivation, however, cannot be correct, for Onguiaahra, and its counterpart Ongiara, were in use as names of the river and falls long before the Seneca village in question was in existence. The Neutral Nation, from whose language the words were taken, lived on *both* borders of the Niagara until they were exterminated by the Senecas in 1643. It is far more probable the Nyah'-gaah' is a reappearance of Ongiara in the Seneca dialect, and this view is strengthened by the fact that the former, unlike most Iroquois names, is without meaning, and as the aborigines do not confer arbitrary names, it is an evidence that it has been borrowed or derived from a foreign language. The conclusion then is, that the French derived Niagara from Ongiara, and the Senecas, when they took possession of the territories of the Neutral Nation, adopted the name Ongiara, as near as the idiom of their language would allow, and hence their name Nyah'-gaah'.

Chapter IX

Niagara under Three Flags

THE abdication of De Nonville at Niagara marks, as nothing else perhaps can, the rise of English influence along the Lakes and among the crafty Iroquois. Slowly but surely this influence made itself felt among the Six Nations in the attempt to swing the entire current of the fur trade from the north-west through the Long House to New York.

With the destruction of the little fort built by De Nonville, however, it becomes clear that when on the same basis the English were no match for the French, so far as winning the redskins to their interests was concerned; it may be that with the withdrawal of the French there followed a natural diminution of English anxiety and activity in the matter: whether this was true or not there immediately ensued a notable increase of French attention to the Six Nations who, after all, controlled the destinies of this key of the continent. As days of war and days of peace came and went the governors both of New York and Quebec sought permission to fortify the Niagara River, but the eighteenth century dawned with no step taken by either side, though each had most jealously been watching the other.

It was characteristic of Frenchmen, however, to

meet and mingle with the Indians as the English seldom did; it was not wholly out of the common, indeed, for them to adopt Indian dress and customs and be, in turn, adopted into some Indian tribe. Through the fortunate influence exerted by one of these adopted sons of the wilderness was New France now able to refortify the strategic Niagara region, temporarily besting England in the contest for the supremacy here. Chabert Joncaire, taken prisoner by the Senecas and adopted into their tribe, married an Indian woman and became an important factor among the warriors and war councils of the western end of the Long House. In the year 1700 Joncaire became a missionary for the French political cause, and he seems to have managed affairs so diplomatically that he in no wise lost caste among the Iroquois, for six years later they suggested to him "to establish himself among them, granting him liberty to select on their territory the place most acceptable to himself for the purpose of living and in peace, even to remove their villages to the neighbourhood of his residence in order to protect him."[1]

In the next decade France made considerable headway in undoing the miserable work of De Nonville by disarming the hostility of the Iroquois, especially with the Senecas who held the Niagara frontier, through Joncaire, who in 1719 was sent to "try the minds of the Seneca nation and ascertain if it would permit the building of a French house in their

[1] *Colonial Documents of New York*, vol. ix., p. 773; in the history of the French régime at Niagara special acknowledgment must be made to Porter's *Brief History of Old Fort Niagara* (Niagara Falls, 1896), which is particularly rich in references to the important sources of information concerning the French along and at the mouth of the Niagara River.

country." As a result, in 1720, Joncaire built a bark cabin at Lewiston which he called "Magazine Royal." In November of that year, according to English report, which was undoubtedly exaggerated through prejudice, the "cabin" is described as a blockhouse forty feet in length and thirty in width, enclosed with palisades, musket-proof and provided with port-holes. The location of this post signifies of itself alone the larger strategic nature of Niagara geographically, for it was not at the mouth of the river but at the beginning of the portage around the Rapids and Falls, at Lewiston, just where La Salle's storehouse, built in 1679, had stood. It is believed that the former building had disappeared by this time. Charlevoix, who came here the next year, 1721, confounds the sites of De Nonville's fort and the "Magazine Royal." Mr. Porter brings out well the office of Joncaire's cabin, in which, by the way, a few soldiers were maintained as "traders" by saying:

. . . The trade in furs was brisk, the Indians from the north, west, and south coming there to barter. The chain of friendship with the Senecas was kept bright by friendly intercourse with their warriors, who constantly came there; French trading vessels came often to its rude wharf bringing merchandise to Frontenac and returning laden with furs. Thus the English for the first time failed to overcome the French, while the English in New York did not delay their expostulations regarding what they called French incroachment at Niagara; but so far were they from being successful that the French were able within four years to begin a more important fortification on the site of the "Magazine Royal."

American history furnishes many illustrations of the genius of the French *coureurs-de-bois* for winning

Stones on the Site of Joncaire's Cabin under Lewiston Heights, where the Magazine Royal was Erected in 1719.

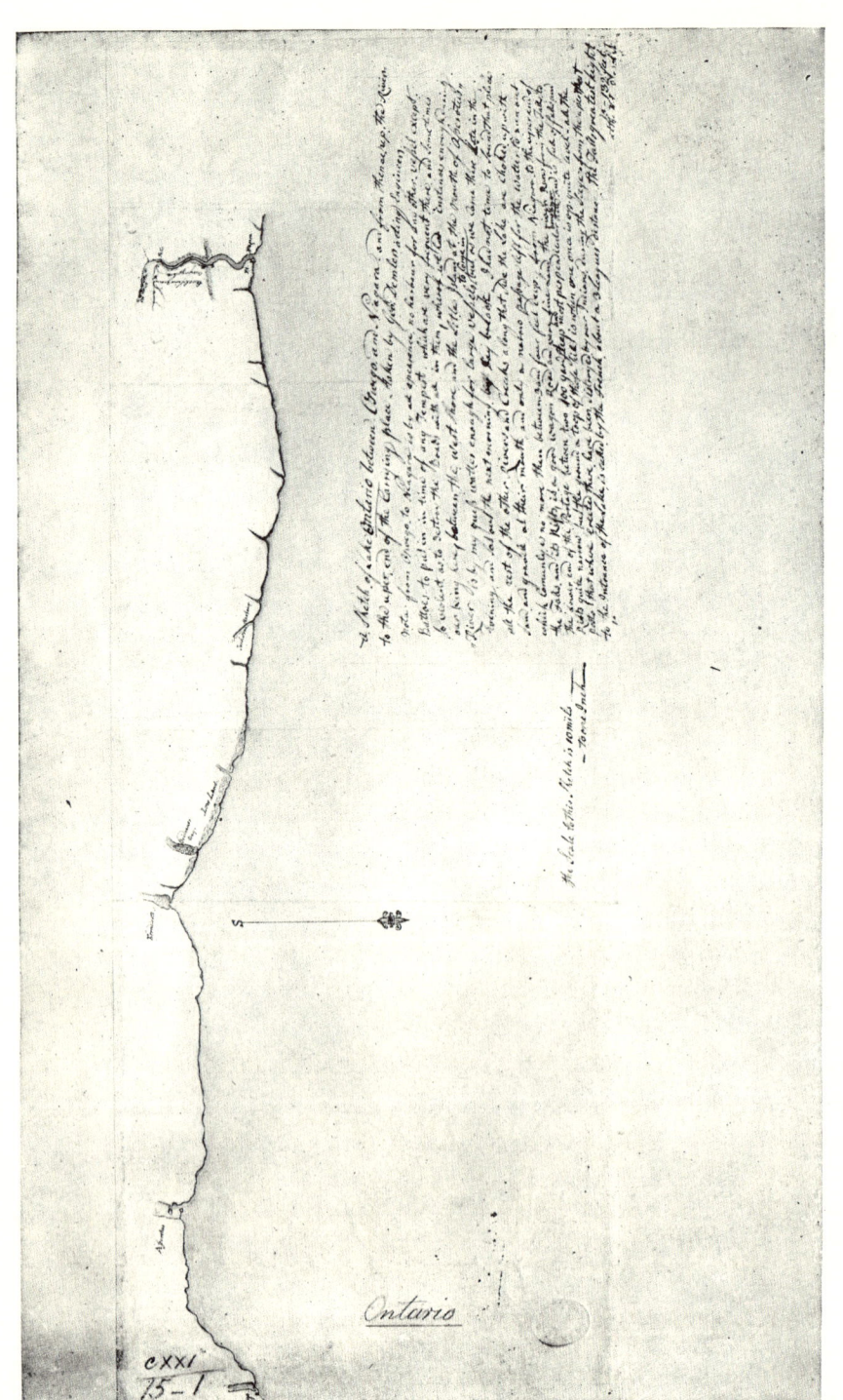

Specimen Manuscript Map of Niagara Frontier of Eighteenth Century.
From the original in the British Museum

to themselves the friendship of the Indians, but perhaps there is no specific illustration of this more clear than this reabsorption of the Niagara region after having once abandoned it. Said Sir Guy Carleton:

> France did not depend upon the number of her troops, but upon the discretion of her officers who, learned the language of her natives, distributed the king's presents, excited no jealousy, entirely gained the affections of an ignorant, credulous, but brave people, whose ruling passions are independence, gratitude, and revenge.

Governor Duquesne once said to a deputation of Indians:

> Are you ignorant of the defence between the king of France and the English? Look at the forts which the king has built; you will find that under their very walls the beasts of the forests are hunted and slain; that they are, in fact, fixed in places most frequented by you merely to gratify more conveniently your necessities.

M. Garneau, the historian, frankly acknowledges that the Marquis accurately stated the route of Indian admiration for the Frenchmen they saw; but it should not be overlooked that the French also were "the most romantic and poetic characters ever known in American frontier life. Their every moment attracts the rosiest colour of imagination"; all this helps to fascinate the savage.

In 1725, the Marquis De Vaudreuil proposed the erection of a storehouse at Niagara, and soon the agent met the council of the Five Nations and got their permission to build what was really a fort at Niagara, which was to cost $5592; one hundred men were instantly sent to begin the work.[1] Thus the historic pile known

[1] *Colonial Documents of New York*, vol. ix., pp. 952, 958.

as the "Mess House" or "Castle" was begun in 1725 and completed in 1726; at a council fire at Niagara the Senecas gave their final ratification to this project, July 14, 1726.

Joncaire's "Magazine Royal" was permitted to fall into decay, being abandoned in 1728 despite the fact that Louis XV. gave his approval to a plan for spending twenty thousand livres for its repair although approving strongly the erection of the castle, as it would prevent the English from trading on the north shore of Lake Ontario as well as getting a foothold on the Niagara River. Mr. Porter brings out well the service of Joncaire's "Magazine Royal" by saying:

> That building had done good service; it had given the French the desired foothold on the Niagara River; it had held and fostered the trade in furs; it had established French supremacy in this region, and furnished them with the key to the possession of the Upper Lakes and the Ohio Valley; and last, and most important of all, it had been the means of France obtaining a real fortress at the point where her diplomats and armies had been waiting to erect one; for over half a century it had served its purposes; a fort had been built at the mouth of the river, its usefulness was ended, and it was abandoned forever.

The story that the foundations of the castle were laid within a gigantic wigwam at a time when the French had induced the Indians to go on a hunting expedition is probably no less true than most legends of the kind with which our history is filled; and if it is not literally true, the spirit of it undoubtedly is, for there must have been a fine story of stratagem and diplomacy in the conception and the erection of this massive old building upon which the tourist looks to-day with much interest. It is also a legend that the stone for the fort was brought from Fort Frontenac; this in a way threatens the authenticity of the former legend of the magical erection of the building. De Witt Clinton writing in 1810 explains that as the stones about the windows are different and more handsome than those in the rest of the building it is possible that they were brought from Kingston; he gave the measurements of the building as 105 by 47 feet.

It is interesting and informing to observe from whence the fort here at the mouth of the Niagara received, first and last, its armament; it appears that upon the capture of Oswego twenty-four guns "of the largest calibre" were sent to Fort Niagara, and we know that during the final siege in 1759 some of the guns trained upon Johnson's army were lost by Braddock away down in the forests beside the Monongahela River. The position held by Fort Niagara in the French scheme of western occupation is clearly suggested by these facts.

The modern tourist looking upon the massive, picturesque "Mess House" must not forget that "Fort Niagara" was a thing of slow growth. The first work here was undoubtedly the foundation and first story of the Mess House, surrounded by the common picket wall always found around the frontier fort. The first picket wall was falling down by 1739, when it was repaired. At this time Niagara was fast losing its hold on western trade because of the enforcing of the policy of not selling the Indians liquor; however, in 1741, the Governor of New York affirmed that he held the Six Nations only by presents and that Fort Niagara must be captured. In 1745, when the

French policy regarding the Indians was changed, Fort Niagara contained only a hundred men and four guns. It is said that the fort had been used to some extent as a State prison; surely few French prisons, at home or abroad, had a more gloomy dungeon than that in Fort Niagara which is shown visitors to-day; the apartment measures six by eighteen feet and ten feet in height, of solid stone with no opening for light or air. The well of the castle was located here, and many a weird story attaches, especially of the headless trunk of the French general that haunted the curbstone moaning over his sorry lot. This dungeon is one of the places named as the scene of imprisonment of the anti-Masonic agitator William Morgan in later days.

As the middle of the eighteenth century drew on France and England turned from the European battlefields to America to settle their immemorial quarrel for the possession of the continent. It is interesting to note that the opening of the struggle occurred not in the North or East, as would naturally be expected, but in the West to which Niagara offered "the communication."

In 1747 the Ohio Company was formed in Virginia and received its grant of land beyond the Alleghanies from the British King. With the exception of Lederer, whose explorations did not reach westward of Harper's Ferry, and Batts, who had visited the Falls of the Great Kanawha, the English colonies knew little or nothing of the West, save only the fables brought back by Spottswood's *Knights of the Golden Horseshoe*. But the doughty Irish and Scotch-Irish traders had pierced the mountains and made bold to challenge the trade of the French with the western nations. Immediately Celoron was sent from Montreal on the long voyage by way of Niagara to bury his leaden plates on the Ohio to re-establish the brave claim incised on La Salle's plate buried at the mouth of the Mississippi in 1682, which vaunted French possession of all lands drained by waters entering the Gulf of Mexico through the mouth of the Mississippi.

Celoron's expedition is interesting because this was the first open advance upon the Ohio Valley by France, leading to the building of a chain of forts westward from the key position, Fort Niagara. Celoron's Journal reads:

I arrived at Niagara on the 6th of July, where I found him [Mr. Labrevois]; we conferred together, and I wrote to the Chevalier de Longnaiul that which I had learned from Mr. de la Nardiere, and desired him, that if these nations of Detroit were in the design to come and join me, and not delay his departure, I would give the rendezvous at Strotves[1] on the 9th or 10th of August; that if they had changed their mind I would be obliged to him to send me couriers to inform me of their intentions, so that I may know what will happen to me. On the 7th of July, I sent M. de Contrecœur, captain and second in command of the detachment, with the subaltern officers and all my canoes to make the portage. I remained at the fort, to wait for my savages who had taken on Lake Ontario another route than I had; having rejoined me I went to the portage which M. de Contrecœur had made, on the 14th of the same month we entered Lake Erie; a high wind from the sea made me camp some distance from the little rapid; there I formed three companies to mount guard, which were of forty men commanded by an officer.

Returning from the Ohio trip Celoron reached Niagara again the 19th of February, 1750, and Montreal

[1] Logstown?

the 10th of March. At last reaching Quebec the frank leader of this spectacular expedition rendered his report concerning French possession of the West. "All that I can say is, that the [Indian] nations of these places are very ill-disposed against the French," were his words, "and entirely devoted to the English. I do not know by what means they can be reclaimed." Then followed one of the earliest suggestions of the use of French arms to retain possession of the great interior. "If violence is employed they [Indians] would be warned and take to flight . . . if we send to trade with them, our traders can never give our merchandize at the price the English do . . . people our old posts and perpetuate the nations on the Belle Riviere and who are within the reach of the English Government."

The plates of lead along the Ohio had very little effect in retarding the Ohio Company of Virginians, and Celoron had hardly left the Ohio Valley when Christopher Gist entered it to pick out and mark the boundaries of the Ohio Company's grant of land. This was in 1750. The Quebec Government, too, acted. If leaden plates would not hold the Ohio, then forts well guarded and manned would accomplish the end sought; and English spies on watch at Fort Oswego now saw a strange flotilla crossing Lake Ontario and knew something extraordinary was in the air. It was Marin's party on its way to fortify Celoron's route by building a chain of posts from Fort Niagara to the present site of Pittsburg at the junction of the Allegheny and Monongahela rivers. After a rest at Niagara the fort-building party proceeded along Lake Erie to Presqu' Isle, now Erie, Pennsylvania. There they built Fort Presqu' Isle; at Watertown Fort La Bœuf was erected and Fort Machault at Franklin on the Allegheny, and Fort Duquesne at the junction of the Allegheny and Monongahela. All this between 1752 and 1754, despite the message sent by Governor Dinwiddie of Virginia by the hand of Major Washington requesting that the French withdraw from the Ohio Valley. In the latter year Washington marched westward to support the party of Virginian fort-builders who had been sent to fortify the strategic position on the Ohio, but was forced to capitulate by the French army, which drove back the English and on their beginnings erected Fort Duquesne.

The line of forts from Quebec to Fort Duquesne was now complete, and of them Fort Niagara was the key. To wrest from the French this western empire it was necessary to strike Fort Niagara, but, with the rare lack of foresight characteristic of the government headed by the impossible Newcastle, the great campaign of 1755 was as poorly conceived as it was executed. It was composed of three spectacular advances on this curling line of French forts that hemmed in the colonies; one army, under Sir William Johnson, should attack the forts on Lakes George and Champlain; Governor Shirley of Massachusetts should leap at Fort Niagara, and General Braddock, formerly commander of Gibraltar, should lead an army from Virginia across the mountains upon Fort Duquesne, after capturing which he should then join forces with Shirley for the conquest of Niagara if that post had not been previously reduced.

From almost any view-point the scheme of conquest seems a glaring inconsistency, but from what is this so conspicuous as by looking upon this French line of fortresses as a serpent whose head was Quebec, whose heart was Fort Niagara, and whose tail rattled luringly on the Ohio at Fort Duquesne? The chief expedition, on which the eyes of the ministry were centred, was the one which launched at this serpent's tail. Moreover, in addition to being wrongly directed it was improperly routed, since there were both waggons and wheat in Pennsylvania but comparatively none in Virginia, and the ill-fated commander of the expedition, General Edward Braddock, was the victim of the lethargy and indifference of the colonies.

It is pitifully interesting to observe in the letter of instruction issued by Cumberland to Braddock that the latter seemed to have held the view that his most proper course was to strike at Niagara at the outset, undoubtedly appreciating the significant fact that to capture that key position of communication was to doom the Allegheny line of forts to starvation itself. "As to your design," read those instructions, "of making yourself master of Niagara, which is of the greatest consequence, his Royal Highness recommends you to leave nothing to chance in the prosecution of that enterprise." In all that was planned for this grand campaign those words give us the only hint of Braddock's own notion.[1] Those instructions also advise that if the Ohio campaign should progress slowly Braddock was to consider whether he should not give over the command of that campaign to another officer and proceed to Niagara. Nothing could illustrate more clearly than this the importance of the position of Niagara in the old French War. But

[1] In the author's *Historic Highways of America*, vol. iv., chap. 2, this whole problem is discussed and Cumberland's instructions quoted.

as Braddock did not deem it wise to give over the command of the Ohio campaign, Governor Shirley was left in charge of it.

The Northern campaigns, however, were of little more success than that of the ill-fated Braddock. True, Johnson won his knighthood beside the lake to which he gave his master's name, but the victory was as much of an accident as was Braddock's defeat, and was not followed up with the capture of the forts on Lake Champlain which was the object of the campaign. Shirley, on the other hand, made an utter failure of his *coup*, after reaching Oswego with incredible hardship; the news of Braddock's defeat demoralised whatever spirit was left in his sickly army; and Fort Niagara was not even threatened. We note here again the interdependence of the Braddock and Shirley campaigns, and the pity that the two armies could not have been combined for a strong movement against Fort Niagara. The Ohio fortress could not have existed with the line of communication once cut, and Braddock's as well as Forbes's campaigns, costing such tremendous sums, would have been unnecessary—or Prideaux's in '59 either, for that matter.

And yet the English campaigns of this year played their part in awakening the French to the situation; and Niagara was taken in hand at once, as though the presentiment was plain that the flag of the Georges would wave over the Niagara some day. Writes Mr. Porter:

> The contemplated attack on Fort Niagara, in 1755, under Shirley, had told the French that that fort must be further strengthened, and Pouchot, a captain in the regiment of Bearn,

and a competent engineer, was sent to reconstruct it. He reached the fort with a regiment in October, 1755. Houses for these troops were at once constructed in the Canadian manner. These houses consisted of round logs of oak, notched into each other at the corners, and were quickly built. Each had a chimney in the middle, some windows, and a plank roof. The chimneys were made by four poles, placed in the form of a truncated pyramid, open from the bottom to a height of three feet on all sides, above which was a kind of basket work, plastered with mud; rushes, marsh grass or straw rolled in diluted clay were driven in between the logs, and the whole plastered. The work of strengthening the fort was pushed on all winter, 300 men being in the garrison, and in March, 1756, the artillery taken from Braddock arrived. By July, 1756, the defences proposed were nearly completed, and Pouchot left the fort. Vaudreuil stated that he [Pouchot] "had almost entirely superintended the fortifications to their completion, and the fort, which was abandoned and beyond making the smallest resistance, is now a place of considerable importance in consequence of the regularity, solidity, and utility of its works." Pouchot was sent back to Niagara, as commandant, with his own regiment, in October, 1756, and remained there for a year. He still further strengthened the fort during this period, and when he left he reported that "Fort Niagara and its buildings were completed and its covered ways stockaded." On April 30, 1759, he again arrived at Niagara to assume command and "began to work on repairing the fort, to which nothing had been done since he left it. He found the ramparts giving way, the turfing all crumbled off, and the escarpment and counter escarpment of the fosses much filled up. He mounted two pieces to keep up appearances in case of a siege." From the general laudatory tone of his own work we are led to feel that Pouchot overpraised his own work of fortifying Niagara in 1756 and 1757, when no immediate attack was looked for, otherwise it could hardly have been in so poor a condition eighteen months afterwards (1759, as just quoted), unless, as is very likely, he foresaw defeat when attacked, as he was advised it would be, and wanted to gain special credit for a grand defence under very disadvantageous conditions. By July Pouchot had finished repairing the ramparts. He

A Drawing of Fort Niagara and Environs Showing Plan of English Attack under Johnson.

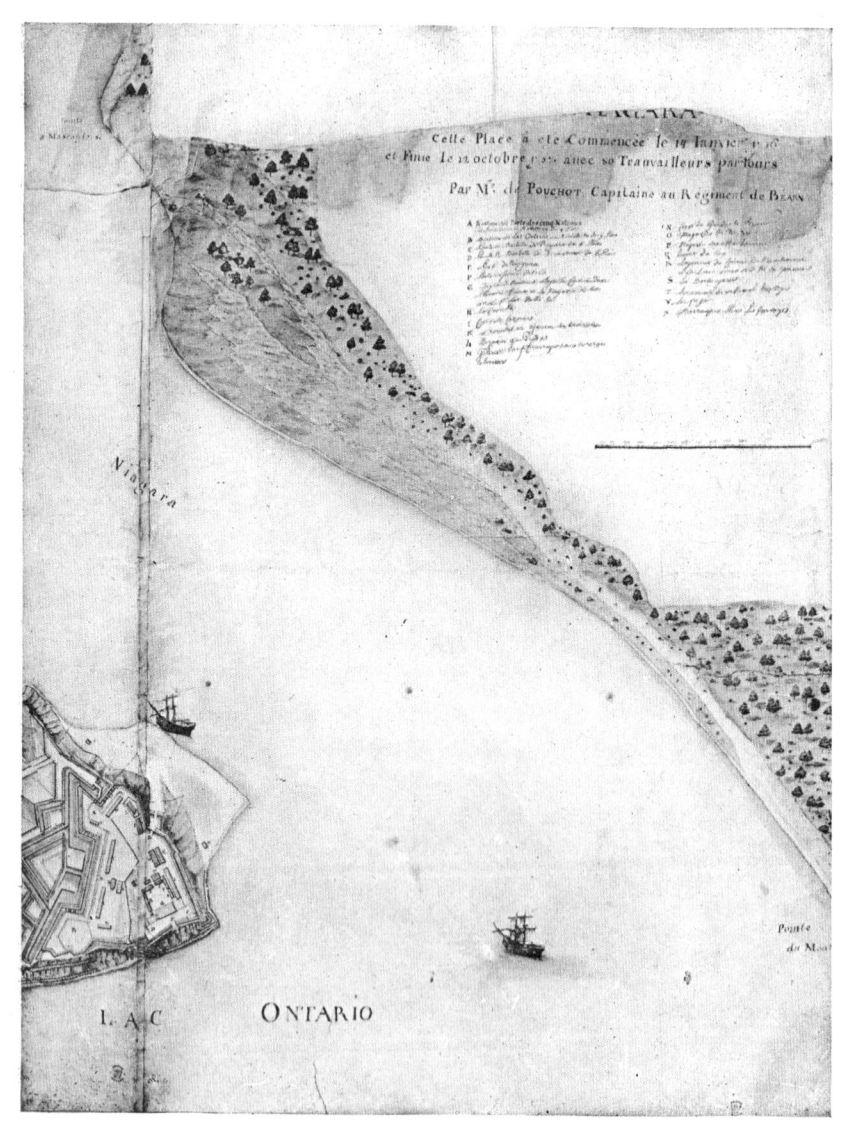

A Sketch of Fort Niagara and Environs; by the French Commander Pouchot, Showing Improvements of 1756–1758.

gives this description of the defence: "The batteries of the bastions which were in barbette had not yet been finished. They were built of casks and filled with earth. He had since his arrival constructed some pieces of blindage of oak, fourteen inches square and fifteen feet long, which extended behind the great house on the lake shore, the place most sheltered for a hospital. Along the faces of the powder magazine, to cover the wall and serve as casemates, he had built a large storehouse with the pieces secured at the top by a ridge. Here the guns and gunsmiths were placed. We may remark that this kind of work is excellent for field-forts in wooded countries, and they serve very well for barracks and magazines; a bullet could only fall upon an oblique surface and could do little harm, because this structure is very solid." Pouchot says that the garrison of the fort at this time consisted of 149 regulars, 183 men of colonial companies, 133 militia and 21 cannoniers. A total of 486 soldiers and 39 employees, of whom 5 were women or children. These served in the infirmary, as did also two ladies, and sewed cartridge bags and made bags for earth. There were also some Indians in the fort, and the officers may not have been included in this number. The fort was capable of accommodating 1000 men.

The great campaigns of 1759 were planned by the new commander-in-chief, Sir Jeffrey Amherst. The Niagara attack was placed in the hands of General John Prideaux, who was ready to sail from Oswego to his death at Fort Niagara on the 1st of July, 1759, with twenty-two hundred regulars and provincials and seven hundred of the Six Nations, brought very quickly to their senses after the successes of British arms in the year previous when Fort Duquesne was captured, under Sir William Johnson. On the 6th of July a hunter brought word to Pouchot that the English were at the doors of Niagara, the army having landed down the shore of the lake at a distance of four miles.

The commander, realising that the crucial moment had come, sent a messenger post-haste to Little Fort Niagara, at the upper end of the portage, and on to the forts in the West for aid; Niagara had assisted Fort Duquesne and the Allegheny forts in their days of trial and it was now turn for them to help her. Little Fort Niagara, or, more properly, Fort du Portage, previously mentioned, was erected probably about ten years before this to defend the portage landing. It was now commanded by the Joncaire—son of the famous French emissary among the Senecas who had given New France a foothold at Niagara—who had proved such a diplomatic guide to Celoron in his western trip; Pouchot ordered him to move the supplies at Fort du Portage across to the mouth of the Chippewa Creek and hasten to Fort Niagara. It is worth while to pause a moment to observe that we have here one of the first references to that shadowy western shore of the Niagara, where Forts Erie, George, and Mississaga were soon to appear; though the town of Newark, or Niagara-on-the-Lake, as it is known to-day, was the first settlement on this side of the river, it is clear that there was at least a storehouse at Chippewa Creek in 1759; unquestionably the portage path on the western shore of the river was a well-worn highway long before even Fort Niagara itself was proposed, for we know that it was the northern shore of Lake Erie that was the common route of the French rather than the southern from the record left by the Celoron expedition and Bonnecamp's map.

Prideaux forced the siege by digging a series of trenches toward the fort, each one in advance of the last. Finally, just before merited success was achieved,

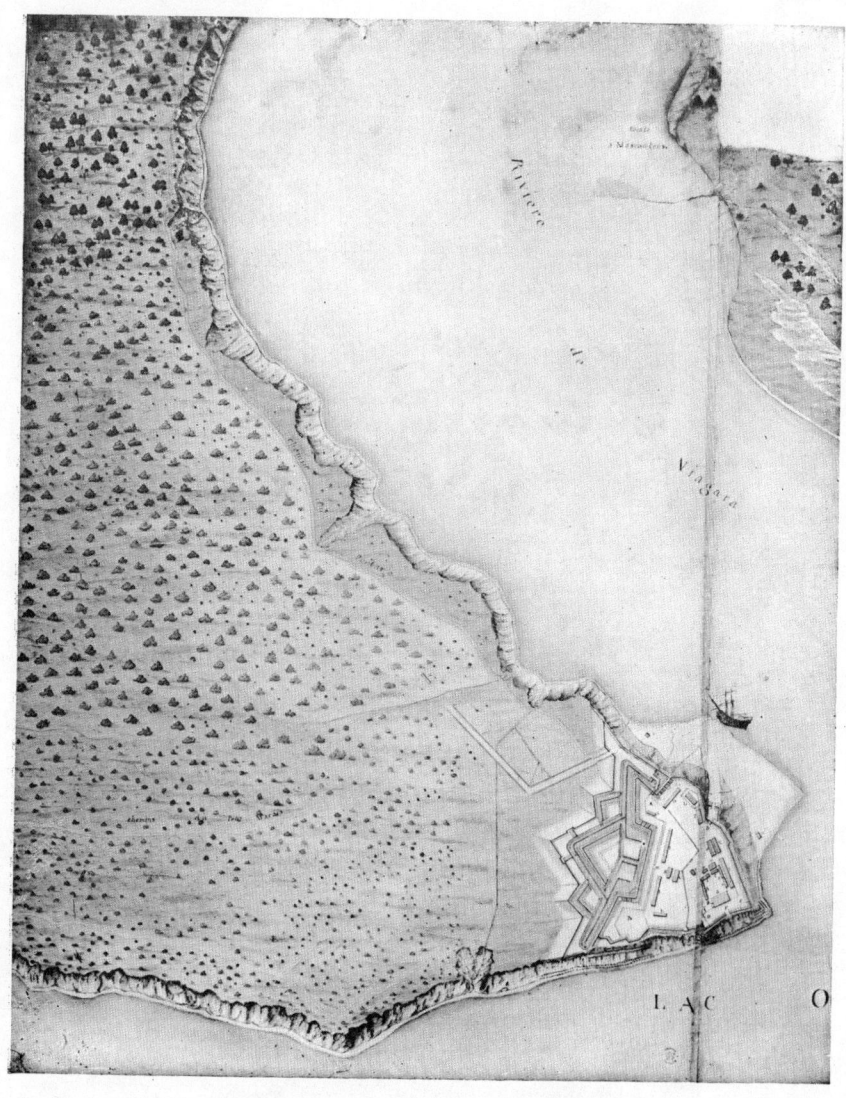

A Sketch of Fort Niagara and Environs; by the French Commander Pouchot, Showing Improvements of 1756-1758.

Canadian Trapper, from La Potherie.

a bursting cohorn killed Prideaux and thrust the command upon that deserving but lucky son of fortune, Sir William Johnson. The siege was pressed most diligently—as though Johnson was fearful that the honour thrust upon him would escape him through the arrival of General Gage, who was on his way to assume command. The fort was completely hemmed in, and its surrender was peremptorily demanded. Johnson was more than a match for the intriguing French Indians who attempted to alienate his Iroquois. He likewise played the clever soldier in handling the relieving army that was already on its way from the West. Three of the four messages sent by Pouchot had been intercepted by the English commander's scouts. The one that went through successfully accomplished its purpose and twelve hundred recruits were en route for the besieged fortress. The scouts told of their progress, to which captured letters from the commanding officers, D'Aubrey and De Lignery, to General Pouchot, gave added information. Descending the Niagara from its head to Navy Island, the reinforcements awaited the commands of their general. The order was to hasten on. Johnson redistributed his force to meet the crisis, at once detailing a sufficient part to cope with the relieving party and retaining a sufficient quota to prevent a sortie from the rapidly crumbling fort, which at best could not hold out longer unless succoured. At an eighth of a mile from the fort, in olden times called *La Belle Famille*, now within the limits of the beautiful village of Youngstown, the clash occurred that settled the fate of the brave Pouchot. With the Iroquois posted in hiding on either flank and the regulars waiting behind slight breastworks, the French force rushed headlong to the attack within the carefully laid ambuscade. After the opening fire of the Indians, the English troop made a savage charge—and the affair was over; the retreating French were followed and nearly a hundred and fifty were captured, including the officers.

Sir William Johnson used his leverage thus gained upon the commander of the doomed fortress with alacrity and success, sending with the officer who went to demand its surrender some of the prisoners captured at the scrimmage up the river, who told the story of their defeat and rout. Had they known it, they might have added that the terror-stricken fugitives from that field of strife hastened to the fleet of boats (in which they had descended the Niagara) and, steering them all into what is called even to this day Burnt Ship Bay, on the shore of Grand Island, set fire to the entire flotilla, lest the English secure an added advantage; and from this fact may we not draw the conclusion that these French hoped to hold the remainder of the great western waterway even if Fort Niagara fell? They could not use those boats very well on the lower Niagara, though with them once in hand they could easily strike at Presqu' Isle and Detroit.

Poor Pouchot demanded the best terms that he dared; it was agreed that the garrison should retain arms and baggage and one cannon as they marched out of the battered shell of a fort they had endeavoured to hold, and, upon laying down their arms, should be transported, in vessels furnished by the English, to New York; it was also demanded that they should be protected from the insults of the redskin allies of the

Niagara under Three Flags

English. That the latter stipulation was agreed to and honestly enforced illustrates the genuine hold Johnson had upon his brown brethren of the Long House. The articles were signed on the night of July 24th and on the 25th the flag of England rose to the breeze that fanned the lake and the wide-sweeping Niagara frontier —the second flag that had dominated that strategic spot in the century. The garrison numbered over six hundred men and eleven officers; the French total loss was about two hundred including the action at Youngstown; the English loss was sixty killed and 180 wounded. Forty-three iron cannon were found within the fort, fifteen hundred round shot, forty thousand pounds of musket-balls, five hundred hand grenades, and many tools, etc. The important result, however, was the removal of French domination over the warlike Seneca nation in this region and the natural inheritance that came with Niagara, the trade of which it was the centre. Near the site of the destroyed Fort du Portage, at the upper end of the portage, Captain Schlosser erected Fort Schlosser. Fort Niagara itself was improved; the present "bakehouse" was built in 1762. The Niagara of this time has been well described by Mr. Porter:

It was the head centre of the military life of the entire region, the guardian of the great highway and portage to and from the West; and hereabouts, as the forerunners of a coming civilisation and frontier settlement, the traders were securing for themselves the greatest advantages. To the rude transient population—red hunters, trappers, Indianised bush-rangers— starting out from this centre, or returning from their journeys of perhaps hundreds of miles, trooping down the portage to the fort, bearing their loads of peltries, and assisted by Indians who here made a business of carrying packs for hire, Fort

Niagara was a business headquarters. There the traders brought their guns and ammunition, their blankets, and cheap jewelry, to be traded for furs; there the Indians purchased, at fabulous prices, the white man's "fire water," and many, yes, numberless were the broils and conflicts in and around the fort, when the soldiers under orders tried to calm or eject the savage element which so predominated in the life of the Garrison.

Pontiac's rebellion came fast on the heels of the old French War, so fast indeed that we cannot really distinguish the line of division except for the fact of English occupation of Fort Niagara; with astonishing alacrity the incorrigible Senecas took up Pontiac's bloody belt, especially disgruntled with English rule in the Niagara country because the carrying business at the Niagara portage had been taken away from them upon the introduction of clumsy carts which carried to Fort Schlosser what had before been transported on the backs of Seneca braves. The retaliation for this serious loss of business was the terrible Devil's Hole Massacre of September 14, 1763, which occurred on the new portage road between Fort Schlosser and Lewiston at the head of what is known as Bloody Brook, in the ravine of which at the Gorge lies the Devil's Hole. Here a party of five hundred Senecas from Chenussio, seventy miles to the eastward of Niagara, waylaid a train of twenty-five waggons and a hundred horses and oxen, guarded, probably indifferently, by a detachment of troops variously estimated from twenty-five to three hundred in number, on its way from Lewiston to the upper fort. But three seem to have escaped that deadly ambuscade, and a relieving party, coming hurriedly at the instance of one of the survivors, ran into a second ambush, in which all but eight out of

Youngstown, N. Y., from Paradise Grove.

The Stone Redoubt at Fort Niagara, Built in 1770.
From the original in the British Museum.

two companies of men escaped. On the third attempt the commander of the fort hastened to the bloody scene with all of the troops at his command except what were needed to defend the fort. But the redskins had gone, leaving eighty scalped corpses on the ground. The first convoy probably numbered about twenty-five and the relieving party probably twice that number. The Indians had thrown or driven every team and all the whites surviving the fire of their thirsty muskets over the brink of the great ravine in which lies the Devil's Hole, fitly named.

At the great treaty that Sir William Johnson now held at Niagara with all the western Indians—one of the most remarkable convocations ever convened on this continent—the Senecas were compelled to surrender to the English Government all right to a tract four miles wide on each side of the Niagara River from Fort Niagara to Fort Schlosser. When it came time to sign the articles agreeing to this grant, Johnson, at the suggestion of General Bradstreet, who had in mind a fortification of the present site of Fort Erie, asked to extend the grant to include all land bordering the entire river from mouth to source and for four miles back. To this the Senecas agreed, but signed the treaty, as it were, with their left hands, never intending to keep it. However, it is to this date that we trace first actual white man's ownership of the first foot of land on the Niagara frontier, save perhaps the enclosure at Fort Niagara. Until this agreement was reached Sir William refused to deal with the gathered host of Indians from the West; thus was the Devil's Hole Massacre avenged.

Over two thousand Indians had met to treat

with the now famous Indian Commissioner for the Crown, coming from Nova Scotia in the East and the head streams of the Mississippi River in the West; that Niagara should have been the chosen meeting-place illustrates again its geographical position on the continent. Shrewd at this form of procrastinating business, Sir William laid down the policy of treaty with each tribe separately and not with the nations as such, and this, added to the formality observed, tended to make the procedure of almost endless duration. But Johnson knew his host and it is said on good authority that the vast sum now invested by the Crown paid good interest; the congress cost about ten thousand dollars in New York currency, and about two hundred thousand was distributed in presents to the vast assemblage. "Though this assemblage consisted of peace-desiring savages, their friendly disposition was not certain. Several straggling soldiers were shot at, and great precautions were taken by the English garrison to avert a rupture." Writes the graphic Parkman: "The troops were always on their guard, while the black muzzles of the cannons, thrust from the bastions of the fort, struck a wholesome awe into the savage throng below."

The Fort Niagara of that day little resembled the sight that greets the tourist's eye at that point to-day. When the French built the "Mess House" or "Castle" they built one story only, but afterward added a second, the walls of which probably extended above the roof to serve as a breastwork for gunners. The present roof is an English addition, comparatively modern. The French built also the two famous block-houses, the walls of which also protruded from the ancient roof for the same purpose as on the "Mess House," and these were used as late as the War of 1812. The old Magazine was built by the French, but its present-day roof is, of course, of modern construction, being in reality nothing but a covering over the stone arch which was the ancient roof. So far as appearance goes the waters of the hungry lake have probably done more altering of the natural aspect than has the hand of man. The fantastic "castle" now stands close to the water's edge, whereas, in the olden time there were upwards of thirty rods of ground between the "Mess House" and the lake, supporting an orchard. The present stone wall was erected in 1839, and the brick walls constructed outside the old line of breastworks in 1861; four years later the lighthouse was established in the upper story of the "Castle"; in 1873 the present lighthouse was erected.

No serious conflict now marked England's rule in her new territory, and the people of Canada, and especially of the Niagara region, had now comparatively a few years' repose, but then came one of the most important periods in its history. Their country was invaded, and for a time seemed on the point of passing under the control of the Congress of the old Thirteen Colonies, now in rebellion against England. Only the genius of an able governor-general saved the valley of the St. Lawrence to the British Crown.

In the year 1774, Parliament intervened for the first time in Canadian affairs, and passed what was known as the "Quebec Act," which greatly extended the boundaries of the province of Quebec, as defined by the Proclamation of 1763. On one side the province now extended to the frontiers of New England, Pennsylvania, New York Province, the Ohio, and the left bank of the Mississippi; on the other to the Hudson's Bay Territory; Labrador, Anticosti, and the Magdalen Islands, annexed to Newfoundland by the Proclamation of 1763, were made part of the province of Quebec. The "Quebec Act" created much debate in the House of Commons. The Earl of Chatham, in the House of Lords, described it as a "most cruel and odious measure." The opposition in the province was among the British inhabitants, who sent over a petition for its repeal or amendment, their principal grievance being that it substituted the laws and usages of Canada for English law. The "Act of 1774" was exceedingly unpopular in the English-speaking colonies, then at the commencement of the Revolution, on account of the extension of the limits of the province so as to include the country long known as the "Old North-west" in American history, and the consequent confinement of the Thirteen Colonies between the Atlantic coast and the Alleghany Mountains, beyond which the hardy and bold frontiersmen of Virginia and Pennsylvania were already passing into the great valley of the Ohio. Parliament, however, appears to have been influenced by a desire to adjust the government of the province so as to conciliate the majority of the Canadian people at the critical time.

The advice of Sir Guy Carleton, afterwards Lord Dorchester, who succeeded General Murray as Governor-General, had much to do with the liberality of the "Quebec Act" towards the French Canadians. He crossed the Atlantic in 1769 and remained absent from Canada for four years. He returned to carry out the "Quebec Act," which was the foundation of the large political and religious liberties which French Canada has ever since enjoyed. The "Act" aroused the indignation of the older American colonies, and had considerable influence in directing the early course of the Revolution which ended in the establishment of a federal republic. To it the Declaration of Independence refers as follows: "Abolishing the free system of English laws in a neighbouring province, establishing therein an arbitrary government, and enlarging its boundaries so as to render it at once an example and fit instrument for introducing the same absolute rule in other colonies." During the Revolution the Continental Congress attempted to secure the active alliance of Canada, and to that end sent a commission made up of Franklin, Chase, Charles Carroll, and John Carroll to Quebec; but the province remained loyal throughout. It will be noticed in another chapter that General Brock, in answering the "Proclamation" issued by Hull in 1812, voiced the belief that Canada was the price the American Colonies had promised to pay France in return for her valuable aid in the Revolution!

It is not necessary to dwell here on the events of a war the history of which is so familiar to every one.[1] When the first Continental Congress met at

[1] The record of these bloody years is hinted in the number of prisoners brought to Niagara. On this topic Frank H. Severance writes * :

"Just how many American prisoners were brought into Fort Niagara

* In *Old Trails on the Niagara Frontier*, pp. 89–91. Mr. Severance, Secretary of the Buffalo Historical Society, has ably taken the place of the eminent scholar of the Niagara country O. H. Marshall. In his volume above quoted Mr. Severance provides a most interesting, scholarly series of papers which no one who loves New York's old frontier should miss. Our story of the famine at De Nonville's fort was written with Mr. Severance's book open before us.

Philadelphia on September 5, 1774, the colonies were on the eve of independence as a result of the coercive measures forced on Parliament by the King's pliable ministers led by Lord North. The "Declaration," however, was not finally proclaimed until nearly two years later, on July 4, 1776, when the Thirteen Colo-

during this period I am unable to say, though it is possible that from the official correspondence of the time figures could be had on which a very close estimate could be based. My examination of the subject warrants the assertion that several hundred were brought in by the war-parties under Indian, British, and Tory leaders. In this correspondence, very little of which has ever been published, one may find such entries as the following:

"Guy Johnson wrote from Fort Niagara, June 30, 1781:

"'In my last letter of the 24th inst. I had just time to enclose a copy of Lieut. Nelles's letter with an account of his success, since which he arrived at this place with more particular information by which I find that he killed thirteen and took seven (the Indians not having reckoned two of the persons whom they left unscalped). . . . '

"Again:

"'I have the honour to transmit to Your Excellency a general letter containing the state of the garrison and of my Department to the 1st inst., and a return, at the foot, of the war parties that have been on service this year, . . . by which it will appear that they have killed and taken during the season already 150 persons, including those last brought in. . . . '

"Again he reports, August 30, 1781:

"'The party with Capt. Caldwell and some of the Indians with Capt. Lottridge are returning, having destroyed several settlements in Ulster County, and about 100 of the Indians are gone against other parts of the frontiers, and I have some large parties under good leaders still on service as well as scouts towards Fort Pitt. . . . '

"Not only are there many returns of this sort, but also tabulated statements, giving the number of prisoners sent down from Fort Niagara to Montreal on given dates, with their names, ages, names of their captors, and the places where they were taken. There were many shipments during the summer of '83, and the latest return of this sort which I have found in the archives is dated August 1st of that year, when eleven prisoners were sent from the fort to Montreal. It was probably not far from this time that the last American prisoner of the Revolution was released from Fort Niagara. But let the reader beware of forming hasty conclusions as to the cruelty or brutality of the British at Fort

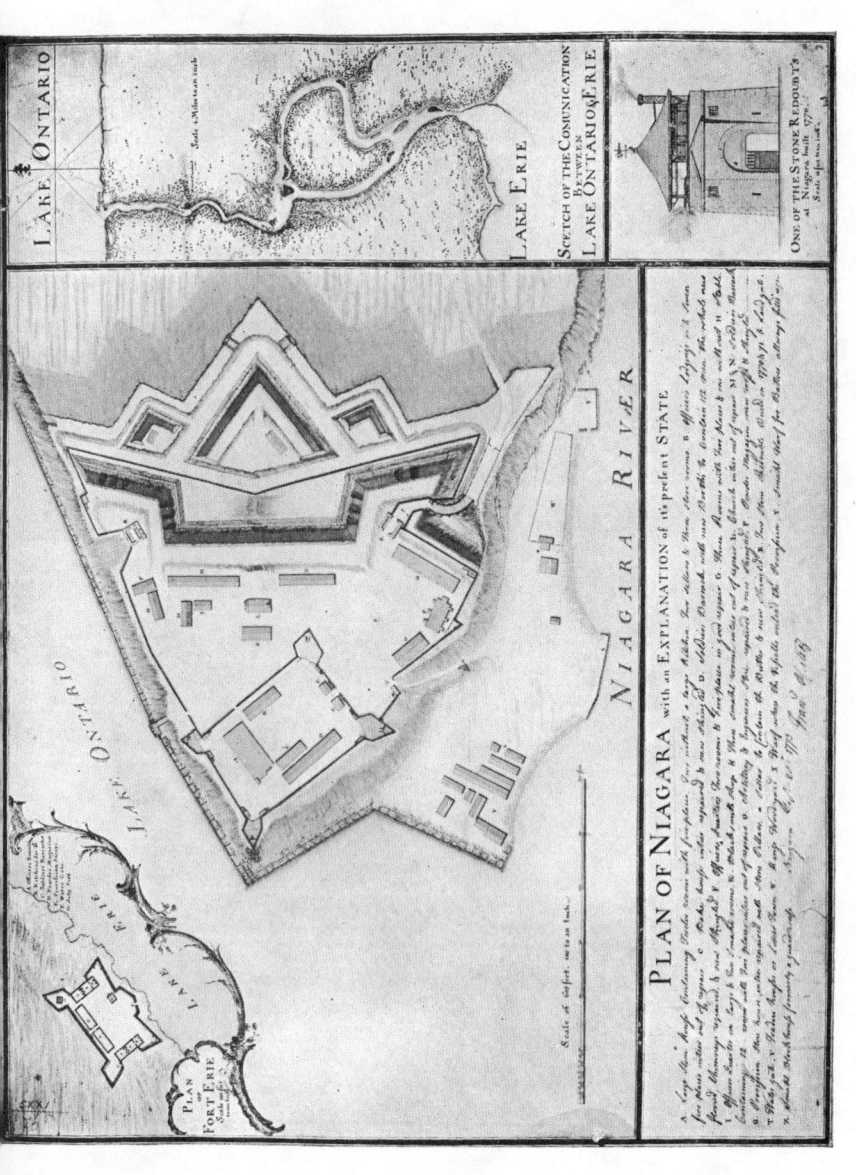

Pfister's Sketch of Fort Niagara and the "Communication," Two Years before the Outbreak of the Revolutionary War.

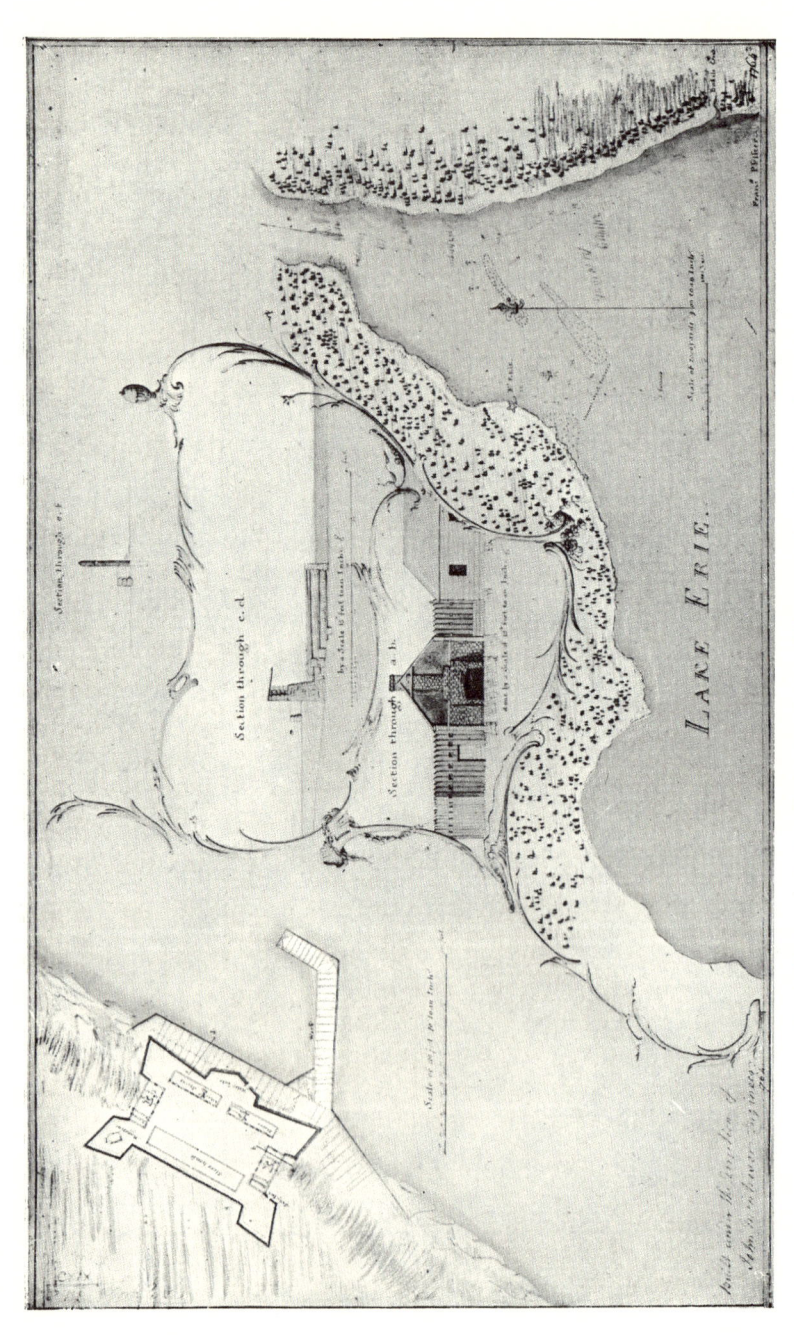

Fort Erie and the Mouth of the Niagara, by Pfister, in 1764.
From the original in the British Museum.

nies declared themselves "free and independent States," absolved of their allegiance to the British Crown. But many months before this great epoch-making event, war had actually commenced on Lake Champlain. On an April day, in the now memorable year 1775, the "embattled farmers" had fired at Concord

Niagara. In the first place, remember that harshness or kindness in the treatment of the helpless depends in good degree—and always has depended—upon the temperament and mood of the individual custodian. There were those in command at Fort Niagara who appear to have been capable of almost any iniquity. Others gave frequent and conspicuous proofs of their humanity. Remember, secondly, that the prisoners primarily belonged to the Indians who captured them. The Indian custom of adoption—the taking into the family circle of a prisoner in place of a son or husband who had been killed by the enemy—was an Iroquois custom, dating back much further than their acquaintance with the English. Many of the Americans who were detained in this fashion by their Indian captors, probably never were given over to the British. Some, as we know, like Mary Jemison, the White Woman of the Genesee, adopted the Indian mode of life and refused to leave it. Others died in captivity, some escaped. Horatio Jones and Jasper Parrish were first prisoners, then utilised as interpreters, but remained among the Indians. And in many cases, especially of women and children, we know that they were got away from the Indians by the British officers at Fort Niagara, only after considerable trouble and expense. In these cases the British were the real benefactors of the Americans, and the kindness in the act cannot always be put aside on the mere ground of military exchange, prisoner for prisoner. Gen. Haldimand is quoted to the effect that he 'does not intend to enter into an exchange of prisoners, but he will not add to the distresses attending the present war, by detaining helpless women and children from their families.'"

In justice to Col. Guy Johnson's administration at Fort Niagara, as well as to give one of the clearest (if biased) views of the trials and perplexities of those hard days, we reproduce a "Review of Col. Johnson's Transactions"; as Mr. Severance notes, this review shows "the real state of affairs at Fort Niagara towards the close of the Revolutionary War" better than does almost any other document *:

"MONTREAL, 24th March, 1782.

"Before Colonel Johnson arrived at Niagara in 1779 the Six Nations lived in their original possessions the nearest of which was about 100 and the farthest about 300 miles from that post. Their warriors were

* I quote Mr. Severance's copy from *Canadian Archives*, Series B, vol. 106, p. 122, *et seq.*

and Lexington, the shots "heard round the world," and a few weeks later the forts at Crown Point and Ticonderoga, then defended by very feeble garrisons, were in the possession of colonial troops, led by Ethan Allen and Seth Warner, the two "Green Mountain Boys" who organised this expedition. Canada was at this time in a very defenceless condition. Burgoyne was

---

called upon as the service required parties, which in 1776 amounted to about 70 men, and the expenses attending them, and a few occasional meetings ought to have been and he presumes were a mere Trifle when compared with what must attend their situation when all [were] driven to Niagara, exposed to every want, to every temptation, and with every claim which their distinguished sacrifices and the tenor of Soloman [solemn] Treaties had entitled them to from Government. The years 1777 & 1778 exhibited only a larger number occasionally employed and for their fidelity and attachment to Government they were invaded in 1779 by a rebel army reported to be from 5 to 600 men with a train of Artillery who forced them to retire to Niagara leaving behind them very fine plantations of corn and vegetables, with their cloathing, arms, silver works, Wampum Kettles and Implements of Husbandry, the collection of ages of which were destroyed in a deliberate manner and march of the rebels. Two villages only escaped that were out of their route.

"The Indians having always apprehended that their distinguished loyalty might draw some such calamity towards them had stipulated that under such circumstances they effected [expected] to have their losses made up as well as a liberal continuation of favours and to be supported at the expence of Government till they could be reinstated in their former possessions. They were accordingly advised to form camps around Niagara which they were beginning to do at the time of Colonel Johnson's arrival who found them much chagrined and prepared to reconcile them to their disaster which he foresaw would be a work of time requiring great judgment and address in effecting which he was afterwards successful beyond his most sanguine expectations, and this was the state of the Indians at Colonel Johnson's arrival. As to the state and regulation of Colonel Johnson's officers and department at that period he found the duties performed by 2 or three persons the rest little acquainted with them and considered as less capable of learning them, and the whole number inadequate to that of the Indians, and the then requisite calls of the service, and that it was necessary after refusing the present wants of the Indians to keep their minds occupied by constant military employment, all which he laid before the Commander in Chief who frequently honoured his conduct with particular approbation."

defeated at Saratoga, and his army, from which so much was expected, made prisoners of war. This great misfortune of the British cause was followed by the alliance of France with the States. French money, men, and ships eventually assured the independence of the Republic, whose fortunes were very low at times despite the victory at Saratoga. England was not well served in this American war; she had no Washington to direct her campaign, and Gage, Burgoyne, and Cornwallis were not equal to the responsibilities thrown upon them. Cornwallis's defeat at Yorktown, October 19, 1781, was the death blow to the hopes of England in North America.

Had General Sullivan's campaign of 1779, as planned, been successful, he would have attacked Fort Niagara, but disaster overtook him, though he led an expedition against the Iroquois, routed a force of Indians and Tories at Newtown, near the present Elmira, and wrought wide devastation in the country of the Cayugas and Senecas.

Yorktown led to the Treaty of Versailles and independence, but oddly enough it was almost a generation before a third flag arose above the historic "Castle" at the mouth of the Niagara. In 1784 the United States came into the control of the territory extending from Nova Scotia (which then included New Brunswick) to the head of the Lake of the Woods and to the Mississippi River in the West, and in the North from Canada to the Floridas in the South, the latter having again become Spanish possessions. The boundary between Nova Scotia and the Republic was so ill defined that it took over fifty years to fix the St. Croix and the Highlands which were, by the treaty, to divide the two countries. In the Far West the line of division was to be drawn through the Lake of the Woods "to the most north-western point thereof, and from thence on a due west course to the River Mississippi"—a physical impossibility, since the head of the Mississippi, as was afterwards found, was a hundred miles or so to the south! In later times this geographical error was corrected, and the curious distortion of the boundary line that now appears on the maps was necessary at the Lake of the Woods in order to strike the forty-ninth parallel of north latitude, which was subsequently arranged as the boundary line as far as the Rocky Mountains.

A strip of land one mile wide along the American shore from Lake Ontario to Lake Erie had been exempted when New York ceded the ownership of what is now the western part of this State to Massachusetts, which ownership New York subsequently reacquired. Finally the Indians, who, in spite of their former cessions to England, still claimed an ownership, ceded to New York, for one thousand dollars and an annuity of one thousand five hundred dollars, their title to all the islands in the Niagara River. The State of New York patented the mile-strip to individuals, commencing in the first decade of the nineteenth century.

In spite of the Treaty of Versailles in 1783, as noted, neither Niagara nor Detroit was surrendered by the British until 1796. Both forts were held as English outposts and strengthened. We have shown that the boundary-line between Canada and the United States was improperly conceived; but it is a fact that during the Revolutionary War the people of the North-west had been warned from Niagara and Detroit to take up arms in behalf of the Americans. Nothing aggressive, however, had been accomplished. The wilderness of three hundred miles between Detroit and the Eastern States made an attack upon the posts by the Americans impracticable; moreover, most of the fighting in this region was done by the British and the Indians and the people of Pennsylvania and Ohio.

It is due to the statesmanship of John Jay that the posts still garrisoned by British troops in the United States, contrary to the stipulations of the Treaty of Paris, were finally evacuated in 1796. Jay had been sent by President Washington to go to Great Britain in 1794 as special envoy to settle differences growing out of the failure of that country to keep the obligations of the Treaty of 1784, differences which had aroused a strong war-spirit all over the States. It was easy to foresee, as Jay recognised, that the outcome of the situation would in all probability be unpopular with the people, but he did not hesitate to meet the responsibility that Washington believed he could meet better than any other man, partially because of the reputation he had established in England while negotiating the Treaty of 1784. Jay set sail on May 12, 1794 in the ship *Ohio*, with his son Peter Augustus, and with John Trumbull as secretary. On June 8th he landed at Falmouth and at once entered into relation with Lord Grenville, the Secretary of Foreign Affairs, who was commissioned by the King to treat with Mr. Jay. The sincerity and candour of the two negotiators soon led to a degree of mutual confidence that both facilitated and lightened their labours. A treaty resulted known on this side of the ocean as

"Jay's Treaty," which settled the eastern boundary of Maine, recovered for illegal captures by British cruisers $10,000,000, secured the surrender of the western forts still garrisoned by the British, and contained an article about the West India trade. With the exception of the latter article, the treaty was approved by the President and ratified by the Senate. But many were not satisfied, and denounced Jay with tongue and pen, and even burned him in effigy in Boston, Philadelphia, and at his own home in New York. How different was the homecoming from that after the negotiation of the other treaty, when the freedom of the city was presented to him in a golden box, and each one seemed to vie with every other in extending a welcome! In a letter to a friend, Jay said at that time, "Calumny is seldom durable, it will in time yield to truth," and he bore himself at that time as one having full confidence that he had acted both wisely and skilfully, and expected the people to realise it in time. The British, however, would not evacuate Niagara and the other forts without a semblance of fighting on paper. They held, amongst other reasons, that they were yet justified in maintaining a garrison on American soil because "it was *alleged* by divers merchants and others, His Majesty's subjects," that they had sustained various losses by the legal impediments they had experienced in collecting debts in America due to them before the war. Mr. Jay, however, with great diplomacy, removed this obstacle by the appointment of Commissioners of Award, and as the British finally were deprived of all pretence for maintaining the posts, it was agreed that they should be surrendered on or before the first of June, 1796. This was finally done and the third and last flag floated lazily in the Lake Ontario breezes over the historic point. The settlers and traders within the jurisdiction of the posts were permitted to remain and to enjoy their property without becoming citizens of the United States unless they should think proper to do so.

Anthony Wayne's army now took full possession of the Niagara region. With the exception of a small strip of land on the river and lake, all the present State of Michigan was occupied by Indians—Pottawattomies, Miamis, Wyandots, Chippewas, Winnebagoes, and Ottawas. The first American commander of the post was Colonel John Francis Hamtramck, who died in 1803. At that period Detroit was headquarters of the Western Army, but the whole garrison only consisted of three hundred men.

Niagara-on-the-Lake may be called the Plymouth Rock of upper Canada. It was once its proud capital. Variously known in the past as Loyal Village, Butlersbury, Nassau, and Newark, it had a daily paper as early as 1792, and was a military post of distinction at the same period, its real beginnings, however, being contemporaneous with the War of Independence. Here, within two short hours' ride of the most populous and busy city of western New York, typical of the material forces that have moulded the nineteenth and twentieth centuries, we come upon a spot of intensest quiet, in the shadow of whose ivy-mantled church tower sleep trusted servants of the Georges, Loyalists and their Indian allies.

The place has been overtaken by none of that unpicturesque commercial prosperity which further up the frontier threatens to destroy all the natural beauties of the river-banks.

The Welland Canal and the Grand Trunk and Great Western Railway systems diverted the great part of the carrying trade, and with it that growth and activity which have signalised the neighbouring cities of Canada. "Refuse the Welland Canal entrance to your town," said the Commissioners, "and the grass will grow in your streets." Here General Simcoe opened the first Upper Canadian Legislature; and later, from here the noble Brock planned the defence of Upper Canada. While the cities of western New York, which have now far eclipsed it, were rude log settlements, at "Newark" some little attempt was made at decorum and society.

Here landed in 1783–'84 ten thousand United Empire Loyalists, who, to keep inviolate their oaths of allegiance to the King, quitted their freeholds and positions of trust and honour in the States to begin life anew in the unbroken wilds of Upper Canada. History has made us somewhat familiar with the settlement of Nova Scotia and New Brunswick by the expatriated Loyalists. Little has been written of the sufferings and privations endured by the "makers" of Upper Canada. Students and specialists who have investigated the story of a flight equalled only by that of the Huguenots after the revocation of the Edict of Nantes have been led to admire the spirit of unselfish patriotism which led these one hundred thousand fugitives to self-exile. While the Pilgrims came to America leisurely, bringing their household goods and their charters with them, the United Empire Loyalists, it has well been said, "bleeding with the wounds of seven years of war, left ungathered the crops of their rich farms on the Mohawk and in New Jersey, and, stripped of every earthly possession, braved the terrors of the unbroken wilderness from the Mohawk to Lake Ontario." Inhabited to-day by the descendants of these pioneers, the old-fashioned loyalty and conservatism of the Niagara district is the more conspicuous by contrasting it with neighbouring republicanism over the river.

Here, over a century ago, near Fort George, stood the first Parliament House of Upper Canada. Here, seventy years before President Lincoln's Emancipation Proclamation, the first United Empire Loyalist Parliament, like the embattled farmers at Concord, "fired a shot heard round the world." For one of the first measures of the exiled patricians was to pass an act forbidding slavery. Few readers know that at Newark, now Niagara, was enacted that law by which Canada became not only the first country in the world to abolish slavery, but, as such, a safe refuge for the fugitive slaves from the Southern States.

General Simcoe, the first governor, was born in 1752 and died in 1806. A landed gentleman of England and likewise a member of the British House of Commons he voluntarily relinquished all the luxuries of his beautiful English home and estates to bury himself in the wilderness of Canada and the Niagara region. As governor-general he exemplified the extremest simplicity. His guard consisted of four soldiers who came from Fort George, close by, to Newark, every morning and returned thither in the evening. Mrs. Simcoe not only performed the duties of wife and mother, but also acted as her husband's secretary. The name of Simcoe is indelibly entered in the history of the development of the Niagara, and it is doubly appropriate that her interesting drawings should illustrate a volume dealing with this region she loved.

Here Cooper is said to have written his admirable novels of border and Indian life, novels which have been devoured by me and millions of readers; it is fair to predict that the stories will be read for another century to come.[1] Many other interesting characters have at different periods made Fort George their abode. In 1780, a handsome house within its enclosure was occupied by General Guy Johnson.

[1] Here, the story runs, the brother of Sir Walter Scott concocted the plots and outlines of Sir Walter's famous novels and sent them on to England to be polished up for publication—a story worthy of a Hennepin.

Chapter X

The Hero of Upper Canada

GENERAL ISAAC BROCK, the Hero of Upper Canada, was the kind of man men delight to honour—honest, capable, ambitious, faithful, kind. Nothing less than a tremendous gorge, such as separates Queenston from Lewiston Heights, could keep the people of one nation from knowing and loving this hero of another; since Brock's day this gorge has been spanned by beautiful bridges, and it is full time now, as the centennial of the second war with England approaches, that the appreciation of the characters of the worthy, patriotic heroes of that olden day o'erleap the chasm of bitter rivalry and hostility and become common and genuine to the northward and the southward of the Niagara.

Isaac Brock was the eighth son of John Brock, Esq., born on the sixth day of October, 1769, in the parish of St. Peter-Port, Guernsey—the famous birth-year of Wellington and Napoleon. Tall, robust, and mentally conspicuous as a lad, Isaac followed his elder brother into the British Army, purchasing the ensigncy in the 8th, or King's Regiment, in 1785. His promotion was the result of merit in addition to possessing the means to purchase higher office; in 1790 we find him a lieutenant in the 49th Regiment, advancing to his majority in 1795 and two years later becoming senior lieutenant-colonel. Supplanting now an officer accused of peculation who had brought the whole regiment into public notice, Brock exerted an influence that seemed to transform the regiment, making it "from one of the worst," said the Duke of York himself, "one of the best regiments in the service."

The opportunity of active service soon came, as the 49th was thrown into Holland, Brock being wounded at Egmont-op-Zee, or Bergen. His simple statement concerning being struck in the breast by a spent bullet is interesting: "I got knocked down soon after the enemy began to retreat," he remarks, "but never quitted the field, and returned to my duty in less than half an hour."[1] Here Brock fought under Sir John Moore and Sir Ralph Abercrombie; in 1801 he was second in command of the land forces at Copenhagen and saw Lord Nelson on the *Elephant* write his famous letter to the Crown Prince of Denmark. During the next year the 49th was sent to Canada and was quartered at Fort George near Newark, the present Niagara-on-the-Lake. The character of Brock's management of the troops under him is well illustrated in the case of a strange mutiny that came near to breaking out at this time at Fort George due to the useless annoyance, or alleged actual severity, which so exasperated the men that an almost inconceivable plot to kill the officers was discovered. After the crime the soldiers were to cross the river into the United States and escape. One of the confederates was sent by the com-

[1] *The Life and Correspondence of Major-General Sir Isaac Brock, K.B.*, by Ferdinand Brock Tupper, p. 16. This most interesting volume has furnished very much of the material for this chapter. D. B. Read's *Life and Times of General Brock* is an excellent book for popular use and will be found quoted herein.

Major-General Brock.

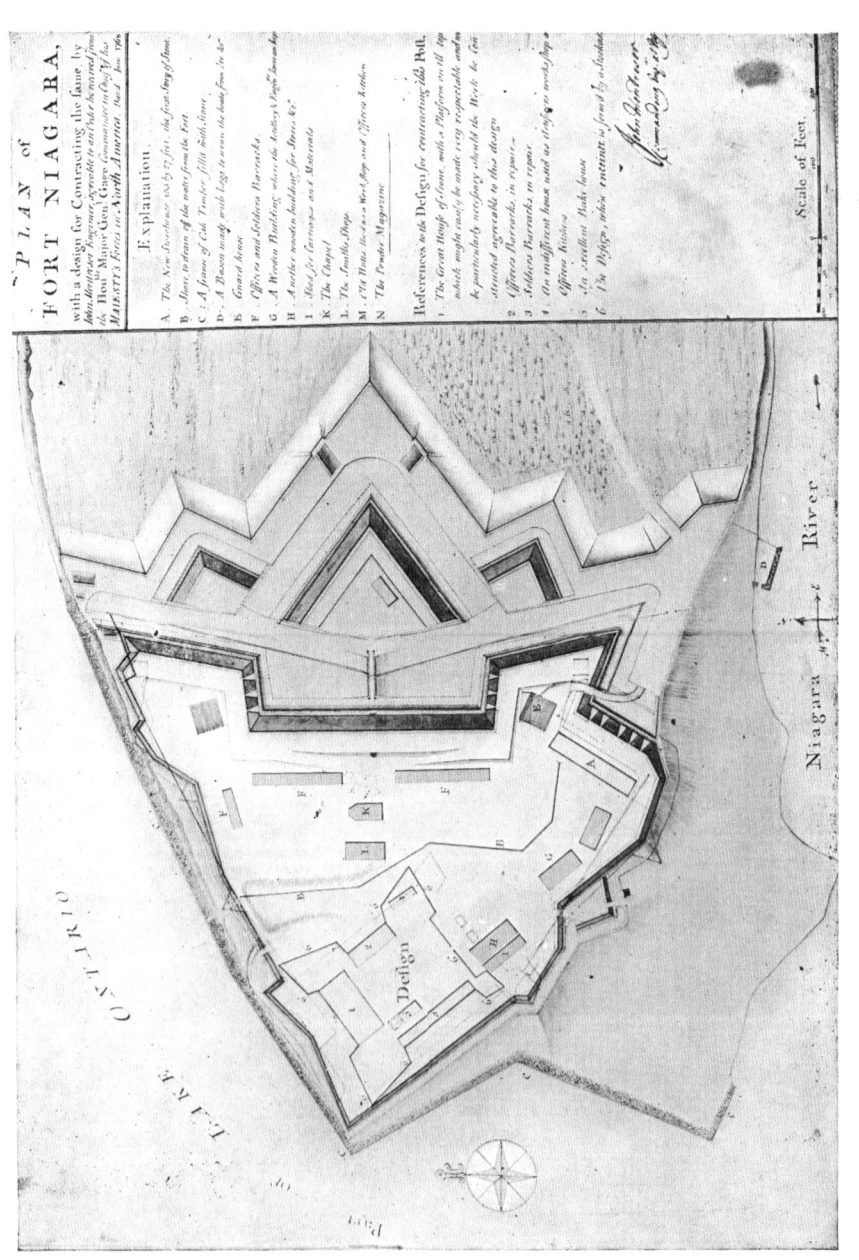

A Plan of Fort Niagara after English Occupation, by Montresor.

manding officer to Brock at York with a letter describing the horrifying discovery. The incensed commander compelled the soldier at the point of a musket to disclose the chief conspirators. Hastening to Fort George the ringleaders were apprehended at the dinner table and hurried off to Quebec, where they were summarily shot. As a result Brock himself was ordered to make Fort George his headquarters, whereupon all trouble seems to have ceased.

In 1805 Brock received his colonelcy and with it leave of absence. While at home he made a report to the commander-in-chief which throws an interesting light on affairs at that period, favouring the formation of a veteran battalion for service in Upper Canada. He wrote:

> The artifices employed to wean the soldier from his duty, conspire to render almost ineffectual every effort of the officers to maintain the usual degree of order and discipline. The lures to desertion continually thrown out by the Americans, and the facility with which it can be accomplished, exacting a more than ordinary precaution on the part of the officers, insensibly produces mistrust between them and the men, highly prejudicial to the service.
>
> Experience has taught me that no regular regiment, however high its claim to discipline, can occupy the frontier posts of Lower and Upper Canada without suffering materially in its numbers. It might have been otherwise some years ago; but now that the country, particularly the opposite shore, is chiefly inhabited by the vilest characters, who have an interest in debauching the soldier from his duty; since roads are opened into the interior of the States, which facilitate desertion, it is impossible to avoid the contagion. A total change must be effected in the minds and views of those who may hereafter be sent on this duty, before the evil can be surmounted.[1]

[1] One cause of desertion seems to have been the ubiquitous American girl. In a later letter Brock wrote:

Such was the warlike tenor of despatches now at hand from Canada that Brock, eager to be at the post of duty at a critical time, hastened from London in June, 1806, cutting short his leave of absence. Throughout that year and its successor he was actively engaged in studying his province with regard to military demands that might suddenly be made upon it; it is noteworthy that the commander feared that in case of an outbreak between England and America a considerable part of the inhabitants of Upper Canada (Loyalists) would prove friendly to the young Republic. Discussing a new militia law he wrote as follows to the Council:

> In thus complying with the dictates of his duty, Colonel Brock was not prepared to hear that the population of the province, instead of affording him ready and effectual support, might probably add to the number of his enemies; and he feels much disappointment in being informed by the first authority, that the only law in any degree calculated to answer the end proposed was likely, if attempted to be enforced, to meet with such general opposition as to require the aid of the military to give it even a momentary impulse.

If such were the apprehensions of the commanding officer in Canada little wonder General Hull, in later days, counted on the co-operation of many of the inhabitants of the trans-Niagara country. In September, 1807, Brock, who was acting-governor in Canada pending the arrival of Sir James Craig, was fortifying Quebec in anticipation of an immediate outbreak of the impending war. In this connection a little incident

---

"Not a desertion has been attempted by any of the 49th for the last ten months, with the exception, indeed, of Hogan. He served Glegg, who took him with him to the Falls of Niagara, where a fair damsel persuaded him to this act of madness, for the fellow cannot possibly gain his bread by labour, as he has half killed himself with excessive drinking; and we know he cannot live upon love alone."

displays his character. He had caused to be erected at Quebec a very powerful battery, and of it he wrote his brothers:

> I erected ... a famous battery, which the public voice named after me; but Sir James, thinking very properly that anything so very pre-eminent should be distinguished by the most exalted appellation, has called it the King's Battery, the greatest compliment, I conceive, that he could pay to my judgment.

The true modesty of the really great man shines out in these charming words.

As the war cloud seemed to dissipate toward the close of 1808, General Brock seems to have set his eyes toward Europe in the hope of opportunity of active service; on November 19th he writes quite despondently:

> My object is to get home as soon as I can obtain permission; but unless our affairs with America be amicably adjusted, of which I see no probability, I scarcely can expect to be permitted to move. I rejoice Savery [Brock] has begun to exert himself to get me appointed to a more active situation. I must see service, or I may as well, and indeed much better, quit the army at once, for no one advantage can I reasonably look to hereafter if I remain buried in this inactive, remote corner, without the least mention being made of me.

It is exceedingly noticeable that Brock now seems to pin all his hope to being recalled in order that he might win his laurels in the tremendously spectacular campaigns against Napoleon in Spain. From his letters we learn that the French-Canadians looked for the Corsican's ultimate triumph and his final possession of Canada itself, and adds that under like circumstances Englishmen would be even more restless under French rule than the French-Canadians were under English;

"Every victory which Napoleon has gained," he observes, "for the last nine years has made the disposition here to resist more manifest."

In the middle of July Brock writes his sister-in-law, Mrs. William Brock, that the die is cast and that he is ordered to Upper Canada. If it is character, rather than mere performance that, in the last analysis, gives every man his historic position in the annals of the world, the truth is nowhere better shown than here in the case of this splendid Canadian hero. Could his Governor have spared him Brock would have, ere this, been at home or en route to Spain and fame; but the conditions demanded a strong, diplomatic officer at Fort George, and there was nothing for it but that Brock must go; and there followed war—and bloody Queenston Heights. "Since I cannot get to Europe," are his gloomy words, "I care little where I am placed."

By September 13th he is writing his brothers from Fort George, but still hinting of his hopes to get leave to return to England eventually. What an out-of-the-way place for fame to seek and find a man—a man repining that he cannot go in search of her! Yet he writes: "I should stand evidently in my own light if I did not court fortune elsewhere." The attitude of Sir James Craig in the matter of his transfer to the European service was candidly stated by a letter from Colonel Baynes as follows:

In reply to an observation of mine, that you regretted the inactive prospect before you, and looked with envy on those employed in Spain and Portugal, he said: "I make no doubt of it, but I can in no shape aid his plans in that respect; I would not, however, be the means of preventing them, and although from his local knowledge I should regret losing him in this country, yet I would not oppose it if he could obtain an appointment to the staff on service; but in that case I would ask for another general officer being sent in his place immediately to Upper Canada." I tell you this, my dear general, without reserve, and give you, as far as I can recollect, Sir James's words. If he liked you less, he might, perhaps, be more readily induced to let you go; as matters stand, I do not think he will, although I am convinced that he will feel very sincere regret in refusing you on a subject upon which you appear to be so anxious.

In his correspondence we now and then get a glimpse of the General's tastes and inclinations; that he was not a frugal entertainer we have considerable proof,[1] likewise evidence of his temperate tastes. In his lonely life by the Niagara he had recourse to such books as were to be found.

But books are scarce [he writes], and I hate borrowing. I like to read a book quickly, and afterwards revert to such passages as have made the deepest impression, and which appear to me most important to remember—a practice I cannot conveniently pursue unless the book be mine. Should you find that I am likely to remain here, I wish you to send me some choice authors in history, particularly ancient, with maps, and the best translations of ancient works. I read in my youth Pope's Translation of Homer, but till lately never discovered its exquisite beauties. As I grow old, I acquire a taste for study. I firmly believe that the same propensity was always inherent in me, but, strange to tell, although many were paid extravagantly, I never had the advantage of a master to guide and encourage me. But it is now too late to repine. I rejoice that my nephews are more fortunate.

[1] A letter from Colonel Kempt runs: "I have just received a long letter . . . giving me an account of a splendid ball given by you to the *beau monde* of Niagara and its vicinity, and the manner in which she speaks of your liberality and hospitality reminds me of the many pleasant hours I have passed under your roof. We *have no such parties now*, and the indisposition of Sir James having prevented the usual public days at the castle, nothing more stupid than Quebec now is can be imagined."

Colonel Vesey, writing to Brock, states that he regrets not having a daughter of marriageable age. "You should be married," runs the letter, "particularly as fate seems to detain you so long in Canada—but pray do not marry there." In another letter, dated Portsmouth, June 10, 1811, the same correspondent refers to Brock's appointment as Major-General. Oddly enough General Vesey says, referring to his friend's probable future: "It may perhaps be your fate to go to the Mediterranean, but the Peninsula is the most direct road to the honour of the Bath, and as you are an ambitious man, that is the station you should prefer. . . ." Only sixteen months from the day this letter was written Brock was gazetted Knight of the Bath—the lonely, patient, splendid man winning the great honour in the very land he was longing so sincerely to leave. On October 17th a communication from Lieutenant-Colonel Torrens gives General Brock permission to return to England, but it was too late; both honour and necessity demanded his presence in Canada as the exciting days of 1812 drew on apace.

At the outbreak of hostilities in this year the United States embraced an immense territory, extending from the St. Lawrence to Mexico, excepting Florida—which remained in the possession of Spain until 1819—and from the Atlantic indefinitely westward to the Spanish possessions on the Pacific coast, afterwards acquired by the United States. The total population of the United States was upwards of eight million souls, of whom a million and a half were negro slaves in the South. Large wastes of wild land lay between the Canadian settlements and the thickly populated sections of New England, New York, and Ohio. It was

The Hero of Upper Canada

only with great difficulty and expense that men, munitions of war, and provisions could be brought to the frontier during the contest.

The principal causes of the war are quite intelligible to the historical student. Great Britain was engaged in a great conflict at the beginning of the nineteenth century, not only for her own national security but also for the integrity of Europe, then threatened by the insatiable ambition of Bonaparte. It was on the sea that her strength mainly lay. To ensure her maritime supremacy England reserved the right of searching neutral, especially American, vessels. This so-called right meant that wherever an English warship met American merchantmen or war-vessels, the latter were required to stop, order their men on deck, and permit as many sailors to be seized and forced into the English service as were unable to prove their nationality. It was maintained that only deserters from the English navy were wanted; but in the period from 1796 to 1802, nearly two thousand American seamen were pressed into the English naval service on the plea that they were deserters. Likewise England became jealous of American trade. French, Spanish, and even English traders raised the American flag in order to get the advantages of neutrals. Thus it appeared that English commerce would fall into the hands of her rivals. It cannot be denied that illicit trade and outrages were really committed and brought back to American doors. The Lion roared. English vessels were stationed just outside the ports of more or less importance to the United States. British cruisers virtually blocked the Atlantic coast from Maine to Georgia. Then happened the *Chesapeake* affair. On June 27, 1803, the British war-vessel *Leopard* signalled the *Chesapeake* to stop as she was leaving Norfolk Harbour. An officer was sent on board, but Commodore Barron refused to muster his men. The *Leopard* thereupon opened fire, took the *Chesapeake* by surprise, three men being killed and eighteen wounded. One Englishman was found when the search was completed; nevertheless, three American sailors (one being a negro) were taken away. This affair excited the American people almost beyond precedent. Indignation meetings were held all over. War soon became the cry. President Jefferson sent an agent to England to demand reparation for the attack on the *Chesapeake*, but England paid no attention to the President's representations.

The Embargo Act of President Jefferson and similar measures solved none of the difficulties they were intended to solve. The South suffered much hardship, tobacco and wheat shrinking to one-half their former value.

Then came the *Little Belt* affair, when, in May, 1811, the United States frigate *President* encountered the British sloop *Little Belt*, and, after a hot chase of several hours practically annihilated her. Never was news more welcome to American ears, and the *Chesapeake* affair had been revenged. But the incident did not help to improve the situation. Lastly it was generally believed that England instigated the Indian attacks which led to the battle of Tippecanoe, where the Americans, under General William Henry Harrison, gained a complete victory, to which our readers' attention will be directed later.

All these causes would, perhaps, have been ineffective but for the revolution in the following year which took place in the American Republican party—the controlling party since 1801. Henry Clay of Kentucky, and John S. Calhoun of South Carolina, advocated war; others followed and President Madison joined them. They hoped to compel Europe to respect the American flag; they had confidence in the young Republic; they dreamed, perhaps, of an alliance with France, of an annexation of Canada. After long and stormy debates war was declared June 18th, the invasion of Canada had already begun!

The War of 1812 officially commenced on June 18th. Great Britain, indeed, had extended a reconciliatory hand but it was too late. The army of the United States numbered at that time 6744 regulars. Congress had authorised its increase to 25,000, and provided, at least by law, for a second volunteer army of 50,000 men. The militia of several States was likewise called on to co-operate with the regulars and the volunteers. But the result was very unsatisfactory. The regular army during the war never reached 10,000; the volunteers appeared only in small numbers, and the militia offered to serve only for short terms and preferably in their own States. The Treasury, with its "sinews of war", was in a precarious condition. The Union had to resort to loans to which the capitalists did not respond with alacrity. On the other hand the British troops in Canada numbered barely seven thousand men; their line of defence was one thousand miles long. England was contending in Europe with her great enemy, Napoleon. The English Navy was, however, the undisputed mistress of all the seas; the British North Atlantic Squadron counted three battleships, twenty cruisers, and fifty smaller ships.

The mind of the man who had been unwittingly awaiting the impossible in the Upper Province for so many gloomy months is well displayed now in a letter written to headquarters at the first intimation of the declaration of war which reached him through roundabout sources:

FORT GEORGE, July 3, 1812.

I have been anxiously expecting for some days to receive the honour of your excellency's commands in regard to the measures the most proper to be pursued on the present emergency.

The accounts received, first through a mercantile channel, and soon after repeated from various quarters, of war having been declared by the United States against Great Britain, would have justified, in my opinion, offensive operations. But the reflection that at Detroit and Michilimakinack the weak state of the garrisons would prevent the commanders from accomplishing any essential service, connected in any degree with their future security, and that my means of annoyance on this communication were limited to the reduction of Fort Niagara, which could easily be battered at any future period, I relinquished my original intention, and attended only to defensive measures. My first object has been the calling out of the flank companies of militia, which has produced a force on this line of about eight hundred men. They turned out very cheerfully, but already show a spirit of impatience. The king's stores are now at so low an ebb, that they scarcely furnish any article of use or comfort. Blankets, hammocks, and kettles, are all to be purchased; and the troops, when watching the banks of the river, stand in the utmost need of tents. Mr. Couche has adopted the most efficacious means to pay the militia in paper currency. I cannot positively state the number of militia that will be embodied, but they cannot exceed throughout the province four thousand men.

The Americans are very active on the opposite side, in the erection of redoubts; we are not idle on our part, but unfortunately having supplied Amherstburg with the guns which that post required from Fort George, depending upon getting others from Kingston to supply their place, we find ourselves at this moment

The Hero of Upper Canada

rather short of that essential arm. I have, however, every reason to think that they are embarked on board the *Earl Moira*, which vessel, according to Major M'Pherson's report, was to have sailed on the 28th ultimo. The Americans have, I believe, about 1200 regulars and militia between Fort Niagara and Black Rock, and I consider myself at this moment perfectly safe against any attempt they can make. About one hundred Indians from the Grand River have attended to my summons; the remainder promise to come also, but I have too much reason to conclude that the Americans have been too successful in their endeavours to sow dissension and disaffection among them. It is a great object to get this fickle race interspersed among the troops. I should be unwilling, in the event of a retreat, to have three or four hundred of them hanging on my flank. I shall probably have to sacrifice some money to gain them over, and the appointment of a few officers with salaries will be absolutely necessary.

The Americans make a daily parade of their force, and easily impose on the people on this side in regard to their numbers. I do not think they exceed 1200, but they are represented as infinitely more numerous.

For the last fortnight every precaution has been taken to guard against the least communication, and to this day we are ignorant whether the President has sanctioned the war resolutions of the two houses of Congress; that is, whether war be actually declared.

I have not been honoured with a line from Mr. Foster,[1] nor with all my endeavours have I been able to retain information of any consequence. The *Prince Regent* made her first voyage this morning, and I purpose sending her to Kingston this evening, to bring such articles as are absolutely necessary, which we know have arrived from Quebec. I trust she will out-sail the *Oneida* brig.

The arrival of General Hull at Detroit and his "invasion" of Canada followed hard on the declaration of war; as a preliminary step previous to invasion he issued the Proclamation for which he was afterward

[1] British Ambassador to the United States.

so roundly scored. The proclamation was really an invitation to all disaffected persons in the Upper Provinces to join Hull's army. That it had no more success than it did, was due, it may be believed, to the personal magnetism of the able man in control of affairs —to the trust that the people had as a whole in General Brock. To counteract Hull's proclamation Brock replied in one of his own, and it contains several statements of interest as displaying the character of its author:

The unprovoked declaration of war by the United States of America against the United Kingdom of Great Britain and Ireland, and its dependencies, has been followed by the actual invasion of this province, in a remote frontier of the western district, by a detachment of the armed force of the United States.

The officer commanding that detachment has thought proper to invite his majesty's subjects, not merely to a quiet and unresisting submission, but insults them with a call to seek voluntarily the protection of his government.

Without condescending to repeat the illiberal epithets bestowed in this appeal of the American commander to the people of Upper Canada, on the administration of his majesty, every inhabitant of the province is desired to seek the confutation of such indecent slander in the review of his own particular circumstances. Where is the Canadian subject who can truly affirm to himself that he has been injured by the government, in his person, his property, or his liberty? Where is to be found, in any part of the world, a growth so rapid in prosperity and wealth, as this colony exhibits? Settled not thirty years, by a band of veterans, exiled from their former possessions on account of their loyalty, not a descendant of these brave people is to be found, who, under the fostering liberality of their sovereign, has not acquired a property and means of enjoyment superior to what were possessed by their ancestors.

The unequalled prosperity would not have been attained by the utmost liberality of the government, or the persevering in-

"Navy Hall Opposite Niagara."
A drawing on bark by Mrs. Simcoe.

Queenston and Brock's Monument,
From a photograph by Wm. Quinn, Niagara-on-the-Lake.

dustry of the people, had not the maritime power of the mother-country secured to its colonists a safe access to every market, where the produce of their labour was in request.

The unavoidable and immediate consequences of a separation from Great Britain must be the loss of this inestimable advantage; and what is offered you in exchange? To become a territory of the United States, and share with them that exclusion from the ocean which the policy of their government enforces; you are not even flattered with a participation of their boasted independence; and it is but too obvious that, once estranged from the powerful protection of the United Kingdom, you must be re-annexed to the dominion of France, from which the provinces of Canada were wrested by the arms of Great Britain, at a vast expense of blood and treasure, from no other motive than to relieve her ungrateful children from the oppression of a cruel neighbour. This restitution of Canada to the empire of France, was the stipulated reward for the aid afforded to the revolted colonies, now the United States; the debt is still due, and there can be no doubt but the pledge has been renewed as a consideration for commercial advantages, or rather for an expected relaxation in the tyranny of France over the commercial world. Are you prepared, inhabitants of Canada, to become willing subjects, or rather slaves, to the despot who rules the nations of continental Europe with a rod of iron? If not, arise in a body, exert your energies, co-operate cordially with the King's regular forces to repel the invader, and do not give cause to your children, when groaning under the oppression of a foreign master, to reproach you with having so easily parted with the richest inheritance of this earth—a participation in the name, character, and freedom of Britons!

The same spirit of justice, which will make every reasonable allowance for the unsuccessful efforts of zeal and loyalty, will not fail to punish the defalcation of principle. Every Canadian freeholder is, by deliberate choice, bound by the most solemn oaths to defend the monarchy, as well as his own property; to shrink from that engagement is a treason not to be forgiven. Let no man suppose that if, in this unexpected struggle, his majesty's arms should be compelled to yield to an overwhelming force, the province will be eventually abandoned; the endeared relations of its first settlers, the intrinsic value of its commerce, and the pretensions of its powerful rival to possess the Canadas, are pledges that no peace will be established between the United States and Great Britain and Ireland, of which the restoration of these provinces does not make the most prominent condition.

Be not dismayed at the unjustifiable threat of the commander of the enemy's forces to refuse quarter, should an Indian appear in the ranks. The brave bands of aborigines which inhabit this colony were, like his Majesty's other subjects, punished for their zeal and fidelity, by the loss of their possessions in the late colonies, and requited by his Majesty with lands of superior value in this province. The faith of the British government has never yet been violated—the Indians feel that the soil they inherit is to them and their posterity protected from the base arts so frequently devised to over-reach their simplicity. By what new principle are they to be prohibited from defending their property? If their warfare, from being different to that of the white people, be more terrific to the enemy, let him retrace his steps—they seek him not—and cannot expect to find women and children in an invading army. But they are men, and have equal rights with all other men to defend themselves and their property when invaded, more especially when they find in the enemy's camp a ferocious and mortal foe; using the same warfare which the American commander affects to reprobate.

This inconsistent and unjustifiable threat of refusing quarter, for such a cause as being found in arms with a brother sufferer, in defence of invaded rights, must be exercised with the certain assurance of retaliation, not only in the limited operations of war in this part of the King's dominions, but in every quarter of the globe; for the national character of Britain is not less distinguished for humanity than strict retributive justice, which will consider the execution of this inhuman threat as deliberate murder, for which every subject of the offending power must make expiation.

Few men ever had the task that General Brock now essayed thrown upon their shoulders. With some fifteen hundred men he had to occupy the forts St.

Joseph, Amherstburg (Malden), Chippewa, Erie, and George, together with York (Toronto) and Kingston; maintain British supremacy, if possible, on three great lakes; preserve the long communication and defend a frontier eight hundred and more miles in length. And it is to be remembered that even in time of peace there had been no little trouble in keeping the British regulars from deserting to the American side of the Niagara—probably to take advantage of the splendid agricultural and commercial opportunities in the West just then being thrown open to the pioneer hosts and to which Easterners were flocking "in shoals," as one observer put it. His position was the more peculiar because of the nature of the larger portion of the inhabitants of the upper province, the loyalists. Having fled from the United States in the hours of the Revolution, fancy now the thoughts of these honest people as they faced the prospect of their land of refuge being invaded by an army from the land below the lakes! Seldom did a people have more cause for apprehension; seldom did the inhabitants of an invaded land look less for commiseration on the part of the invaders. The result was that a very few fled back again to the land of their birth; but the vast majority resolved to trust the issue to Providence—and these looked to General Brock to preserve the land.

The situation was unique and gave the man at the helm a singular opportunity to prove himself and win the deathless devotion of a whole people. Little wonder that the man who proved himself equal to this critical hour will forever be known as "The Hero of Upper Canada."

Brigadier-General Hull had advanced into Upper

Canada from Detroit early in July, but it was not until the capture of Hull's despatches by Colonel Proctor in the affair near Brownsville when Van Horne's party was ambushed that Brock planned to execute the daring advance which ended in the astonishing capture of Detroit and Hull's entire army. On the 6th of August Brock departed from York, with five hundred additional volunteers, largely sons of loyalists, who were very true to their adopted country in this crisis— or, perhaps we should say, loyal to this brave leader in whom were suddenly found the qualities required by the extraordinary occasion. Being compelled to leave a part of the little force he was leading westward along the Niagara River, General Brock reached Amherstburg (Malden) in five days and nights with some three hundred followers. It is plain on this showing that whatever the result of the bold enterprise there was now no hesitation in carrying it out. Tecumseh's salute in his honour was suppressed as quickly as possible, such was the scarcity of powder! There is something pathetically interesting in two despatches issued by Brock on two successive days,—August 14th and 15th. One was an appeal to his troops to prevent desertion among the country folk who felt it imperative to get in their crops; the other was an ultimatum to Hull summoning him to surrender. The incongruity of the two epistles is almost amusing, especially when it is remembered that the British had very little powder and a force smaller than that opposed to it beyond the Detroit River. And yet the bombastic order reads:

> The force at my disposal authorises me to require of you the immediate surrender of Fort Detroit. It is far from my inclination to join in a war of extermination; but you must be aware

that the numerous body of Indians who have attached themselves to my troops will be beyond my control the moment the contest commences. You will find me disposed to enter into such conditions as will satisfy the most scrupulous sense of honour. Lieut.-Colonel M'Donell and Major Glegg are fully authorised to conclude any arrangement that may lead to prevent the unnecessary effusion of blood.

An answer of bold and frank tenor from Hull was received by the desperate Brock, who immediately chose his course; there was nothing for it but to retreat or attack the enemies' position; he could not sit still; he was in George Rogers Clark's shoes at Kaskaskia a generation before when Hamilton had captured Vincennes—he must capture Hull or be captured by Hull. It was true to the kind of man he was that Brock should spurn the advice of his officers to retreat and should determine, despite their objections, to put his threat into execution. On Sunday, the 16th of August, Brock's determined men were crossing the Strait. His force included less than four hundred regulars and about that many militia supported by some six hundred Indians. The American troops numbered upwards of two thousand. As is well known Brock received notification as his force was moving upon the fort that General Hull was ready to treat with him. The resolute deportment of the desperate Brock had won for him and his King a bloodless conquest that will go down in history as one of the most heroic on the part of one commander and most despicable on the part of the other to be found in the annals of warfare. Congressmen who had been boasting in debate that it was unnecessary to even send troops into the Canadas since officers alone, by appearing there, could rally armies of disaffected persons about them, now read that one determined man, acting against the advice of his officers had appeared at the gates of Detroit with half an army and taken its keys as readily as though they were voted to him by the city fathers and brought to him on a silver salver. "We have the Canadas," rang the silvery voice of Henry Clay in Congress, "as much under our command as Great Britain has the ocean; and the way to conquer her on the ocean is to drive her from the land." No one could have more completely misjudged an enemy or his own country as did the great Kentuckian in this instance.

It is interesting in the extreme to survey the man who had won a signal triumph as he now marches back to York and Fort George where he had spent so many useless, fruitless years, as it seemed to him—yearning in season and out of season for the opportunity to get away to the Peninsula, or somewhere where fame might be achieved. Brock's success is a great lesson to all ambitious men. Doing the humble drudgery of the duty that lay next his hand, despite the regret and even pain occasioned by lack of opportunity, this man suddenly came into a fame world-wide and the honour of the Bath that he thought could come to him only in sunny Spain. On the 10th of the following October General Brock's brother William was asked by his wife why the park and tower guns were saluting. "For Isaac, of course," he answered, playfully; "don't you know that this is Isaac's birthday?" A little later he learned that the news of the surrender of Detroit had just been received, and that his playful answer was very near the truth after all!

It is fruitless to imagine what might have been the

The Hero of Upper Canada 251

trend of events in Canada but for the daring decision made by Brock to move upon Detroit; his courage in running in the teeth of the wind and trusting to Providence to fetch the quay by hook or crook, is the very quality of the human heart that mankind most delights to honour; it is remarkable that the imbecility of Hull could have so completely blinded our American eyes to this display of splendid daring of Brock's, which ranks with Clark's bold march through the drowned lands of the Wabash, or Wayne's attack on Stony Point. The capture of Hull and Detroit unquestionably saved Upper Canada to England; for though American arms were successful to some degree beyond the line, as we shall see, the successes did not count toward conquest and annexation as would have been the case, perhaps, had they come at the outbreak of the war. All Canada felt the heartening effect of Brock's inexplicable victory; thousands who had feared instant and ruthless invasion now felt strong to repel any and all invaders; and the effect extended to the Indian allies and across the ocean to the home-country, as well. Had Clay's theory been true and the war had to be settled by land battles, Detroit would have delayed the end for many years; but America was soon to show a power on the sea as surprising as the stupidity of some of her commanders on shore and play England at her own sea-dog game with her own weapons and gain the victory.

The General's letter to his brothers is interesting as exhibiting the man's private views on his great success:

> I have received [he writes] so many letters from people whose opinion I value, expressive of their admiration of the exploit, that I begin to attach to it more importance than I was at first inclined. Should the affair be viewed in England in the light it

is here, I cannot fail of meeting reward, and escaping the horror of being placed high on a shelf, never to be taken down. Some say that nothing could be more desperate than the measure; but I answer, that the state of the province admitted of nothing but desperate remedies. I got possession of the letters my antagonist addressed to the secretary of war, and also of the sentiments which hundreds of his army uttered to their friends. Confidence in the General was gone, and evident despondency prevailed throughout. I have succeeded beyond expectation. I crossed the river, contrary to the opinion of Colonel Proctor, . . . etc.[1]; it is, therefore, no wonder that envy should attribute to good fortune what, in justice to my own discernment, I must say, proceeded from a cool calculation of the *pours* and *contres*.

General Brock, along with most other British leaders who operated along the American frontier, has been accused of using the savages to fight in savage ways the battles of white men against fellow whites. Rossiter Johnson, in his *War of 1812*, to cite one of the careful students who has thus referred to Brock, in speaking of the minute-guns fired on the American shore during Brock's funeral, says:

> There was perhaps no harm in this little bit of sentiment, though if the Americans remembered that two months before, in demanding the surrender of Detroit, General Brock had threatened to let loose a horde of savages upon the garrison and town, if he were compelled to capture it by force, they must have seen that their minute-guns were supremely illogical, not to say silly.[2]

One who has any reason to know how much basis Washington had for his sweeping remark that most of the trouble the United States had with the western

[1] In the face of the fact here divulged concerning Proctor's attitude toward Brock's determination to move upon Detroit it is interesting to remember Brock's very high praise of Proctor in his report of the capture. His words, so characteristic of the gentleman, were: "I have been admirably supported by Colonel Proctor. . . ."
[2] P. 60.

Indians was due to the demeanour of British officers to them, could only with difficulty become prejudiced in favour of any British officers who had actual dealings with the Canadian Indians and actually led them in person to battle. And yet the present writer has found sufficient ground in Brock's correspondence for holding that Brock was above reproach personally on this score —that he was a gentleman here as elsewhere, a true nobleman. We cannot here enter into a lengthy discussion of such a difficult problem. A letter extant, written by Brock to General Prevost, shows his attitude in this delicate matter during those desperate days when Harrison was fighting the wily Tecumseh:

> My first care, on my arrival in this province, was to direct the officers of the Indian department at Amherstburg to exert their whole influence with the Indians to prevent the attack which I understood a few tribes meditated against the American frontier. But their efforts proved fruitless, as such was the infatuation of the Indians, that they refused to listen to advice.

It will always be an open question how much control the responsible men, either American or British, had over their red-skinned "brothers" compared with their half-renegade, forest-running underlings who dispensed the powder, blankets, and fire-water and directed affairs much as they pleased.

Before the outbreak of the war Brock wrote to his superiors concerning his province as follows:

> The first point to which I am anxious to call your excellency's attention is the district of Amherstburg. I consider it the most important, and, if supplied with the means of commencing active operations, must deter any offensive attempt on this province, from Niagara westward. The American government will be compelled to secure their western frontier from the inroads of the Indians, and this cannot be effected without a very considerable

force. But before we can expect an active co-operation on the part of the Indians, the reduction of Detroit and Michilimakinack must convince that people, who conceive themselves to have been sacrificed, in 1794, to our policy,[1] that we are earnestly engaged in the war. The Indians, I am made to understand, are eager for an opportunity to avenge the numerous injuries of which they complain. A few tribes, at the instigation of a Shawnese, of no particular note, have already, although explicitly told not to look for assistance from us, commenced the contest. The stand which they continue to make upon the Wabash, against about two thousand Americans, including militia and regulars, is a strong proof of the large force which a general combination of the Indians will render necessary to protect so widely extended a frontier.

Again, Brock was in a very different position from the British commanders during the Revolution; his province was being invaded and the Indians who had settled under the auspices of the British Government in that province were threatened with destruction as seriously as the loyalists or the native Englishmen transplanted from the mother-country. Surely, no one would expect Indians whose homes lay in the upper province to remain neutral when that province was invaded. Indeed, in February, 1812, we find Brock complaining to his superior of the lax attention that was paid by the Government to the Indians settled in the province he had been sent to govern.

Divisions are thus uninterruptedly sowed among our Indian friends [he wrote, meaning, of course, sowed by Americans], and the minds of many altogether estranged from our interests. Such must inevitably be the consequence of our present inert and neutral proceedings in regard to them. It ill becomes me to determine how long true policy requires that the restrictions imposed upon the Indian department ought to continue; but this I will venture to assert, that each day the officers are restrained

[1] The reference here is to the failure of the British to assist the Indian confederacy withstand General Wayne's invasion of the Maumee Valley which ended in the victory of Fallen Timber.

from interfering in the concerns of the Indians, each time they advise peace and withhold the accustomed supply of ammunition, their influence will diminish, till at length they lose it altogether.

Nothing shows better the activity of the American officers in seeking to line the Indians up on the side of the fighting Republic than Brock's letters to his superiors. We have already seen that Brock had, as late as July 3d, little hope of keeping the Indians of the Grand River true to him because of the American influence exerted over them by active agents. And we have seen, in his counter-proclamation answering that issued by General Hull, that Brock places the employment of the Indians on the ground of territorial rights: "By what new principle," he asks, "are they to be prohibited from defending their property?"

The ominous words used by General Brock in his summons to Hull to surrender have, it must be admitted, all the ring of a threat; but, for one, I do not take them to be that primarily, but rather the honest, frank words of a gentleman. In case of the sacking of Detroit Brock could not have controlled those redskins of his, and he knew it. In like circumstances what general had been able to control the Indians attached to him? In the single instance of Sir William Johnson at the fall of Fort Niagara, we find an illustration of approximate control, yet nothing in the world but the power of that great man would have answered under the circumstances. I would believe that Brock knew he could not control his Iroquois allies,[1] whether in victory or in defeat, and made a plain statement to Hull to that effect. That he told the truth I think no one can

---

[1] That Brock feared the Indians when acting in unison, that is, when not "interspersed" among the troops, is perfectly plain from his letter to General Prevost of July 3d.

doubt after examining the situation; whether he would have told the truth if the truth had not carried a threat may be questioned. The truth usually answers a gentleman's purposes, and Brock was that to the marrow of his bones.

Brock had not overestimated the effect and influence of his bloodless victory upon the English, but, by strange caprice of Fate, was not permitted to live to receive the high honours bestowed upon him. On the thirteenth of the following October, in the battle of Queenston Heights, elsewhere described, while reforming the broken British ranks for a second time, a bullet in the breast cut short a life that promised very high attainment. As was his custom the General had arisen before daybreak on this fatal day and had left Fort George at the first sound of the battle on the heights. His conspicuous presence, bright uniform, and animated deportment in attempting to reform the broken lines, made him a plain target for Wool's heroic men, who had climbed up a pathway steeper than any Wolfe's troops ever saw at Quebec. "Push on the York volunteers," were the words of the brave man's last order; but as he lay in the arms of his aides he begged that his injury might not be noticed by the troops or disconcert their advance; and with one half-understood wish concerning a token of love to be given to his sister, Isaac Brock fell dead.

It is not given to many notable men to fall in the very midst of spectacular success; it can easily be believed that General Brock, being the man we know him to have been, would have made the best use of his triumph, and that it would have been but a stepping-stone to enlarged opportunities where each duty in its turn would have received the same decent, earnest attention that the man gave to his work throughout those half-unhappy days when he felt marooned in the wilds of a dreary ocean, where no one could prove his merit, calibre, or knowledge. And so, after all is said for this fine man, I, for one, like best to go back to those days of impatient longing for opportunity amid the dull grind of routine at Fort George, and see the real spirit of Brock who, in all truth, deserves the honourable title of "Hero of Upper Canada"; and when you have caught the spirit displayed by him in those dispiriting days, realise his careful faithfulness in the humdrum life he was asked to live, while his schoolmates of war were winning great glory on the epoch-making European battlefields, join to it that sudden burst of splendid grit and heroism that provoked the Detroit attack despite the advice of the staff officers, and you have a combination that thrills the heart of friend and enemy —of all who love patient doing of duty and real displays of undiluted heroism.

Some of the best tributes to Brock, were, as should have been the case, those paid by persons who knew of his place in the hearts of the people of his adopted land of service:

> The news of the death of this excellent officer [observed the Quebec *Gazette*] has been received here as a public calamity. The attendant circumstances of victory scarcely checked the painful sensation. His long residence in this province, and particularly in this place, had made him in habits and good offices almost a citizen; and his frankness, conciliatory disposition, and elevated demeanour, an estimable one. The expressions of regret as general as he was known, and not uttered by friends and acquaintances only, but by every gradation of class, not only by grown persons, but young children, are the test of his worth.

Such, too, is the only eulogium worthy of the good and brave, and the citizens of Quebec have, with solemn emotions, pronounced it on his memory. But at this anxious moment other feelings are excited by his loss. General Brock had acquired the confidence of the inhabitants within his government. He had secured their attachment permanently by his own merits. They were one people animated by one disposition, and this he had gradually wound up to the crisis in which they were placed. Strange as it may seem, it is to be feared that he had become too important to them. The heroic militia of Upper Canada, more particularly, had knit themselves to his person; and it is yet to be ascertained whether the desire to avenge his death can compensate the many embarrassments it will occasion. It is indeed true that the spirit, and even the abilities, of a distinguished man often carry their influence beyond the grave; and the present event furnishes its own example, for it is certain notwithstanding General Brock was cut off early in the action, that he had already given an impulse to his little army, which contributed to accomplish the victory when he was no more. Let us trust that the recollection of him will become a new bond of union, and that, as he sacrificed himself for a community of patriots, they will find a new motive to exertion in the obligation to secure his ashes from the pestilential dominion of the enemy.

A Montreal newspaper of the day also contained the following observations:

The private letters from Upper Canada, in giving the account of the late victory at Queenstown, are partly taken up with lamentations upon the never-to-be-forgotten General Brock, which do honour to the character and talents of the man they deplore. The enemy have nothing to hope from the loss they have inflicted; they have created a hatred which panteth for revenge. Although General Brock may be said to have fallen in the midst of his career, yet his previous services in Upper Canada will be lasting and highly beneficial. When he assumed the government of the province, he found a divided, disaffected, and, of course, a weak people. He has left them united and strong, and the universal sorrow of the province attends his fall. The father, to his children, will make known the mournful story.

The Hero of Upper Canada 259

The veteran, who fought by his side in the heat and burthen of the day of our deliverance, will venerate his name.

And the sentiments of the British Government, on the melancholy occasion, were thus expressed in a despatch from Earl Bathurst, the secretary of state for the colonies, to Sir George Prevost, dated December 8, 1812:

His Royal Highness the Prince Regent is fully aware of the severe loss which his Majesty's service has experienced in the death of Major-General Sir Isaac Brock. This would have been sufficient to have clouded a victory of much greater importance. His Majesty has lost in him not only an able and meritorious officer, but one who, in the exercise of his functions of provisional lieutenant-governor of the province, displayed qualities admirably adapted to awe the disloyal, to reconcile the wavering, and to animate the great mass of the inhabitants against successive attempts of the enemy to invade the province, in the last of which he unhappily fell, too prodigal of that life of which his eminent services had taught us to understand the value.

The body of the fallen hero lay in state at the government house until the 16th of October, when, with that of Colonel McDonell, it was buried with due honours in a cavalier bastion of Fort George, at the spot now marked by the tablet indicating the first burial-place. On the 13th of October, 1824, the remains were moved to the summit of the heights, whereon a beautiful monument had been erected by the Provincial Legislature, 135 feet in height, bearing this "splendid tribute to the unfading remembrance of a grateful people":

UPPER CANADA
HAS DEDICATED THIS MONUMENT

TO THE MEMORY OF THE LATE
MAJOR-GENERAL SIR ISAAC BROCK, K.B.
PROVISIONAL LIEUT.-GOVERNOR AND COMMANDER OF THE FORCES
IN THIS PROVINCE
WHOSE REMAINS ARE DEPOSITED IN THE VAULT BENEATH
OPPOSING THE INVADING ENEMY
HE FELL IN ACTION NEAR THESE HEIGHTS
ON THE 13TH OCTOBER, 1812
IN THE 43D YEAR OF HIS AGE
REVERED AND LAMENTED
BY THE PEOPLE WHOM HE GOVERNED
AND DEPLORED BY THE SOVEREIGN
TO WHOSE SERVICE HIS LIFE HAD BEEN DEVOTED.

The following description of this interesting pageant portrays the genuine feeling of devotion felt for the "Hero of Upper Canada" that filled the hearts of his countrymen:

There is something so grand and imposing in the spectacle of a nation's homage to departed worth, which calls for the exercise of so many interesting feelings, and which awakens so many sublime contemplations, that we naturally seek to perpetuate the memory of an event so pregnant with instruction, and so honourable to our species. It is a subject that in other and in older countries has frequently exercised the pens, and has called forth all the descriptive powers of the ablest writers. But here it is new; and for the first time, since we became a separate province, have we seen a great public funeral procession of all ranks of people, to the amount of several thousands, bearing the remains of two lamented heroes to their last dwelling on earth, in the vaults of a grand national monument, overtopping the loftiest heights of the most magnificent section of one of the most magnificent countries in the world.

The 13th of October, being the anniversary of the battle of Queenstown, and of the death of Brock, was judiciously chosen as the most proper day for the removal of the remains of the general, together with those of his gallant aide-de-camp, Lieutenant-Colonel M'Donell, to the vaults prepared for their reception on Queenstown Heights.

Brock's Monument.

"Queenston or Landing near Niagara."
A drawing on bark by Mrs. Simcoe.

The Hero of Upper Canada

The weather was remarkably fine, and before ten o'clock a very large concourse of people, from all parts of the country, had assembled on the plains of Niagara, in front of Fort George, in a bastion of which the bodies had been deposited for twelve years.

One hearse covered with black cloth, and drawn by four black horses, each with a leader, contained both the bodies. Soon after ten, a lane was formed by the 1st and 4th regiments of Lincoln militia, with their right on the gate of Fort George, and their left extending along the road towards Queenstown, the ranks being about forty paces distant from each other; within this line was formed a guard of honour of the 76th Regiment, in parade order, having its left on the fort. As the hearse moved slowly from the fort, to the sound of solemn music, a detachment of royal artillery began to fire the salute of nineteen guns, and the guard of honour presented arms.

On moving forwards in ordinary time, the guard of honour broke into a column of eight divisions, with the right in front, and the procession took the following order:

A Staff Officer.
Subdivision of Grenadiers.
Band of Music.
Right Wing of 76th Regiment.
THE BODY.
Aide-de-Camp to the late Major-General Sir Isaac Brock.
Chief Mourners.
Commissioners for the Monument.
Heads of Public Departments of the Civil Government.
Judges.
Members of the Executive Council.
His Excellency and Suite.
Left Wing of the 76th Regiment.
Indian Chiefs of the Five Nations.
Officers of Militia not on duty—Junior Ranks—First Forward.
Four deep.
Magistrates and Civilians.
With a long Cavalcade of Horsemen, and Carriages of every description.

On the 17th of April, 1840, a miscreant by the name of Lett laid a train to a quantity of gunpowder secreted beneath the monument to General Brock and fired it, partially wrecking both the base and the pillar. The criminal had been compelled to flee the country during the rebellion then just over, and, returning, took this outrageous method of gratifying his malice. As we look upon the beautiful monument that stands above Brock's remains to-day it is with a feeling almost of pleasure that such a wretched deed was necessary to result in the fine pillar that is one of the scenic beauties of the Niagara country to-day. This fine shaft bears the following inscription:

The Legislature of Upper Canada has dedicated this Monuument to the very distinguished, eminent, civil, and military services of the late Sir Isaac Brock, Knight of the Most Hon. Order of the Bath, Provisional Lieutenant-Governor, and Major-General commanding the Forces in this Province, whose remains are deposited in the vault beneath. Having expelled the Northwestern Army of the United States, achieved its capture, received the surrender of Fort Detroit, and the territory of Michigan, under circumstances which have rendered his name illustrious he returned to the protection of this frontier; and advancing with his small force to repel a second invasion of the enemy, then in possession of these heights, he fell in action, on the 13th of October, 1812, in the forty-third year of his age, honoured and beloved by the people whom he governed and deplored by his Sovereign, to whose service his life had been devoted.

Chapter XI

The Second War with England

WE have explained the influence of the life and death of General Brock in the upper province sufficiently for the reader to conceive, perhaps, an unusual interest in the course of the war that soon was raging, in reality or in burlesque, as it sometimes appeared, along the northern border; no one can take any interest in Brock's career without wondering whether his province was invaded or conquered despite the sacrifices of this undefeated but dead hero.

Upon Brock's return from Detroit he found General Stephen Van Rensselaer commanding the American shore of the river, preparing, according to report, to begin the conquest of the upper province. There was much cause for delay, which in turn provoked criticism and unrest, but as October of 1812 drew near it was considered necessary and possible to execute the advance upon Brock's positions along the river and on Queenston Heights and Fort George. The first attempt to advance on the night of the 10th proved abortive through the treachery of an irresponsible lieutenant. Instead of quieting the ardour of the army this disgusting mishap made the troops the more eager for the conflict, and a new plan was very secretly arranged, with such success that it is pretty sure that

General Brock was in doubt up to the last moment where the attack was to be made. A strong force had been kept at Fort Niagara, and this, with the stationing of Colonel Chrystie's troops at Four Mile Creek, caused Brock to believe that the attack was to be made on Fort George.

The night of the twelfth was set as the time for the second attempt to cross the Niagara. Soon after dark, Chrystie with his three hundred men marched from Fort Niagara by interior routes to Lewiston, reaching his destination before midnight. Re-enforcements had also come from the Falls, as well as Colonel Scott who had just arrived at Schlosser, aroused by the information that a battle was soon to be fought and glory to be won. Scott presented himself to the General asking permission to take part in the engagement, and though Van Rensselaer could not change his plans he offered to let Scott take position on Lewiston Heights and co-operate with the rest of the army as he saw fit.

Solomon Van Rensselaer was again placed in command but Colonel Chrystie was allowed to lead an equal force, thus recognising his rank. Three o'clock in the morning, October 13th, was the time set for crossing the river. The night was very dark. The plan was for Chrystie and Van Rensselaer to cross and storm the heights, when the rest of the army should follow on the second trip and attack Queenston. The boats, however, would not carry more than half the desired number; these with their leaders landed on the Canadian shore not more than ten minutes after leaving Lewiston landing, at the very spot aimed at, at the foot of the cliff under Lewiston suspension bridge. The British were found very much on the alert and opened fire from the heights the moment the boats touched land. Lovett's battery on Lewiston Heights immediately opened fire in answer, and this, with a charge by the regulars of the Thirteenth under Wool, soon drove the enemy backward toward Queenston. Wool took position just above Queenston when orders were given him to storm the heights. Eager and anxious for the struggle, his troops were immediately put in motion, but he soon received orders countermanding the first just as he was moving rapidly toward the heights. No sooner had his men taken position in accord with it than the right flank was fiercely attacked by Dennis's full force. At the same moment the British opened fire upon the little body from the heights. Wool immediately, without tarrying for orders, faced about and poured such a fierce fire into Dennis's command that it was compelled to fall back. In the meantime Van Rensselaer had come up with his command and taken position on Wool's left. In this short engagement, the Americans suffered most severely. Van Rensselaer was so severely wounded that he was forced to relinquish the command, and Wool had been wounded though refusing to leave the field.

The British on the heights kept up a continual fire on the Americans, which from their position could not be returned with effect, and the little invading army fell back to the shore below the hill where they occupied a more sheltered position.

Daybreak had now come, and a storm which had raged all morning had ceased with the retreat of the Americans; but the storm of lead was soon to break more furiously than before, although the little army was in a sorry plight. Wool was only twenty-three years old. The commanding officer, Solomon Van Rensselaer, was forced to retire. What was to be done? Wool had asked for orders. The heights must be taken or the enterprise abandoned; Wool was ordered to storm the heights and Lush commanded to follow and shoot the first man that wavered—for signs of disaffection were already showing themselves. No sooner did Wool receive his orders than, fired by the frenzy of the battle, forgetting wounds and all else, he sprang forward to its execution. Up the ascent the men rushed, protected from fire to a degree by bushes and rocks. Many parts of the hill were so steep that there was nothing for it but to pull themselves along by the roots and shrubs. General Brock, in the meantime, hardly knew what to expect. He was at Fort George and seems to have had a determined suspicion that the main attack would be made upon Fort George from Fort Niagara. He heard the early cannonading but supposed that it was only a feint to conceal the point of real movement. However, the true soldier mounted his horse and raced away immediately to the scene of action and death. On arriving and taking a view of the field Brock considered affairs favourable to the British; however, he had hardly dismounted at the redan battery than Wool's men scrambled upon the heights and opened up a galling fire. So hot was the attack that the Canadians were immediately forced from their stronghold; a few moments later the flag of the Union waved there.

Brock immediately sent to Fort George for reenforcements, rallied the disorganised force, and with Williams's and Dennis's commands attempted to turn the American right flank; Wool perceived the move and tried to anticipate it by sending fifty men to its protection. These were forced back by superior numbers, and the whole command was compelled to give ground until the edge of the precipice was reached with the rushing river flood two hundred feet below. It seemed that they must either surrender or perish; one captain attempted to raise a white flag but was stopped by Wool, who, having addressed a few hurried words to his men, led them to the charge with such fierce zeal that the British in turn gave back. The brave Brock saw this movement in dismay; with a stinging rebuke, which called every man back to a realisation of his duty, the General placed himself at the head of the column to lead it back to victory. His tall form, towering above that of the soldiers around him, made a conspicuous mark for the American sharpshooter, and he was soon struck in the wrist but bravely pressed on; shortly after a ball entered his breast and passed out of his side, inflicting a death wound. He scarcely had time to make a few last requests when he died. As soon as the soldiers knew of their commander's death, they became infuriated. The column charged up the hill toward the Americans. Wool's little command, doubtful of victory, spiked the cannon in the redan. The struggle was fierce for a few moments; but the British were again made to retire, leaving Wool master of Queenston Heights.

Re-enforcements were slowly crossing the river. Colonel Scott had arrived early in the morning and had placed his cannon to protect the crossing as far as possible. Later he received permission to cross over as a volunteer. Having met with Wadsworth of the New York militia, that officer unselfishly waived his rank on account of Scott's superior military experience, and allowed him to take command of regulars and militia, amounting in all to some six hundred. While Scott was superintending the unspiking of the cannon in the redan his command on the heights was assailed by a band of Indians under John Brant, son of the famous Mohawk chieftain. So furious and unexpected was their attack that the pickets were driven in immediately and the main body began to draw back. This was shortly after one o'clock in the afternoon. The militia, unused to being under fire, were beginning to break away when Scott appeared and by his commanding presence and steady nerve led the men back to order. A charge was immediately ordered, which was executed so fiercely that the Indians retired; however, they kept up a fire on the Americans from sheltered positions until Scott ordered a general assault and drove them from the heights. Lieutenant-Colonel Chrystie then appeared on the field for the first time and ordered Wool to the American shore to have his wounds dressed.

General Sheaffe now arrived from Fort George with re-enforcements and took command of the British forces; these now numbered about thirteen hundred while the Americans could not count over six hundred. Scheaffe marched to the east to St. Davids and by brilliantly counter-marching gained the rear of the American army. Van Rensselaer was on the heights at this time; seeing these movements he returned to send over re-enforcements. But to his surprise, and their own eternal disgrace, the American militia, which had been crying out so long for action, refused to budge. He, as well as others, threatened, entreated, and implored; all in vain. The men who but a few hours before had demanded to be led to the war, now, at sight of blood and the smell of gun-powder, refused to help their comrades threatened with destruction on the heights across the river. Van Rensselaer transmitted this information to Wadsworth and promised boats if he wished to retreat, but he could not even make this promise good, as the frightened boatmen refused to raise an oar. Nothing was left for the little band on the heights but surrender or death! It has been offered in extenuation of the action of the militia that there had been gross mismanagement of the boats, only one or two being at hand, necessitating their being sent across the river in dangerously small parties. Wherever the blame should be placed, there was enough of it to go around and to make any patriot blush. The militia were within their legal rights in refusing to pass beyond the boundaries of their State, and may have been entirely right in refusing to attempt the crossing if it could not be made in force.

The final engagement of the battle of Queenston Heights was inaugurated about four o'clock in the afternoon by General Sheaffe directing a large body of Indians and regulars against the American right. The superior numbers, together with the impetuous advance, threw the Americans into confusion. Scheaffe ordered an advance along the whole line and the American ranks were soon broken, most of those fleeing toward the city being cut off by the Indians; some few escaped by letting themselves down the steep hill by roots and bushes. Several attempts were made to surrender, but it is said that even those bearing the flag were shot down by the Indians. Colonel Scott was attacked by two savages while on this mission, but was valiantly rescued by a British officer. On reaching headquarters terms were soon agreed upon by which all the Americans on the Canada side became prisoners of war.

Thus ended this, the spectacular battle of Queenston Heights. In many ways it was typical of so many battles in American military annals; the eagerness of hot-headed militia to hear the guns popping, the daring attack, the heroism of cool, undaunted officers, the loss of enthusiasm as the struggle wore on, the final conflict of regular and militia, the seemingly inexcusable lack of interest on the part of the non-combatants, the flight and surrender—all are typical.

The death of the noble Brock has thrown a halo over the Niagara frontier for Briton and American alike. As you wander to-day across the pleasant commons at Niagara-on-the-Lake to the site of old Fort George, or scramble up the steep sides of beautiful Queenston Heights, you will find yourself thinking of the heroic leaders at the battle of Queenston—Brock, Wool, Chrystie, and the impetuous Scott; to one rambler, at least, amid these striking scenes, the battle, as such, quite faded out of the perspective, leaving the fine military figure of the British commander looming up alone beside that of the twenty-three-year-old boy Wool, who had jumped from his law books down in New York to come here as captain of militia and give the world another clear picture of absolute daring not surpassed in any point by Wolfe's at Quebec; the young Scott appears too, so willing to be in the fracas across the river that he crosses as a private soldier. Had the faltering militia caught his spirit there would have been, perhaps, another story to tell of the outcome of the battle! It is to be hoped that the year 1912 will not pass without seeing raised on Lewiston Heights a monument to these noble men equal in point of beauty to the splendid shaft raised across the river to the memory of Brock.

On the 17th of November, a bombardment was opened on Black Rock from batteries which had been constructed across the river. The firing was kept up all day; but little damage was done to the Americans, and almost none to the British, as few cannon were mounted against them. On the 21st of November a fierce cannonade was opened from a number of batteries which had been erected opposite Fort Niagara. At the same time the guns of Fort George, and all those of the vicinity which could be brought to bear, directed their fire against Fort Niagara, and kept up all day. The fort was fired several times by red-hot shot as were also the works of the enemy. Two Americans were killed and two by the bursting of a cannon, while four were wounded; night ended the fight and it was not renewed.

General Smyth had succeeded in the command of the American forces in Van.Rensselaer's place after the engagement at Queenston. He had given it as his opinion that the invasion should have taken place at some point between Black Rock and Chippewa Creek and was now in position to carry out his own plans. After a number of boastful proclamations, orders were given the army on the 25th to be ready to march at a moment's notice. The line of advance was planned and the whole campaign marked out. Boats sufficient for men and artillery were provided, and Lieutenant-Colonel Boerstler was to cross in the darkness and destroy a bridge about five miles below Fort Erie, capture all men and supplies possible, and return to the American shore. Captain King was to cross higher up the river and storm the batteries. But the enemy was not to be caught napping; Smyth's idle boasts and proclamations, together with his statements as to the proper place for crossing, had put the British on their guard with the result that the whole upper river was well guarded.

The advance parties embarked at three o'clock on the morning of the 29th. Of King's ten boats only four were able to effect a landing. His small command jumped ashore into the very thickest of the fire and almost immediately captured two batteries. Angus and his seamen who had accompanied King rushed upon the Red House, captured the field-pieces stationed there, spiked them, and threw them and the caissons into the river. Angus returned to the river, and, not knowing that the other six boats had been unable to land, supposed King had either returned or been taken prisoner. It being too dark to reconnoitre, he struck away to the American shore in the four boats, leaving King and his handful of men helpless in Canada. King, on the other hand, not receiving re-enforcements, returned to the landing and found all the boats gone, and passing down the river about two miles he discovered two boats in which he placed his prisoners and half his command, and started them for the American shore. Only a few moments later he and all with him were taken prisoners.

The firing had roused the British all along the line. A number of Boerstler's boats were not able to find the point designated as their landing-place, and of those that did all were driven off but Boerstler's own. In

Lieutenant Pierie's Sketch of Niagara, 1768.
From an old print.

Old View of Fort Mississagua.

the face of a hot fire, he landed, forced back the enemy to the bridge, but when he attempted to destroy that structure he found that in the excitement the axes, militia-like, had been left behind, so that his work was only partly accomplished. While thus engaged he received the interesting intelligence that the whole force at Fort Erie were only five minutes distant. In the darkness the enemy could not be seen; but their advancing tramp could be easily heard. Boerstler, addressing his subordinates as field officers, succeeded in deceiving the British as to the size of his command. The Americans fired one volley and then charged with such spirit that the British fell back, and the little command recrossed the river without being further molested.

It was late in the afternoon before all was in readiness for a general advance and the enemy were on the alert ready to give a warm reception. Smyth had not been seen all day. When finally all was prepared orders came to disembark and dine and, as nothing could be done, the soldiers retired to their quarters.

A council was called, but no agreement could be reached. Smyth ordered another advance on the 30th which never took place. Disagreements between officers and insubordination among the soldiers soon led to the abandonment of the plan entirely. General Porter openly attributed the failure to Smyth, which shortly led to a duel in which neither was injured and each one's honour was vindicated.

While these absurd pantomime war measures were transpiring on land the little American navy covered itself with glory. By hard work Lieutenant Oliver H. Perry had gotten ready nine vessels and fifty-five guns at Erie, Pennsylvania, to oppose six vessels and sixty-three guns under the English commander Barclay. After a careful cruise of the Lake, Perry met the enemy in ill condition for a battle near Put-in-Bay on the 10th of September, 1813. The completeness of his victory was described in his famous despatch to Harrison: "We have met the enemy and they are ours; two ships, two brigs, one schooner, and one sloop."

Shortly before the victory on Lake Erie, Gen. W. H. Harrison, who now commanded the North-western army, accompanied by Johnson and his Kentucky rifles, crossed into Canada and during the last week of August and the first week of September was kept busy by the enemy. Proctor did not, however, seem anxious to fight but kept falling back before the Americans, much to the disgust of the famous Shawanese chieftain Tecumseh, who was anxious for a battle. The army at last took position on the Thames River on the 5th of August. Here they were attacked by Harrison's forces, Johnson's Kentuckians leading the successful charge. In a few minutes the British army with its Indian allies was routed and Tecumseh killed. The North-west was relieved of further danger; and much that was lost by Hull was regained with something in addition.

The Army of the North under General Dearborn, during the year of 1813 was to co-operate in the invasion of Canada, and on the 27th of April, 1813, the American army crossed Lake Ontario to York, now Toronto, and were entirely successful in capturing that point, as more fully noted in our chapter on that city.

It was part of Dearborn's plan on capturing York to press on over the thirty miles to the River Niagara and

The Second War with England

take Fort George. On account of unfavourable weather the army did not leave York until the 8th of May, the fleet being under command of Chauncey and being joined in the evening of the 25th by Perry, who had come hastily from Erie. The attack was to be made on the morning of the 27th. Dearborn was himself sick, being confined to his bed most of the time, but his orders were faithfully carried out by his under officers. An attempt to launch several boats on the evening of the 26th brought on a cannonade from the batteries along both shores as well as from Fort George and Fort Niagara. Darkness, however, came on and the preparations were made by the Americans under its cover without further molestation. The morning was somewhat foggy but a light breeze soon dissipated this and revealed a fine sight for friend and foe alike. The waters of the lake were covered with boats large and small, crowded with guns and soldiers, all advancing bravely on the British position.

As soon as the fog lifted the batteries of both sides began a brisk fire. Colonel Scott was in command of the landing party, assisted by Chauncey with four hundred seamen to be used if necessary. Lieutenant Brown directed such a hot fire against the battery at the landing that it was finally silenced and Perry then, being in command of the boats, rushed in despite a somewhat rough sea, to effect a landing, many of the troops in their eagerness leaping into the water before the boats touched land. The landing party was assailed by a heavy, well-directed musketry fire from a neighbouring ravine, which caused them to scurry for shelter under the bank. Perry seemed everywhere present, urging the gunners on the boats to greater efforts and cheering on the landing parties with words of confidence. In attempting to scale the bank, the Americans were several times hurled back to the beach, but Scott was finally successful in gaining a sheltered position in a neighbouring ravine where a sharp conflict ensued for several minutes, but between the execution of the American rifles and a well-directed cannonade from one of the vessels the doughty British were compelled to retreat.

General Vincent, being persuaded that Fort George could not be saved, ordered its destruction, which information reached Scott by two escaped prisoners. He immediately attempted to save it if possible, but a short distance from its walls one magazine blew up, though he reached his destination in time to extinguish two other fuses and save the remainder of the fort. He then continued his pursuit but was ordered to return and had to give up what he thought half the glory of the contest.

Hearing that Colonel Proctor was coming from the West to help regain the Niagara region, General Winder was sent in pursuit of Vincent. On the 5th he was joined by Chandler with five hundred men, who took the chief command. At Forty-mile Creek they encountered a body of the enemy and drove them off; twice now they drove the pickets in on the main body of the army, causing no little alarm, but finally on account of treacherous negligence in the American camp the British effected a night attack so well planned and brilliantly executed that the force was in the heart of the American camp while the soldiers were still sleeping. In the confusion that followed, the Americans several times attacked their own men. The British loss was the heavier, and they were compelled to retire, but the victory was felt to be a decided one from the fact that they captured two American generals.

The Americans, fearing a renewal of the attack, began to retreat. Near Forty-mile Creek they were joined by Colonel Miller with reinforcements, and retreat was continued with a fleet watching them from the lake and a small army of regulars and a body of savages following in the rear. The army finally reached Fort George after having lost several prisoners who had been picked up in the rear. For several days the vessels were a continual menace to the passage of American supplies, but on the 20th the squadron sailed for Oswego. Not daring to make an attack here, they again turned westward and took position off Niagara River.

While the operations were going on against the Niagara frontier, a British squadron appeared against Sacketts Harbour. On the morning of May 29th the attack was made, but so vigilant a defence was made by General Brown with his raw militia that the enemy were forced to withdraw.

General Dearborn, now at Fort George, sent a force to attack the enemy at Beaver Dam and Ten-mile Creek, by way of St. Davids, on June 23d. It was annoyed for a greater part of the way by Indians, and when near the enemy's camp, having been deceived as to the opposing force, the whole command was surrendered. The British, emboldened by this success, suddenly retook Queenston and shortly after invaded Fort George, General Dearborn being relieved of command by the still more incompetent General Wilkinson.

The British, encouraged by their success, now began

to make raids into the American territory. One of these expeditions was directed against Black Rock on July 11th. The expedition put to flight the American guards with almost no fighting, took the city and supplies, and obtained a large amount of booty. General Porter, however, rallied a small body of the retreating militia and with these and reinforcements which had arrived from Buffalo and about fifty citizens he fell with such force upon the invaders that they retreated precipitately to their boats. During the remainder of the summer little fighting was done in the vicinity of Fort George except by foraging parties.

Most of the troops had been withdrawn from the fort in the early winter, leaving only about sixty men within its walls; news was being continually received of forces marching to the Niagara region and, fearful of losing the fort, McClure, its commander, determined to destroy it and retreat to Fort Niagara. The fort was partially demolished, December 10th, but Newark was wantonly fired, leaving hundreds of people homeless in the severest weather and rousing the British to a revenge which they now visited on the Americans.

On the 12th, Fort Niagara was invested. So negligent were the officers that on the morning of the 13th one of the gates was found open, and the enemy entered without opposition to a victory which might have been almost bloodless had not the attacking force, incensed by the burning of Newark, been led to revenge; a number of the garrison were bayoneted; Lewiston was sacked, plundered, and almost entirely destroyed. A body of soldiers pressed on to the town of Niagara Falls. They were met on the heights by a small force which was not able to check them and the whole Niagara

The Second War with England

region was laid waste. The Indians were turned loose and many innocent persons perished at their hands. The advance on Buffalo and Black Rock was only temporarily checked and on the 30th these cities were captured and plundered as elsewhere described. Only four houses were left in Buffalo and one in Black Rock. Such was the revenge of the burning of Newark. These were dark days along the Niagara, when hatred never bred in honest warfare flamed up in the hearts of men, and the beginning of the story goes back to the inhuman destruction of old Newark.

Toward the latter part of March the campaign of 1814 was opened by General Wilkinson in the north, but little being accomplished he was soon superseded by General Brown. By the end of June the Northern army was gathered under Brown, once more prepared to carry the war into Canada, Buffalo being the headquarters. On the morning of the 3d of July, before daylight, General Scott crossed the river from Black Rock to invest Fort Erie. General Ripley was to have followed immediately, but he was delayed so long that it was broad day before he reached the Canadian shore. Scott pushed forward and drove the enemy's pickets into the fort. Brown, not waiting for Ripley, pushed into the forest in the rear of the fort, extending his lines so as to enclose the post. Ripley then appeared and took position in connection with Scott's command. The fort was then summoned to surrender, which summons, on account of its weak condition, was soon complied with just as reinforcements were on their way to give aid.

To stop the advance of these troops, Scott was sent with his command down the river. His march of about sixteen miles was a continual skirmish with the British, and finding the enemy in force across the Chippewa Creek he encamped for the night. Before morning of the fifth he was joined by the main body of Brown's army. On the east was the river, on the west a heavy wood, and between the armies the Chippewa and Street's creeks. The British had also received reinforcements during the night, and the battle of Chippewa was opened by each army attempting to test the other's strength.

The American pickets on Scott's left were in trouble by four o'clock and Porter was sent to relieve them; he drove back the British and Indians, but in following up his success found himself suddenly confronted by almost the whole of the enemy's army which attacked immediately. Porter maintained his ground at first but was finally compelled to give the order to retreat and this soon became a panic. General Brown noticed this and correctly supposed that the whole force of the enemy was advancing. Ripley and Scott were immediately rushed to the rescue, Ripley to fall on the rear of the British right by stealing through the wood, Scott to make a frontal attack.

The latter advanced across Street's Creek and the engagement became general along the whole line of both armies. Time and again the British line was broken but it sternly closed and continued the contest. Scott finally decided to take advantage of what he considered the unskilful manœuvres of his foe; advancing, he ordered his forces to charge through an opening in the lines. Almost at the same instant Leavenworth executed a like movement, while Towson's battery poured canister into the British ranks. They were

The Second War with England

completely demoralised and gave back. Jesup on the American left had suffered greatly during the battle; forced to fall back, he finally found a better position, and now poured such a well-directed fire that the troops before him also retired. The British retreat did not stop until the troops were behind their entrenchments below Chippewa and the bridge across its waters destroyed. This stronghold could not be taken by the Americans; the command was given to retreat, and the same relative positions were occupied by the armies the night after the battle as the night before.

On the eighth the whole American force again moved forward. The British broke camp and retreated down the river closely pursued by Brown, who took possession of Queenston on the 10th. The enemy occupied Fort George and Fort Mississaga. Here Brown decided to await reinforcements from Chauncey and his fleet. News, however, soon came of the commander's illness and his blockade in Sacketts Harbour, whereupon Brown on the 23d fell back to the Chippewa. In case Riall did not follow, he expected to unlimber and fight wherever the enemy might be found; the night of the 24th, the army encamped on the battle-ground of the 5th, unconscious of the laurels to be won in a few short hours at far-famed Lundy's Lane.

The morning of the 25th dawned clear and beautiful. Unconscious of the proximity of the enemy, the Americans were enjoying a much-needed rest behind the village of Chippewa, when about noon news came that the British were in force at Queenston and on the heights, and that Yea's fleet had appeared in the river. Next came information that the British were landing at Lewiston and were threatening the supplies at Fort

Schlosser. These reports were partly true. Pearson had advanced, unknown to the Americans, and taken position at Lundy's Lane a short distance from the Falls. Brown seemed impressed with the idea that the British were after the supplies at Schlosser and he was ignorant of the size of the force opposed to him. He at once determined that the best way to recall the British was to threaten the forts at the mouth of the river and Scott was detailed to accomplish this task. Eager for the conflict his whole command was in motion twenty minutes after having received the order. Between four and five o'clock the march of twelve hundred men began toward the forts.

Near Table Rock, Scott was informed that General Riall and his staff had just departed. In fact the Americans saw the troops move off from the house as they were advancing toward it, and the informant also stated that the enemy were in force behind a small strip of woods in front; but so convinced was the American leader that Fort Schlosser was the objective point of the British movement that he would not credit the story. Believing that but a small force was in front, he dashed into the woods to dispel them. Imagine his surprise when he found himself faced at Lundy's Lane by Riall's whole force! Scott's position was indeed perilous. To advance seemed destruction, to stand still would be equally fatal, while to retreat would probably throw the whole army into confusion. With that resource which always distinguished him, he quickly decided to engage the enemy, and if possible deceive them into believing that the whole American army was present while he sent back for reinforcements.

General Brown had been misinformed as to the

enemy's movements. No soldiers had crossed to Lewiston, but the whole force was with Riall preparing for the present move. Scott found himself opposed to fully eighteen hundred men. The English lines extended over the hill in a crescent form with the horns extending forward. In its centre and on the brow of the hill, the strongest point of the position, was placed a battery of seven guns. Into the very centre of this crescent he had unconsciously led his army.

Scott immediately perceived on the enemy's left flank an unprotected space of brushwood along the river and instantly he ordered Major Jesup to seize this and turn the flank if possible. While this move was being accomplished Scott's troops engaged the enemy in front, only hoping to hold the army in check until the reserves arrived.

Jesup was more than successful. He turned the left flank of the enemy, gained his rear, and kept the reinforcements sent to Riall's aid from joining the body of the army. Besides this he had captured Riall himself with a number of his staff. By nine o'clock at night Jesup had accomplished this and in the meantime Scott had beaten back a fierce charge made by the British right; only the centre stood firm now.

Informed of the true state of affairs, and leaving orders for Ripley to make all haste possible with the whole reserve force, Brown mounted his horse and rode to the field, arriving just at this critical juncture. He immediately saw that the hill crowned with cannon was the key to the enemy's position; Ripley was advancing along the Queenston road; Scott's worn men had been recalled. The commander turned to Colonel Miller, saying, "Colonel, take your regiment, storm that work, and take it." "I'll try, Sir," said Miller, and at once moved forward. At this moment the regiment under Lieutenant-Colonel Nicholas, which was to draw the enemy's fire from Miller, gave way. Nothing daunted, the young commander, with three hundred followers, crept up the hill in the shadow of an old rail fence thickly grown over with shrubbery. In this way they reached unobserved a point only several rods distant from the enemy, whom they saw around the guns waiting the order to fire. Resting their pieces across the old fence the little command took deliberate aim, the order was given by Miller in a whisper, a sheet of flame broke from the shrubbery, and not a man was left to apply a match to the British artillery. The men then broke from cover with a shout and rushed forward, and all seven of the cannon were captured. A fierce hand-to-hand contest was waged for a short time with the body of infantry stationed behind the guns, but they were finally forced from the hill. Four different attempts were made to recapture the position but all were unsuccessful.

While these events were taking place Scott was maintaining his position with great difficulty. His regiments were being literally cut to pieces and, finally, he gathered the remnants into one mass, formed in line for storming, and had given the order to move forward when the battery was taken by Miller. Scott countermanded his order and returned to his position at the base of the hill.

Brown and Scott were both severely wounded and the command devolved now on Ripley. When the battle was finally won Brown ordered Ripley to fall back to the Chippewa to give the soldiers a much-

Monument at Lundy's Lane.

Lieutenant-General Simcoe.

needed rest during the night, but to be back at Lundy's Lane by daybreak the next morning to obtain the fruits of the victory. Day came and Ripley had not moved from his quarters, but the British had returned and the two armies occupied almost the same ground as before the battle. Ripley advanced but the enemy's position was too strong to attack, so he discreetly returned to camp. Brown was so disgusted that he sent to Sacketts Harbour for General Gaines to come and assume command.

Generals Brown and Scott's troops were moved from the field supposing that Ripley would at least hold his position. Hardly had they gotten out of sight when Ripley ordered a retreat to Black Rock. Here he was forbidden by Brown to cross the river, so he took up a position above Fort Erie; at the same time the fortifications were strengthened in order to repel the expected siege.

The work on Fort Erie went forward unmolested until the 3d of August. Drummond then appeared before the fort with his army, which had been resting at Lundy's Lane since the battle of the 20th of July. Lieutenant-Colonel Tucker was sent across the river with a body of troops to capture Black Rock and Buffalo. These were met so gallantly by Morgan and his riflemen that they were compelled to return. Drummond at the same time opened fire on the fort; this was discontinued until the seventh, the respite being spent by both parties in preparing for the siege. Gaines arrived on the 5th and assumed command while Ripley returned to the head of his own brigade. On the 6th Morgan and his riflemen attempted to draw the enemy from his trenches but were unsuccessful; the cannonade was opened on the fort on the morning of the 7th and was continued until the 13th. On the next day all the guns possible were brought to bear on the fort, causing its commander to believe that an assault was planned and arrangements were made to receive the enemy. The guns were heavily shotted, vigilance of the guards doubled, and things made ready for the warm reception of the enemy. At midnight of the 14th, all was still quiet; a body of a hundred men under Belknap had been thrown out toward the British army to do picket duty as the night was so dark that the movements of the enemy could not be seen. Their stealthy advance, though cautious, was detected by the sharp ears of the waiting men; an alarm gun was fired and the advance party fell back toward the fort. Fifteen hundred men came charging against Towson's battery on the left, expecting to find the soldiers asleep, but a broad sheet of flame burst from the long twenty-four pounders here which made the line waver in its advance. At the same moment the line of the 21st shone forth in its own light, then all was darkness except as the guns were loaded and fired. Five times the attack was renewed by the two columns; each time they were beaten back.

Almost simultaneous with the attack on the left, another was made on the American right, against the old fort; this was repelled, but Drummond, valiant man, could not be held in check, and under cover of a heavy cloud of smoke, followed by a hundred of the Royal Artillery, he crept silently around the fort and by means of scaling ladders gained the parapet almost unobserved. All attempts to dislodge the enemy failed. Time and again they were charged, but each time they beat back their assailants. Lieu-

The Second War with England

tenant-Colonel Drummond commanded his men to give no quarter, and in a short time he fell, pierced through the heart by a man to whom he refused mercy. Daylight dawned with the enemy repulsed on the left. Reinforcements were brought to the right but there was no room to use them. The Americans were finally gathered for a furious charge, when that part of the fort which the British had seized was blown suddenly a hundred feet into the air and fell in ruins. At the same instant a galling fire was opened from the batteries and the enemy was compelled to retire.

Both armies now received reinforcements and kept preparing for a second engagement. A continual cannonade was kept up, when on the 28th of August General Gaines was so injured by a shell that he had to retire from action. General Brown, though shattered in health then resumed command. The British were continually strengthening their works and he saw that his only hopes lay in a sortie. The weather had been rainy which inconvenienced the enemy as their works were located on the low ground. Their numbers had also been greatly reduced by fever. These facts were learned from prisoners which had been captured. The sortie was planned for the 17th of September, all the officers acquiescing except General Ripley. The plan was laid with great secrecy and was favoured by heavy fog on the morning of the proposed action. The Americans were entirely successful, the enemy being driven from their works and almost all their supplies captured. This victory was hailed with delight by the whole country. This, with the brilliant achievement at Plattsburg, and the repulse of the British from Baltimore caused rejoicing all over the nation, and restored the people from that gloom into which they had been cast by the fall of the national capital.

On the 5th day of October General Izard arrived with reinforcements and took command. With almost eight thousand troops he now prepared to attack Drummond, but all attempts to draw him out of his trenches failed.

Learning that there was a large store of grain at the mill on Lyons Creek, Bissell was sent to destroy it. On the night of the 18th, he was attacked but was successful in driving off the enemy and accomplishing his task. Drummond, now perceiving that he could not hope to cope successfully with the superior forces brought against him, fell back to Fort George and Burlington Heights. General Izard soon removed his whole force from Canada. On the 5th of November Fort Erie was blown up, to keep it from falling again into the hands of the British.

On September 11th, the brilliant victory, mentioned before, was gained by the Americans at Plattsburg and with the opening of winter, the militia was disbanded and the war closed on the Canadian frontier.

In 1837 the Niagara was again the scene of military operations on a slight scale when the Patriot War broke out, an uprising of revolutionists who planned the overturning of the Canadian Government. Navy Island was for a time the headquarters of the ferment, and from here, under the date of December 17th, the leader, William Lyon Mackenzie, issued a proclamation to the citizens of Canada. This strong, misguided man is most perfectly described in Bourinot's *The Story of Canada:*

He had a deep sense of public wrongs, and placed himself

immediately in the front rank of those who were fighting for a redress of undoubted grievances. He was thoroughly imbued with the ideas of English radicalism, and had an intense hatred of Toryism in every form. He possessed little of that strong common-sense and power of acquisitiveness which make his countrymen, as a rule, so successful in every walk of life. When he felt he was being crushed by the intriguing and corrupting influences of the governing class, aided by the lieutenant-governor, he forgot all the dictates of reason and prudence, and was carried away by a current of passion which ended in rebellion. His journal, *The Colonial Advocate*, showed in its articles and its very make-up the erratic character of the man. He was a pungent writer, who attacked adversaries with great recklessness of epithet and accusation. So obnoxious did he become to the governing class that a number of young men, connected with the best families, wrecked his office, but the damages he recovered in a court of law enabled him to give it a new lease of existence. When the "family compact" had a majority in the assembly, elected in 1830, he was expelled five times for libellous reflections on the government and house, but he was re-elected by the people, who resented the wrongs to which he was subject, and became the first mayor of Toronto, as York was now called. He carried his grievances to England, where he received much sympathy, even in conservative circles. In a new legislature, where the "compact" were in a minority, he obtained a committee to consider the condition of provincial affairs. The result was a famous report on grievances which set forth in a conclusive and able manner the constitutional difficulties under which the country laboured, and laid down clearly the necessity for responsible government. It would have been fortunate both for Upper Canada and Mackenzie himself at this juncture, had he and his followers confined themselves to a constitutional agitation on the lines set forth in this report. By this time Robert Baldwin and Egerton Ryerson, discreet and prominent reformers, had much influence, and were quite unwilling to follow Mackenzie in the extreme course on which he had clearly entered. He lost ground rapidly from the time of his indiscreet publication of a letter from Joseph Hume, the English radical, who had expressed the opinion that the improper proceedings of the legislature, especially in expelling Mackenzie, "must hasten the crisis that was fast approaching in the affairs of Canada, and which would terminate in independence and freedom from the baneful domination of the mother-country." Probably even Mackenzie and his friends might have been conciliated and satisfied at the last moment had the imperial government been served by an able and discreet lieutenant-governor. But never did the imperial authorities make a greater mistake than when they sent out Sir Francis Bond Head, who had no political experience whatever.

From the beginning to the end of his administration he did nothing but blunder. He alienated even the confidence of the moderate element of the Reformers, and literally threw himself into the arms of the "family compact," and assisted them at the elections of the spring of 1836, which rejected all the leading men of the extreme wing of the Reform party. Mackenzie was deeply mortified at the result, and determined from that moment to rebel against the government, which, in his opinion, had no intention of remedying public grievances. At the same time Papineau, with whom he was in communication, had made up his mind to establish a republic, *une nation Canadienne*, on the banks of the St. Lawrence.

The disloyal intentions of Papineau and his followers were made very clear by the various meetings which were held in the Montreal and Richelieu districts, by the riots which followed public assemblages in the city of Montreal, by the names of "Sons of Liberty" and "Patriots" they adopted in all their proceedings, by the planting of "trees" and raising of "caps" of liberty. Happily for the best interests of Canada the number of French Canadians ready to revolt were relatively insignificant, and the British population were almost exclusively on the side of the government. Bishop Lartigue and the clergy of the Roman Catholic Church now asserted themselves very determinedly against the dangerous and seditious utterances of the leaders of the "Patriots." Fortunately a resolute, able soldier, Sir John Colborne, was called from Upper Canada to command the troops in the critical situation of affairs, and crushed the rebellion in its very inception. A body of insurgents, led by Dr. Wolfred Nelson, showed some courage at St. Denis, but Papineau took the earliest opportunity to find refuge across the frontier. Thomas Storrow Brown, an American by birth, also made a stand at St. Charles, but both he and Nelson were easily beaten by the regulars. A most unfortunate episode was the murder of Lieutenant Wier, who had been captured by Nelson while carrying despatches from General Colborne, and was butchered by some insurgent *habitants*, in whose custody he had been placed. At St. Eustache the rebels were severely punished by Colborne himself, and a number burned to death in the steeple of a church where they had made a stand. Many prisoners were taken in the course of the rebellious outbreak. The village of St. Benoit and isolated houses elsewhere were destroyed by the angry loyalists, and much misery inflicted on all actual or supposed sympathisers with Papineau and Nelson. Lord Gosford now left the country, and Colborne was appointed administrator. Although the insurrection practically ended at St. Denis and St. Charles, bodies of rebels and American marauders harassed the frontier settlements for some time, until at last the authorities of the United States arrested some of the leaders and forced them to surrender their arms and munitions of war.

The *Caroline* incident most closely connects the immediate Niagara region with the Patriot rebellion. This small steamer was chartered by Buffalo parties to run between that city, Navy Island, and Schlosser, the American landing above the Falls. The Canadian authorities very properly looked upon this as a bold attempt to provide the freebooters on Navy Island with the sinews of rebellion. Colonel Allan McNab was sent to seize the vessel, and the fact that it was found moored at the American shore in no way troubled the determined loyalists. It was about midnight December 29th when the attacking party found the ship. In the melée one man was killed; the boat was fired and set adrift in the river, passing over the Horseshoe Fall while still partly afire.

Chapter XII

Toronto

IT is believed that the word Toronto is of Huron origin, and that it signified "Place of Meeting." This has been contested; in any case it should be spelled *To-ron-tah*. The word is also interpreted as "Oak Trees beside the Lake," a derivation rather divergent from the above version and we must leave this to the learned etymologists.

Glancing over maps of the middle of the eighteenth century designed after the Treaty of Aix-la-Chapelle (1748), we see the names of many forts and posts intended to keep up "the communications" between Canada and Louisiana, and overawe the English colonies then confined to their narrow strip of territory on the Atlantic coast. Conscious of the mistake that they had made in giving up Acadia, the French at this moment claimed that its "ancient limits" did not extend beyond the isthmus of Chignecto—in other words, included Nova Scotia. Accordingly they proceeded to construct the forts of Gaspereau and Beauséjour on that neck of land, and also one on the St. John River, so that they might control the land and sea approaches to Cape Breton from the St. Lawrence, where Quebec, enthroned on her picturesque heights, and Montreal at the confluence of the Ottawa and the St.

Lawrence, held the keys to Canada. The approaches from New England by the way of Lake Champlain and the Richelieu were defended by the fort of St. John, near the northern extremity of the lake, and by the more formidable works known as Fort Frederick or Crown Point—to give the better known English name—on a peninsula at the narrows towards the South. The latter was the most advanced post of the French until they built Fort Ticonderoga or Carillon on a high, rocky promontory at the head of Lake St. Sacrament. At the foot of this lake, associated with so many memorable episodes in American history, Sir William Johnson erected Fort William Henry, about fourteen miles from Fort Edward or Layman, at the great carrying place on the upper waters of the Hudson. Returning to the St. Lawrence and the Lakes, we find Fort Frontenac at the eastern end of Lake Ontario, where the old city of Kingston now stands.

Within the limits of the present city of Toronto, La Gallissonière then built Fort Rouille[1] as an attempt to control the trade of the Indians of the North, who were finding their way to the English fort of Oswego which had been commenced with the consent of the Iroquois by Governor Burnet of New York, and was now a menace to the French dominion of Lake Ontario. At the other extremity lay Fort Niagara. When the French were establishing this chain of forts or posts through the West and down the Mississippi valley Fort Rouille was founded on a site even then commonly

---

[1] Named in honour of a French Minister of Colonies. The *Rouillés* are a celebrated family, later on styled Rouille-de-Marbœuf. The above-named Rouille is highly praised by St. Simon as a statesman of ability and integrity.

called "Fort Toronto." It does not seem ever to have been a dominant strategic point; the probabilities are there was no force stationed here worth mentioning and, possibly, it was a mere dependency of Fort Niagara. It was destroyed in 1756 to prevent its fall into the hands of the English.

Little is known about the region of Toronto prior to Revolutionary times save the above records. It was untrodden wilderness. But when the fort was erected here the district in a general sense appears to have been known as "Toronto." Under French dominion it was a royal trading post and in the course of time the name attached itself to the fort and village at the neighbouring bay, which have grown to be the beautiful Capital City of Ontario. But the Toronto of the river Don and the great bay is strictly of English origin, and had for its Romulus Lieutenant-General Simcoe (1752–1806), first governor of Upper Canada.

When John Graves Simcoe arrived in Canada in 1792, the site of the present city of Toronto was covered by the primeval forest, its only human tenants being two or three families of wandering savages who had happened to select the spot for the erection of their temporary wigwams. One hundred years later we find at that very spot a magnificent city having a population of 250,000 people, a prosperous and enterprising community, possessed of all the comforts and appliances of modern civilisation and refinement,—and, instead of the sombre, impenetrable wilderness, the most wealthy and populous city of Upper Canada, with streets and private dwellings, and public edifices that will compare favourably with those of many other cities which have had centuries for their development.

For its rapid rise to its present eminence Toronto is almost exclusively indebted to its admirable commercial position, its advantages in that respect having been appreciated by the far-seeing sagacity of Governor Simcoe, when selecting the site for a capital.

In 1791, when the former province of Quebec was divided into the provinces of Upper and Lower Canada, Upper Canada contained about ten thousand inhabitants, chiefly Loyalists, who, as noted elsewhere, when the United States threw off allegiance to Great Britain, sought new hope in the wilds of Canada; where, though deprived of many comforts, they had the satisfaction of feeling that they kept inviolate their loyalty to their sovereign and preserved their connection with the beloved mother country.

In 1792 General Simcoe was appointed Lieutenant-Governor of Upper Canada; and in the summer of that year arrived in the colony. In the first instance the Government was established at Niagara, and there the first Legislature of Upper Canada was convened on the 17th of September, 1792. It was seen, however, that from its position on the frontier, Niagara was not well adapted for being the seat of government, and one of the first subjects which occupied the attention of Governor Simcoe was the selection of another site for a capital. On this point he very soon came into collision with the views of the Governor-General, Lord Dorchester, who was in favour of making Kingston the capital on account of its proximity to Lower Canada which he regarded as a matter of the first importance from a standpoint of trade, and also because of its possibility of defence, as, in the event of an invasion, troops from Lower Canada could be more easily forwarded to Kingston than to a more westerly point. Governor Simcoe, however, had visited Toronto Harbour, and had traversed the route thence to Penetanguishene on the Georgian Bay. He perceived that that was the most advantageous route for the then existing Northwest trade,—the vast development of which since his time he may have dimly foreseen—and that so soon as a road was opened up to Lake Simcoe (then *Lacaux Claies*) merchandise from New York for the North-west, would be sent by Oswego to Toronto, and then *via* Lake Simcoe to Lake Huron, avoiding the circuitous passage of Lake Erie. Finally the Lieutenant-Governor's views prevailed, and the site of a town having been surveyed on the margin of Toronto Bay, his first step thereafter was to commence the construction of a road (Yonge Street) to Lake Simcoe. In recent years the idea which thus originated with the first governor has been completely carried out until to-day Toronto is, with Montreal, the chief railway centre and the second city of the Dominion. How long ere it will outrank its rival?

The very next year after his assumption of the government of Upper Canada General Simcoe ordered the survey of Toronto Harbour, and entrusted the task to Colonel Bouchette, the Surveyor-General of Lower Canada, who gives us our first historical glimpse of Toronto a hundred years ago, or so, in the following passage:

It fell to my lot to make the first survey of York Harbour in 1793. Lieutenant-Governor, the late General Simcoe, who then resided at Navy Hall, Niagara, having formed extensive plans for the improvement of the colony, had resolved upon laying the foundation of a Provincial capital. I was at that period in the

"York Harbor."
A drawing on bark by Mrs. Simcoe.

"The Garrison at York."
A drawing on bark by Mrs. Simcoe.

naval service of the lakes, and the survey of Toronto (York Harbour), was entrusted by His Excellency to my performance. I still distinctly recollect the untamed aspect which the country exhibited when first I entered the beautiful basin which thus became the scene of my early hydrographical operations. Dense and trackless forests lined the margin of the lake, and reflected their inverted images in its glassy surface. The wandering savage had constructed his ephemeral habitation beneath their luxuriant foliage—the group then consisting of two families of Missassagas—and the Bay and neighbouring marshes were the hitherto uninvaded haunts of the wild fowl; indeed they were so abundant as in some measure to annoy us during the night. In the spring following, the Lieutenant-Governor removed to the site of the new capital, attended by the regiment of Queen's Rangers and commenced at once the realisation of his favourite project. His Excellency inhabited, during the summer and through the winter, a canvas house which he imported expressly for the occasion, but, frail as was its substance, it was rendered exceedingly comfortable, and soon became as distinguished for the social and urbane hospitality of its venerated and gracious host, as for the peculiarity of its structure.

Governor Simcoe gave the name of York to the capital he had selected, and the rivers on either side received the names of the Don and Humber. His own residence he built at the brow of the hill overlooking the valley of the Don, at the junction of what was a few generations later Saint James Cemetery with the property of F. Cayley, Esq., calling it "Castle Frank," the name which the property still retains.

While the gubernatorial residence was being erected Governor Simcoe returned to Niagara, where he opened the third session of the Upper Canada Parliament on June 20, 1794. In the fall of that year, orders were given for the construction of Parliament buildings at York on a site at the foot of what in 1857 was Parliament Street, adjoining the place where the "gaol stands." In 1795 the Duc de Rochefoucauld was in Upper Canada, and in his published *Travels* alludes to a visit paid to York by some of his companions:

During our stay at Navy Hall, Messrs. Du Petit Thouars and Guillemard, took the opportunity of the return of a gun-boat, to pay a visit to York. Indolence, courtesy towards the Governor (with whom the author was then residing at Navy Hall), and the conviction that I would meet with few objects of interest in that place, combined to dissuade me from this journey. My friends informed me on their return, that this town, which the Governor had fixed upon as the Capital of Upper Canada, has a fine, extensive bay, detached from the lake by a tongue of land of unequal breadth, being in some places a mile, in others only six score yards broad; that the entrance of this bay, about a mile in width, is obstructed in the middle by a shoal or sand-bank, the narrow passages on each side of which may be easily defended by works erected on the two points of land at the entrance, on which two block-houses have already been constructed; that this bay is two miles and a half long, and a mile wide, and that the elevation of its banks greatly increases its capability of defence by fortifications thrown up at convenient points. There have not been more than a dozen houses built hitherto in York, and these are situated in the inner extremity of the bay, near the river Don. The inhabitants, it is said, do not possess the fairest character. One of them is the noted Batzy, the leader of the German families, whom Captain Williamson accuses the English of decoying away from him, in order to injure and obstruct the prosperity of his settlement. The barracks which are occupied by the Governor's Regiment, stand on the bay near the lake, about two miles from the town. The Indians are for one hundred and fifty miles round the sole neighbours of York.

Nothing shows better than this that we must remember that Old World measurements of growth and cultural life cannot be applied to the condition of a new continent where every foot of land had to be taken from the aborigines, a continent in its agricultural infancy, devastated by wars, changing ownership thrice within one hundred years. The Indians in the district one hundred and fifty miles around Toronto have been replaced to-day by a million of people as enterprising as they can be found on the surface of the globe. In lieu of the dozen huts described by our noble writer in 1795, you will find to-day a city of a quarter million inhabitants, steamships, railroads, telegraph, electric light—the "City of Churches."

Toronto, as noted, owes the progress it has made almost entirely to its advantageous commercial position, which was the chief circumstance that originally weighed with General Simcoe in selecting this as a site for the capital of Upper Canada. The city is built on a slope, rising with a very slight inclination from the bay, sufficient to secure its salubrity, and to admit of a complete system of sewerage; but not enough to give its architectural beauties the advantage they deserve to gratify the æsthetic taste which would be disposed to seek on the shores of Lake Ontario for a parallel to the grand old cities of Europe.

Governor Simcoe's amenities and hospitalities, his simplicity, his cares and troubles are all parts of the early history of the province; his administration in Canada has been generally commended, despite the displays of prejudice against the United States. His schemes for improving the province were "extremely wise and well arranged." But his stay was abruptly cut short. It seems to-day that England was fearful he might involve the mother-country in a new war with the young Republic and he was rather hastily recalled to England in 1796, although at the same time promoted a full lieutenant-general in the army.

In 1804 a census of the inhabitants of Toronto was taken, and it was found that they numbered 456. At that time the town was bounded by Berkeley Street on the east, Lot, now Queen Street on the north, and New, now Nelson Street on the west. In 1806, Toronto or York was visited by George Heriot, Esq., Deputy Postmaster-General of British North America, and from the terms in which he speaks of it in his *Travels through the Canadas*, it appears that it had then made considerable progress. He says:

> Many houses display a considerable progress. The advancement of this place to its present condition has been effected within the lapse of six or seven years, and persons who have formerly travelled in this part of the country, are impressed with sentiments of wonder, on beholding a town which may be termed handsome, reared as if by enchantment in the midst of a wilderness.

The Parliament buildings, when Heriot visited Toronto, were two buildings of brick, at the eastern extremity of the town, which had been designed as wings to a centre, and which were occupied as chambers for the Upper and Lower House of Assembly.

In 1807 the inhabitants numbered 1058, and continued slowly to rise till 1813, when the American War brought calamities on to Toronto, from the disastrous effects of which it took more than a decade to recover.

In 1813 the campaigns of the war centred, as we have seen, around Lake Erie. The Navy had lately restored American confidence, and a second invasion of Canada was a principal feature in the programme. At the middle of April Dearborn and Chauncey matured a plan of operations. A joint land and naval expedition was proposed, to first capture York, and then to cross Lake Ontario and reduce Fort George. At the same time troops were to cross the Niagara, from Buffalo and Black Rock, capture Fort Erie and Chippewa, join the fleet and army at Fort George, and all proceed to attack Kingston. Everything being arranged, Dearborn embarked about 1700 men on Chauncey's fleet, at Sacketts Harbour on the 22d of April, and on the 25th the fleet, crowded with soldiers, sailed for York. After a boisterous voyage it appeared before the little town early in the morning of the 27th, when General Dearborn, suffering from ill health, placed the land forces under charge of General Pike, and resolved to remain on board the Commodore's flagship during the attack.

The little village of York, numbering somewhat more than one thousand inhabitants at the time, was then chiefly at the bottom of the bay near a marshy flat, through which the Don, coming down from the beautiful fertile valleys, flowed sluggishly into Lake Ontario, and, because of the softness of the earth there, it was often called "Muddy Little York." It gradually grew to the westward, and, while deserting the Don, it wooed the Humber, once a famous salmon stream, that flows into a broad bay two or three miles west of Toronto. In that direction stood the remains of old Fort Toronto, erected by the French. On the shore eastward of it, between the present new barracks and the city, were two batteries, the most easterly one being in the form of a crescent. A little farther east, on the borders of a deep ravine and small stream, was a picketed blockhouse, some intrenchments with cannon, and a garrison of about eight hundred men under Major-General Sheaffe. On "Gibraltar Point," the extreme western arm of the peninsula, that embraced the harbour with its protecting arm, was a small blockhouse; another stood on the high east bank of the Don, just beyond a bridge at the eastern termination of King and Queen streets. These defences had been strangely neglected. Some of the cannon were without trunnions, others, destined for the war-vessel then on the stocks, were in frozen mud and half covered with snow. Fortunately for the garrison, the *Duke of Gloucester* was then in port, undergoing some repairs, and her guns furnished some armament for the batteries. These, however, only amounted to a few six-pounders. The whole country around, excepting a few spots on the lake shore, was covered with a dense forest.

On the day when the expedition sailed from Sacketts Harbour General Pike issued minute instructions concerning the manner of landing and attack.

> It is expected [he said] that every corps will be mindful of the honour of the American, and the disgraces which have recently tarnished our arms, and endeavour, by a cool and determined discharge of their duty, to support the one and wipe off the other. [He continued:] The unoffending citizens of Canada are many of them our own countrymen, and the poor Canadians have been forced into the war. Their property, therefore, must be held sacred; and any soldier who shall so far neglect the honour of his profession as to be guilty of plundering the inhabitants, shall, if convicted, be punished with death. But the commanding general assures the troops that, should they capture a large quantity of public stores, he will use his best endeavours to procure them a reward from his government.

It was intended to land at a clearing near old Fort Toronto. An easterly wind, blowing with violence, drove the small boats in which the troops left the fleet full half a mile farther westward, and beyond an effectual covering by the guns of the navy. Major Forsyth and his riflemen, in two bateaux led the van, and when within rifle shot of the shore they were assailed by a deadly volley of bullets by a company of Glengary Fencibles and a party of Indians under Major Givens, who were concealed in the woods that fringe the shore. "Rest on your oars! Prime!" said Forsyth in a low tone. Pike, standing on the deck of the *Madison*, saw this halting, and impatiently exclaimed, with an expletive: "I cannot stay here any longer! Come," he said, addressing his staff, "jump into the boat." He was instantly obeyed, and very soon they and their gallant commander were in the midst of a fight, for Forsyth's men had opened fire, and the enemy at the shore were returning it briskly. The vanguard soon landed, and were immediately followed, in support, by Major King and a battalion of infantry. Pike and the main body soon followed, and the whole column, consisting of the Sixth, Fifteenth, Sixteenth, and Twenty-First Regiments of Infantry, and detachments of light and heavy artillery, with Major Forsyth's riflemen and Lieutenant McClure's volunteers as flankers, pressed forward into the woods.

The British skirmishes meanwhile had been reenforced by two companies of the Eighth or King's Regiment of Regulars, two hundred strong, a company of the Royal Newfoundland Regiment, a large body of militia, and some Indians. They took position in the woods, and were soon encountered by the advancing Americans, whose artillery it was difficult to move. Perceiving this, the British, led by General Sheaffe in person, attacked the American flank with a six-pounder and howitzer. A very sharp conflict ensued, and both parties suffered much. Captain McNeil, of the King's Regiment, was killed. The British were overpowered, and fell back, when General Pike, at the head of the American column, ordered his bugler to sound, and at the same time dashed gallantly forward. That bugle blast thrilled like electric fire along the nerves of the Indians. They gave one horrid yell, then fled like frightened deer to cover, deep into the forest. That bugle blast was heard in the fleet, in the face of the wind and high above the voices of the gale, and evoked long and loud responsive cheers. At the same time Chauncey was sending to the shore, under the direction of Commander Elliott, something more effective than huzzas for he was hurling deadly grape-shot upon the foe, which added to the consternation of the savages, and gave fleetness to their feet. They also hastened the retreat of Sheaffe's white troops to their defences in the direction of the village, while the drum and fife of the pursuers were briskly playing *Yankee Doodle*.

The Americans now pressed forward rapidly along the lake shore in platoons by sections. They were not allowed to load their muskets, and were compelled to rely upon the bayonet. Because of many ravines and little streams the artillery was moved with difficulty, for the enemy had destroyed the bridges. By great exertions a field-piece and a howitzer, under Lieutenant Fanning, of the Third Artillery, was moved steadily with the column. As that column emerged from thick woods, flanked by McClure's volunteers, divided equally as light troops under Colonel Ripley, it was confronted by twenty-four pounders on the Western Battery. Upon this battery the guns of some of Chauncey's vessels which had beat up against the wind in range of the enemy's works were pouring heavy shot. Captain Walworth was ordered to storm it with his grenadiers, of the Sixteenth. They immediately trailed their arms, quickened their pace, and were about to charge, when the wooden magazine of the battery, that had been carelessly left open, blew up, killing some of the men, and seriously damaging the defences. The dismayed enemy spiked their cannon, and fled to the next, or Half-Moon, Battery. Walworth pressed forward; when that, too, was abandoned and he found nothing within but spiked cannon. Sheaffe and his little army, deserted by the Indians, fled to the garrison near the Governor's house, and there opened a fire of round and grape-shot upon the Americans. Pike ordered his troops to halt, and lie flat upon the grass, while Major Eustis, with his artillery-battery moved to the front, and soon silenced the great guns of the enemy.

The firing from the garrison ceased, and the Americans expected every moment to see a white flag displayed from the blockhouse in token of surrender. Lieutenant Riddle, whose corps had brought up the prisoners taken in the woods, was sent forward with a small party to reconnoitre. General Pike, who had just assisted with his own hands in removing a wounded soldier to a comfortable place, was sitting upon a stump conversing with a huge British sergeant who had been taken prisoner, his staff standing around him. At that moment was felt a sudden tremor of the ground, followed by a tremendous explosion near the British garrison. The enemy, despairing of holding the place, had blown up their powder magazine, situated upon the edge of the water at the mouth of a ravine, near where the buildings of the Great Western Railway now stand. The effect was terrible. Fragments of timber and huge stone of which the magazine walls were built were scattered in every direction over a space of several hundred yards. When the smoke floated away the scene was appalling. Fifty-two Americans lay dead, and one hundred and eighty others were wounded. So badly had the affair been managed that forty of the British also lost their lives by the explosion. General Pike, two of his aids, and the British sergeant were mortally hurt, while Riddle and his party were unhurt, the missiles passing entirely over them. The terrified Americans scattered in dismay, but they were soon rallied by Brigade-Major Hunt and Lieutenant-Colonel Mitchell. The column was re-formed and the general command was assumed by the gallant Pennsylvanian colonel, Cromwell Pearce, of the Sixteenth, the senior officer. After giving three cheers, the troops pressed forward toward the village, and were met by the civil authorities and militia officers with propositions of a capitulation in response to a peremptory demand for surrender made by Colonel Pearce. An arrangement was concluded for an absolute surrender, when, taking advantage of the confusion that succeeded the explosion, and the time intentionally consumed in the capitulation, General Sheaffe and a large portion of his regulars, after destroying the vessels on the stocks, and some storehouses and their contents, stole across the Don, and fled along Dundas Street toward Kingston. When several miles from York they met a portion of the King's Regiment on their way to Fort George. These turned back, covered Sheaffe's retreat, and all reached Kingston in safety. Sheaffe (who was the military successor of Brock) was severely censured for the loss of York. He was soon afterward superseded in command in Upper Canada by Major-General De Rottenburg and retired to Montreal to take command of the troops there.

On hearing of the death of General Pike, General Dearborn went on shore, and assumed command after the capitulation. At sunset the work was finished; both Chauncey and Dearborn wrote brief despatches to the government at Washington; the former saying: "We are in full possession of the place," and the latter: "I have the satisfaction to inform you that the American flag is flying upon the fort at York." The post, with about two hundred and ninety prisoners besides the militia, the war vessel *Duke of Gloucester*, and a large quantity of naval and military stores, passed into the possession of the Americans. Such of the latter as could not be carried away by the squadron were destroyed. Before the victors left, the public buildings were fired by some unknown hand, and consumed.

Four days after the capitulation, the troops were re-embarked, preparatory to a descent upon Fort George. The post and village of York, possessing little value to the Americans, were abandoned. The British repossessed themselves of the spot, built another blockhouse, and on the site of the garrison constructed a regular fortification.

The loss of the Americans in the capture of York was sixty-six killed and two hundred and three wounded on land, and seventeen killed and wounded on the vessels. The British lost, besides the prisoners, sixty killed and eighty-nine wounded. General Pike was crushed beneath a heavy mass of stones that struck him in the back. He was carried immediately after discovery to the water's edge, placed in a boat, and conveyed first on board the *Pert*, and then to the Commodore's flagship. Just as the surgeons and attendants, with the wounded general, reached the little boat, the huzzas of the troops fell upon his benumbed ears. "What does it mean?" he feebly asked. "Victory," said a sergeant in attendance. "The British union-jack is coming down from the blockhouse, and the Stars and Stripes are going up." The dying hero's face was illuminated by a smile of great joy. His spirit lingered several hours, and then departed. Just before his breath ceased the captured British flag was brought to him. He made a sign for them to place it under his head, and thus he expired. His body was taken to Sacketts Harbour, and with that of his pupil and aid, Captain Nicholson, was buried with military honours within Fort Tompkins there.

It was not till 1821 that the town recovered from these disasters, and then the population only amounted to 1559. In 1830 it was 2860; but in 1834, a strong tide of emigration into Canada having set in, the population increased to 9254. In that year the town was incorporated as a city, and Mr. William Lyon Mackenzie was elected the first mayor of Toronto, April 3, 1834. In 1838 the inhabitants numbered 12,571; in 1848, 15,336; in 1861 they had increased to 44,821; in 1871, to 56,039; in 1881, 86,415; in 1891, 181,220; and finally, in 1903, to 266,989.

In 1821, E. A. Talbot, the author of some works of travel[1] visited the town. He states that the public edifices at that time were a Protestant Episcopal Church ("a wooden building with a wooden belfry"), a Roman Catholic Chapel (a brick building "not then completed, but intended to be very magnificent"—the present St. Paul's Church in Power Street), a Presbyterian Meeting House (a brick building, occupying the site of what is now Knox's Church), a Methodist Meeting House, situated in a field, nearly on the present site of the *Globe* office, the Hospital (the brick building on King Street now known as the Old Hospital, and occupied as Government offices), which Talbot describes as the most important building of the province, "bearing a very fine exterior," the Parliament House (a brick building erected in 1820 on the former site, and destroyed by fire in 1824), and the residence of the

[1] *Five Years' Residence in the Canadas.*

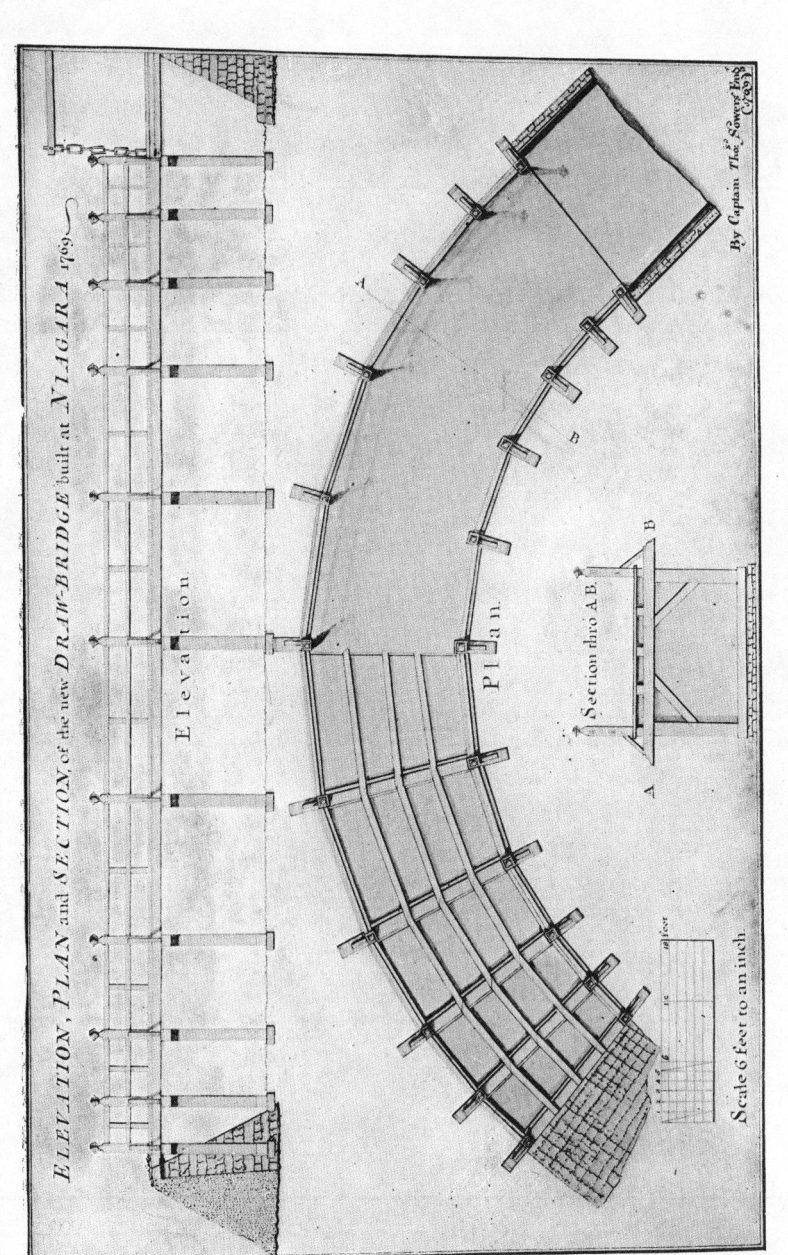

Captain Sowers's drawings of Fort Niagara, 1769.
From the original in the British Museum.

Lieutenant-Governor, a wooden building, "inferior to several private houses of the town, particularly that of Rev. Dr. Strachan," says Talbot. The streets, he adds, are regularly laid out, but "only one of them is in a finished state, and in wet weather those of them which are unfinished, are if possible more muddy than the streets of Kingston."

How different to-day, when Toronto has been called the "City of Churches," because of the large number of fine churches that have been erected in it! The distinctive feature of church architecture in Toronto consists in the fact that all denominations have built a considerable number of fine churches instead of concentrating their efforts on the erection of a few of greater magnificence. The large churches are not confined to the central portion but are found widely distributed throughout. Toronto to-day is the see of both Anglican and Roman Catholic archbishops. The city has suffered from destructive conflagrations, notably in 1890, and in April, 1904, when more than one hundred buildings in the wholesale business section were burned down, some five thousand persons were thrown out of work, and about eleven millions' worth of property was destroyed.

The year 1866 is a memorable one in the history of Toronto as well as all Canada as the year of the Fenian raids. The Toronto regiments of volunteers were promptly sent to drive the Fenians out of the Niagara peninsula. The "Queen's Own" met the enemy at Ridgeway, and sustained a loss of seven killed and twenty-three wounded. The beautiful monument erected to the memory of those who fell at Ridgeway is decorated each year on June 2d by their comrades and by the school children of the city. Another monument in Queen's Park commemorates the loyalty and bravery of Toronto volunteers. It records the gallantry of those who were killed during the North-west rebellion of 1885.

Toronto is a notable educational centre. The university is one of the best equipped in America. The first step towards its establishment was taken as early as 1797, but the university was not founded until 1827, chartered and endowed somewhat later, and opened for students in 1843. Until then it had rather a sectarian character, but nowadays it embraces, besides the four principal faculties, the following institutions: Ontario Agricultural College, Royal College of Dental Surgeons, the College of Pharmacy, the Toronto College of Music, the School of Practical Science, and the Ontario Veterinary College. The students in 1905-06 numbered 2547. The University buildings, it is said, are the best specimen of Norman architecture in America. The most beautiful other public buildings of Toronto are: the new Parliament buildings, the new City Hall, Osgood Hall, the Seat of the Provincial Courts and Law School, Trinity University, McMaster University, the Normal School, Upper Canada College, and the Provincial Asylum.

Toronto is pre-eminently a city of homes. It claims to have a larger proportion of good homes and a much smaller proportion of saloons than any city of its size in America. One of the gratifying features of Toronto that distinguishes it from most large cities is the fact that there is no part of the city that can be fairly regarded as a "slum" district.

The city covers a very large area so that there is

no overcrowding. Working men have no difficulty in obtaining homes with separate gardens, and it is a common practice to use these gardens in growing both flowers and vegetables.

The Park System is extensive and beautiful, possessing about 1350 acres, the chief being Queen's Park, adjoining the university, and the extensive High Park on the west of the city. But the most popular is probably Island Park, on Hiawatha Island, which lies immediately in front of the city in the form of a crescent about three miles in length.

The following great Canadians were born in Toronto: Professor Egerton Ryerson; Sir John MacDonald; Sir Daniel Wilson; Reverend Wm. Morley Puncheon; Hon. George Brown; Sir Oliver Mowat; but the most widely known Toronto citizen is probably Goldwin Smith, the great historian and economist. Toronto has ever shown itself fervently British in sentiment. Its later history has been purely civic without other interest than that attaching to prosperous growth. A pleasant society and an attractive situation make it a favourite place of residence.

In the first quarter of the nineteenth century, there was a certain Mr. Hetherington in Toronto, one of the clerks of St. James. Now the music of those primitive times seems to have been managed altogether after the old country village choirs. Mr. Hetherington was wont, after giving out the Psalm, to play the air on a bassoon; and then to accompany with fantasias on the same instrument, when any vocalist could be found to take the singing in hand. By-and-by the first symptoms of progress are apparent in the addition of a bassviol and clarinet to help Mr. Hetherington's bassoon

—"the harbinger and foreshadow," as Dr. Scadding says, "of the magnificent organ presented in after-times to the congregation of the 'Second Temple of St. James' by Mr. Dunn, but destroyed by fire, together with the whole church, in 1839, after only two years of existence."

Incidents of a different character no less strongly mark the changes which a period of only ninety years has witnessed. In 1811, namely, we find William Jarvis, Esq., His Excellency's Secretary, lodging a complaint in open court against a negro boy and girl, his slaves. The Parliament at Newark had, indeed, enacted in 1793—in those patriarchal days already described, when they could settle the affairs of the young province under the shade of an umbrageous tree—that no more slaves should be introduced into Upper Canada, and that all slave children born after the 9th of July of that year should be free on attaining the age of twenty-five.

But even by this creditable enactment slavery had a lease of life of fully a quarter of a century longer, and the *Gazette Public Advertiser*, and other journals, continue for years thereafter to exhibit such announcements as this of the Hon. Peter Russell, President of the Legislative Council, of date, February 19, 1806: "To be sold: a black woman, named Peggy, aged forty years, and a black boy, her son, named Jupiter, aged about fifteen years." The advertisement goes on to describe the virtues of Peggy and Jupiter. Peggy is a tolerable cook and washerwoman, perfectly understands making soap and candles, and may be had for one hundred and fifty dollars, payable in three years, with interest, from the day of sale. Jupiter, having various acquirements besides his specialty as a good house servant, is offered for two hundred dollars, but a fourth less will be taken for ready money. So recently as 1871, John Baker, who had been brought to Canada as the slave of Solicitor-General Gray, died at Cornwall, Ontario, in extreme old age. But before that the very memory of slavery had died out in Canada; and it long formed the refuge which the fugitive slave made for, with no other guide than the pole-star of our northern sky.

The history of Toronto, as already noted, is necessarily to a great extent that of the province, and of the whole region of Canada.

Upper Canada [says Dr. Scadding], in miniature, and in the space of a century, curiously passed through conditions and processes, physical and social, which old countries on a large scale, and in the course of long ages passed through. Upper Canada had its primeval and barbaric, but heroic age, its mediæval and high prerogative era; and then, after a revolutionary period of a few weeks, its modern, defeudalised, democratic era.

Index

A

Abbott, Francis, the "Hermit of Niagara," 40
Abercrombie, Sir Ralph, Brock under, 232
Allen, Ethan, mentioned, 222
Allen, Sadie, shoots the Rapids, 139
"American Blondin," the, see Calverly
American Canals, Great, see Hulbert
American Civic Association mentioned, 119
Amherst, Sir Jeffrey, campaign of 1759, 209
Anderson, M. B., on first Niagara Commission, 80
"Angevine place," building-site of *Griffon* 181

B

Bakewell's estimate of Niagara's age, 65
Balleni, tight-rope artist, 130
Barton, J. L., reminiscences of early Buffalo, 7
Bath Island, 76
Biddle Stairs, 32
Bird Island, 30, 76
Black Rock, origin of name, 8
Blondin, career of, 123–129; W. D. Howells's description of, 127–128
Blossom, I. A., agent of Holland Land Co., 7
Bourinot, Dr., quoted, 159-160, 288–291
Braddock, plans to capture Ft. Niagara, 206–207
Brock, Gen. Isaac, sketch of life, 231–238; replies to Hull's Proclamation, 244–246; captures Hull, 246–253; relations with the Indians, 252–253; death, 256; eulogies, 257–262; monuments to, 48, 259–262
Brodie, "Steve," goes over the Falls, 137

Browne, G. W., on St. Lawrence, 4, 161; on De Nonville at Niagara, 187–189
Brulé on Niagara frontier, 165
Buckley, A. B., *Fairyland of Science*, cited, 168
Buffalo, N. Y., growth of, 4–8
Buffalo Historical Society mentioned, 6
Burnt Ship Bay, 10, 212
Burton Act for preservation of Niagara, 116–120

C

Calverly, C. M., the "American Blondin," 132
Campbell, W. G., Niagara crank, 149
Canada (Story of the Nations), see Bourinot
Canadian Niagara Falls Power Co., 104, 112, 117
Canals, Great American, see Hulbert
Cantilever bridge, 46
Caroline, the, incident, 291
Cassier's Magazine quoted, 121
Cataract House, the, 75
"Cave of the Winds," the, 28, 31–33
Cayuga Creek mentioned, 10
Céloron at Niagara, 203
Century Magazine quoted, 29, 42–44
Champlain on Niagara frontier, 158–163
Chippewa Creek, 46; battle of, 279 seq.
Chrystie, Col., in War of 1812, 264
Church's "Niagara" mentioned, 14
Clark, George Rogers, compared with Brock, 249
Clark, Dr. John M., on "destruction of Niagara," 117
Colcourt, Henry, Blondin's assistant, 125
Colour of Niagara water explained by Mrs. Van Rensselaer, 42–44

315

Index

Commissioners of N. Y. State Reservation, first report of, 82 *seq.*
Crystal Palace, Blondin at, 128
Cutter, O. W., Niagara committeeman, 89

D

Dallion, Father, at Niagara, 166
"Darting Lines of Spray" explained, 45
Day, D. A., report, 17
Dearborn, Gen., in War of 1812, 274 *seq.*
De Leon, "Prof.," Niagara crank, 131
De Nonville, Gov., on Niagara frontier, 186–194
"Destruction of Niagara" discussed, 110–120
De Troyes at Fort Niagara, 190–194
"Devil's Hole," 49; massacre, 214–215
Dittrick, W., Niagara crank, 148
Dixon, S. J., tight-rope artist, 132
Dogs go over Falls, 151–152
Dorsheimer, William, on first Niagara Commission, 80; presents the park to New York State, 92
Dufferin Islands, 46

E

Electrical Development Co., 117
Ellicott, Andrew, estimates Niagara's age, 63
Erie Canal, importance to Niagara frontier, 6
Evershed, Thomas, devises wheelpits, 101

F

Farini, Signor, tight-rope artist, 129
Flack, R. W., killed in race in Niagara River, 148
Fool-Killer, see Nissen.
Forts: Chippewa, 46; Drummond, 48; du Portage, 15; Erie, 8; battle of, 285 *seq.*; Frontenac, 17, 170; George, 50, 274–276; Niagara, the first, 189–194; building, 197–202; during French War and Revolution, 204–229; Sir William Johnson captures, 278; Rouille, 293; Schlosser, 15
Fuller, Margaret, describes Niagara by night, 12; on Goat Island flora, 18; quoted, 28

G

Galinee on Niagara frontier, 166
Geology of Niagara, 52 *seq.*
Goat Island, 16–19, 25, 29, 40, 74
Golden Book of Niagara, names in the, 79
Gorge of Niagara, its history, 63 *seq.*
Graham, C. D., performs at Niagara, 137
Gravelet, see Blondin
Gray, Dr. Asa, on Goat Island flora, 16
Great Lakes, drainage, 3
Green, A. H., on first Niagara Commission, 80
Green Island, 30
Griffon, the, built at La Salle, N. Y., 180–186. See Remington
Gull Island, 40

H

Hall, Capt. Basil, experiment at Niagara, 34
Hall, Prof. James, survey of Falls, 65
Hardy, J. E., tight-rope artist, 132
Hazlett, George, Niagara crank, 139
"Heart of Niagara," 38, 45
Hennepin, Father, Narrative, quoted, 168, 173–184
Hennepin's View, 21
Heriot, George, quoted, 300
"Hermit of Niagara," see Abbott
"Hermit's Cascade," 40
Hill, Gov. D. B., signs Niagara Reservation Bill, 81
Historic Highways of America, cited, 206
Historic Towns of the Middle West, quoted, 5
Holland Land Co., mentioned, 7
Hooker, Sir J., on Goat Island, 16
Houghton, George, "The Upper Rapids," quoted, 13
How Niagara was Made Free, see Welch
Howells, W. D., quoted, 28, 29, 72–73, 74, 127–128
Hulbert, A. B., *The Ohio River*, cited, 3, 4; *Great American Canals*, cited, 6; *Historic Highways*, cited, 206
Hull, General, surrenders to Brock, 243, 277–279

Index

Hunt, William M., painting of Niagara, 14
Hunter, Colin, view of Niagara rapids, 11

I

Ice Age, Niagara in the, 58–59
Ice Bridge, 39
Inspiration Point, 44
International Railway Co., 117
Iris Island, see Goat Island
Iroquois, dominate Niagara frontier, 153 seq.; Hennepin's embassy to, 177–180

J

Jay's treaty, 225–226
Jenkins, I. J., tight-rope artist, 131
Johnson, Sir William, captures Fort Niagara, 211–213; treaty at Fort Niagara, 215–216
Joncaire, Chabert, erects "Magazine Royale" 197–200

K

Kendall, W. I., swims Niagara rapids, 136
King, Alphonse, performs at Niagara, 136-7

L

La Belle Famille, see Youngstown, N. Y.
La Salle, on Niagara frontier, 170–186
La Salle N. Y., the *Griffon* built at, 183
Lewiston Heights, 50, 264–265
Life and Correspondence of Major-General Sir Isaac Brock, K. B., see Tupper
Life and Times of General Brock, see Read
Luna Island, 31
Lundy's Lane, 46; battle of, 282
Lyell, Sir Charles, estimates Niagara's age, 65

M

Mackenzie, William Lyon, Bourinot describes, 288
"Magazine Royale," Joncaire builds, 197–200

Mahany, R. B., in *Historic Towns of the Middle States*, 5
Maid of the Mist, 44; voyage through lower rapids, 144–146
Manchester, see Niagara Falls, N. Y.
Mars, Tesla's project to signal, 120
Marshall, O. H., mentioned, 157, 187, 194–195, 219
Matheson, James, advocates reclamation of Niagara, 77
Michigan, brig, sent over the Falls, 133
Milet, Father, at Fort Niagara, 193
Mohawk River in the Ice Age, 60
Montresor, Capt., blockhouse, 15
Morgan, William, mentioned, 202

N

Nation, The, on the "desecration of Niagara," 78
Neuter Nation first inhabit Niagara frontier, 156 seq.
Newark, see Niagara-on-the Lake
"New Jerusalem," Major Noah's, 9
New York State Reservation, history of, 77–96
New York Times, on opening of New York Reservation, 94–95
Niagara Book, The, cited, 28
Niagara Falls, N. Y., described, 96–98
Niagara Falls Hydraulic Power and Manufacturing Co., 102, 104, 110, 111–112, 118–119
Niagara Falls Power Co., 101, 104, 111–112, 118–119
Niagara, Lockport, and Ontario Power Co., 114–115
Niagara-on-the-Lake, 50, 227–230
Niagara Reservation Act, 79–82, 84
Niagara River, historic importance, 2; drainage area, 2–4; description of the upper, 8–22; upper rapids of, 10–15; islands of, 12–22; historic sites of upper, 14–16; Falls of, 20 seq.; bridges over, 21 seq.; music of, 24–27; Howells on repose of, 28; air pressure at Falls of, 34–37; when dry, 38; in winter, 39; changes in, 41–42; Mrs. Van Rensselaer on colour of, 42–44; view of, from Queen Victoria Park, 44; a tour around, 20–51; the lower, described, 46–51; the geology of, 52–71; recession of Falls of, 63–71; George Frederick

318　Index

Niagara River—(*Continued*)
Wright on age of, 66–70; during era of private ownership, 72–77; struggle for passage of "Reservation Act," 77–82; *Golden Book of*, names in, 79; as producer of power, 99–122; volume of, 99; tunnel beneath, 106; manufacturing companies, use of,111–113, 117; use of water of, discussed, 111–122; Burton Act concerning, Taft on, 117–120; Blondin, career on, 123–129; performances of cranks on, 129–152 (see Farini, Dixon, Webb, Graham, etc.), *Maid of the Mist* sails lower, 144–146; controlled by Iroquois, 153–156; Neuter Nation inhabit banks of, 156–157; French occupation of, 158–213; Cartier hears of, 165; described by Galinee, 166–167; Hennepin describes, 167 *seq.*; reached by La Salle, 173–186; the *Griffon* built on, 181 *seq.*; first fort built on, 189; sufferings of first French troops on,191–194; name of, discussed by Marshall, 194–195; Joncaire on,197–198; in Old French War, 200 *seq.*; French lose, 209–212; in Revolutionary War, 217–226; fixed as international boundary line, 223–226; Loyalists settle upon, 227 *seq.*; in the War of 1812, 263 *seq.*
Nissen, Peter, exploits at Niagara, 149–151
Noah, Maj. N. N.,"New Jerusalem," 9

O

Official opening of New York Reservation, 85–95
Ohio River, The, see Hulbert
"Old Indian Ladder," 46
Old Stone Chimney mentioned, 15
Olmsted, F. A., on Goat Island flora, 16–18; mentioned, 77–78, 119
Ontario Power Co., 104, 108, 112, 117
Ottawa River, in Ice Age, 63

P

Papineau in Patriot War, 290
Parkman's works quoted, 171, *seq.*
Patch, Sam, jumps at Niagara, 133
Patriot War, Bourinot on the, 288–291

Peere, Stephen, tight-rope artist, 131
Percy, C. A., goes through rapids, 146–149
Perry, Lieut. O. H., captures Fort George, 274–276
Pike at the capture of York, 302 *seq.*
Pittsburg Reduction and Mining Co., 118
Platt, John J., mentioned, 80
Portage, old Niagara, 15, 18
Porter's Bluff, 33
Porter, Judge, 37, 38, 96
Porter, Hon. Peter A., *Guide Book*, 11; *Old Fort Niagara*, 11, 197, 200, 207–209, 213; *Goat Island*, 11, 19; on proposed attack on Fort Niagara in 1755, 207–209; on commercial importance of Fort Niagara, 213–214
Potts, William, Niagara crank, 139
Pouchot, Gen., surrenders Fort Niagara, 209–213
Poughkeepsie Eagle quoted, 80
Power development at Niagara, 99–122
Prideaux, Gen. John, captures Fort Niagara, 209 *seq.*
Prospect Point, 20, 21

Q

"Quebec Act," effect of, 217–218
Queen Victoria Park, 44, 108
Queen's Royal Hotel, 51
Queenston, 50
Queenston Heights, 48; battle on, 263 *seq.*

R

Rapids of Niagara, 11–15, 22, 45, 46, 49–50; Hunter's painting of, 11, 14
Read, D. B., *The Life and Times of General Brock*, cited, 232
Red Jacket, anecdote of, 22
Reed, Andrew, suggests reclamation of Niagara, 77
Remington, C. K., on the building-site of the *Griffon*, 183
Road to Frontenac, The, mentioned, 162
Robb, J. H., on first Niagara Commission, 80
Robinson, Joel, sails the *Maid of the Mist* through lower rapids, 144–146
Rogers, Sherman S., on first Niagara Commission, 80

Index

S

St. Davids, Ont., in the history of geologic Niagara, 63
St. Lawrence drainage, 3
St. Lawrence River, George Waldo Browne on, 4
Schlosser, Capt., 15, 213; see Fort Schlosser
Scott, Gen. Winfield, in War of 1812, 267 seq.
Scribner's Monthly quoted, 25
Senecas dominate Niagara frontier, 5
Severance, F. H., *Old Trails of the Niagara Frontier*, 6, 219-222
Sheaffe, Gen., mentioned, 268 seq.
Ship Island, 30
"Shipyard of the *Griffon*," the, see Remington
Shirley, Gov., plans Niagara attack 207
"Shoreless Sea," the, 45
Silliman, Prof., Basil Hall writes, 34-35
Simcoe, Gov., John Graves, mentioned, 229, 294 seq.
Smyth, Gen., in War of 1812, 271 seq.
Spelterini, Signorina, tight-rope artist, 130
Spencer, J. W., estimates Niagara's age, 66
Spouting Rock, 41
Steadman Bluff, 30
Steadman, John, first owner of Goat Island, 18
Steel arch bridge, built by Roebling, 46
Story of Canada, The, by Bourinot, quoted, 288-291
Sullivan's campaign of 1779, 223

T

Table Rock, 38, 45
Taft, Sec'y William H., on the "destruction of Niagara," 117-120
Talbot, E. A., description of early Toronto, 308
Taylor, Mrs. A. E., barrel-fiend, 141-143
Tempest Point, 104
Terrapin Rocks, 33, 37-38
Terrapin Tower, 33, 37
Tesla, Nikola, on Niagara electrical power, 120
Thayer, Eugene, on the music of Niagara, 25-26

Thompson, Sir William, prophesies era of electricity, 77
Three Sister Island, 40
Tonawanda, N. Y., mentioned, 10
Toronto, Ont., 51; history of, 292-313
Toronto and Niagara Power Co., 104, 105, 112, 121
Tupper, Ferdinand Brock, *The Life and Correspondence of Major-General Sir Isaac Brock, K. B.*, cited, 232
Tyndall, Prof., on Terrapin Rocks, 33

U

United Empire Loyalists, 228
Upper Canada, and Lower, divided, 295

V

Van Rensselaer, Mrs. Schuyler, on Niagara, quoted, 24, 27, 42-44
Van Rensselaer, Col. Solomon, 264-266
Van Rensselaer, Gen. Stephen, 263
Victoria Falls compared with Niagara Falls, 13

W

Wagenfuhrer, Martha E., barrel-crank at Niagara, 140
War of 1812, 263-291
Webb, Capt. Matthew, drowned at Niagara, 134-135
Welch, Thomas V., labours to enfranchise Niagara, 79; *How Niagara was Made Free*, cited, 79-82; mentioned, 81, 89
Whirlpool, the, 47, 50
Whitney, Gen. P., 40
Willard, Maud, Niagara crank, killed, 140
Woodward, Prof., surveys Niagara Falls, 65
Wool, Capt., hero of Queenston Heights, 265 seq.
Wright, Dr. Geo. Frederick, makes new estimate of Niagara's age, 66-70

Y

York, Ont., Americans capture, 300-306
York Harbour, early description, 296-297
Youngstown, N. Y., 50; skirmish at, 211

A HISTORY OF THE ADIRONDACKS

By Alfred L. Donaldson

The long awaited reprint of a scarce book, with a new introduction by John J. Duquette, Saranac Lake Village Historian.

2 volumes, 856 pages; 34 illustrations and maps.

clothbound $39.50

Alfred Donaldson's *History of the Adirondacks* is recognized as the major work about the entire region and as such remains unsurpassed. As the author pointed out in the preface, "The previously recorded history of the Adirondacks lies scattered in the most meager parts of old county histories, in a score of early books on travel, in a few guide-books and pamphlets, in many detached magazine and newspaper articles, and in a long series of rather dry and often technical State Reports." His task was, therefore, to sift and sort this material and to bring it together into a comprehensive and cohesive history, while adding much information from "unmapped sources" and a copious index.

Alfred Donaldson did not live to witness the success of his work. He died two years after its publication. It would probably have surprised him more than anyone that his book would eventually become so scarce that collectors were paying between $100 and $200 for a copy.

Harbor Hill Books is proud to offer this reprint at an affordable price and of a technical quality that far surpasses that of the original edition: acid-free paper and a heavy buckram binding. John J. Duquette, Village Historian of Saranac Lake and himself an expert on Adirondack history, has written an introduction to this new edition, including a biographical sketch of Alfred Donaldson.

Harbor Hill Books, P.O. Box 407, Harrison, N. Y. 10528

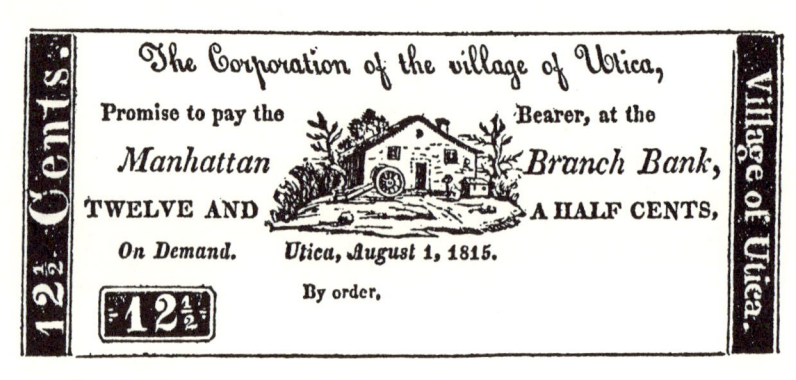

Fractional currency of the Village of Utica, 1815, with wood cuts by William Williams. Reduced size

An Oneida County Printer: William Williams.

Printer, Publisher, Editor.

With a Bibliography of the Press at Utica, 1803-1838.

By John Camp Williams.

214 pages, illus. Reprinted from the 1906 ed.
cloth $12.50

The story of William Williams (1787-1850) whose enterprise made Utica an important publishing center for more than a quarter century. Williams was active in the community in many ways: in addition to being a printer, book binder, paper manufacturer, wood engraver, publisher and bookseller, he was also an Elder in the Presbyterian Church, organizer of the volunteer firefighters, took part as a Captain in the defense of Sackets Harbor in 1812 and led efforts to aid the poor in the cholera epidemic of 1832.

With fine portraits of Williams and of Henry Morgan (of masonic fame) and numerous facsimiles of titlepages of Williams' books. Also of woodcuts engraved by Williams and of fractional currency of the Village of Utica, 1815. — The original edition printed in 160 copies only.

Harbor Hill Books, P.O. Box 407, Harrison, N. Y. 10528

History of the Press in Western New York

from the Beginning to the Middle of the 19th Century.

By Frederick Follett. Preface by Wilberforce Eames.

82 pages, foldout plate. Reprinted from the 1902 edition. cloth $8.50

This is essentially a history of newspapers and periodicals in the counties of Alleghany, Cattaraugus, Cayuga, Chautauque, Chemung, Erie, Genesee, Livingston, Monroe, Niagara, Orleans, Ontario, Seneca, Steuben, Tioga, Tompkins, Wayne, Wyoming, and Yates, of western New York, during the first half of the 19th century. As such it is the earliest attempt to gather information on the subject from many different sources and organize it for publication, by a contemporary newspaper editor who personally knew many of the publishers of the period. The original edition was printed in 102 copies only.

A Brief History of the Printing Press in Washington, Saratoga and Warren Counties.

Together with a Check List of their Publications prior to 1825, and a Selection of Books relating particularly to this Vicinity.

By William H. Hill.

118 pages. Reprinted from the Fort Edward 1930 edition (privately printed) cloth $8.50

This book deals with the history of newspaper and periodical publishing in three New York counties, arranged by individual towns: Salem, Sandy Hill, Cambridge, Whitehall, Greenwich, Fort Edward and Granville, in Washington County; Ballston, Saratoga, Waterford, Schuylerville, Stillwater, Mechanicsville and Crescent, in Saratoga County; and Glens Falls and Caldwell in Warren County.
    By far the most interesting part to book collectors, however, are the checklists of local imprints of those communities. There is a chapter on the early paper mills and a list of books relating to the local history of the three counties. The original edition was printed privately, in an edition of 54 copies only.

Harbor Hill Books, P.O. Box 407, Harrison, N. Y. 10528

Woods and Waters or the Saranacs and Racket.

By Alfred Billings Street.

386 pages, illus. map. Reprinted from the first ed. 1860.

cloth $14.50

Five prominent Albany citizens, two lawyers, a banker, a physician, and the author start out from the state capital one hot day in July in the 1850's, to escape the heat of the city and to experience the thrills, the excitement — and the quiet serenity — of an Adirondack hunting expedition.

Constituting the entire membership of what they term "The Saranac Club," they travel north, via Whitehall, Port Kent and Keeseville, to Baker's Lake House on the Lower Saranac. It is here that they pick up their guides: Harvey Moody, with his brothers and sons, five in all. Together they plan the trip which will take them for a month of hunting and fishing along the Saranac and Raquette Rivers, through the Lower and Upper Saranacs, Round Lake and Tupper Lake, and the numerous ponds to the north.

Street's portrayals of the Adirondack guides have become classics and excerpts from *Woods and Waters* are included in Paul Jamieson's *Adirondack Reader* and in Kenneth Durant's *Guide-Boat Days.*

The Indian Pass and Mount Marcy.

By Alfred Billings Street.

258 pages. Reprinted (with enlarged type) from the first ed. 1869. cloth $9.75

A narrative of a climb during the 1860's in a region now so familiar to Adirondack hikers but unknown then to all but a few mountain guides. Street, along with two guides, set out to penetrate the Indian Pass, starting from Scotts on Elizabethtown road, to the "Upper Works", from there to Lakes Colden and Avalanche, to the top of Marcy, and to the "Keene Flats" and Whiteface. A nostalgia book for those who like to tag along with the Adirondack explorers of the mid-19th century.

Harbor Hill Books, P.O. Box 407, Harrison, N. Y. 10528

Historical Sketches of Northern New York and the Adirondack Wilderness.

By Nathaniel B. Sylvester

324 pages, portr. Reprinted from the 1877 ed. paper $6.95

Alfred Donaldson regarded Sylvester's *Historical Sketches* as the only logical predecessor of his own *History*. He wrote in his preface: "The most notable attempt to tell a consecutive and comprehensive story of the region, was made by Nathaniel Bartlett Sylvester in his *Historical Sketches of Northern New York*, published in 1877. This is a volume of great research and merit...."

For lovers of the Adirondacks there is no more satisfying reading than this collection of 33 short essays on as many different regions and historical incidents of the North Country. The author covers a wide territory and deals with incidents over a great time span. There are stories about Champlain, Cartier and other early explorers, about the Indians, the early trappers and settlers, and personages such as Nat Foster, Sir William Johnson, Joseph Bonaparte and John Brown. There are separate chapters on the High Peaks, the Indian Pass, Lake George, the Manor of Willsboro, the Chazy, Hudson and St. Lawrence Rivers, Tryon County, Smith's Lake, and much more.

The Life and Adventures of Nat Foster, Trapper and Hunter of the Adirondacks.

By A.L. Byron-Curtiss.

286 pages, 20 illus. Reprinted from the first ed. 1897.
cloth $13.95

The best and most complete biography of the famous Adirondack trapper Nathaniel Foster (1767?-1840), a book that has long been a rarity in the antiquarian market. It begins with Nat's childhood, the family's move from New England to New York, the father's exploits during the Revolutionary War and the family's hardships during his years of absence. Above all, it is the story of Foster's life as a trapper and hunter in Herkimer County, his encounters with the Indians and last, but not least, the shooting of Drid at Old Forge and Foster's subsequent trial and acquittal. A book particularly about Herkimer County and the Fulton Chain of Lakes.

Harbor Hill Books, P.O. Box 407, Harrison, N. Y. 10528

GRAVES, Dr. ROSEWELL, d. at New York city, Oct. 28, 1837.
GRAVES, WILLIAM T., d. at Louisville, Ky., Sept. 27, 1848, a. 43; was in congress from Kentucky from 1827 to 1841.
GRAY, MRS. ELIZABETH S., d. in Boston, Mass., Aug. 15, 1842, a. 33; dau. of the late Joseph White, Jr., of Salem.
GRAY, GEORGE, was an active friend of the revolution at Philadelphia, and a member of the convention for amending the constitution; was in the legislature of Pennsylvania, and speaker of the house; d. 1800. (*Simpson's Eminent Philadelphians.*)

Sample from Hough's American Biographical Notes

American Biographical Notes,

being Short Notices of Deceased Persons, chiefly those not included in Allen's or in Drake's Biographical Dictionaries.

By Franklin B. Hough.

442 pages. Reprinted from the orig. ed. Albany, 1875.   cloth $15.00

Franklin Benjamin Hough (1822-1885), the versatile and prolific New York historian, made a remarkable contribution toward American biographical and genealogical research when he published his *American Biographical Notes*. It is a reference book which has been little known to librarians and genealogists, and for a good reason: the original edition was printed in 130 copies only and has been extremely rare.

The book contains, in alphabetical arrangement, the names of some 7000 Americans of lesser prominence and not listed in the two standard biographical dictionaries of the day, nor included in the later dictionaries (Appleton, DAB, etc.). The entries are generally brief and contain, above all, the date and in most cases the place of death and often the age of the deceased. It is obvious that these data are helpful in finding obituaries in local newspaper files.

Although not limited to any geographical area, the scope is weighted toward New York State which was Hough's chief interest during his life-long scholarly endeavors. Since the death-dates fall roughly within the period 1820-1870 it follows that the entries concern persons who lived during the latter part of the 18th and the first half of the 19th centuries. Sources are given, such as the author's own histories of Jefferson, Lewis, St. Lawrence and Franklin counties, Benton's Herkimer Co., Munsell's Historical Collections, Sabine's Loyalists, Documentary Hist. of N.Y., Thompson's Hist. of Long Island, Bradford's N.E. Biogr. and many periodicals and newspapers. The book belongs in every library reference collection.

Harbor Hill Books, P.O. Box 407, Harrison, N. Y. 10528

HISTORY OF THE TOWN OF FLUSHING

By Henry D. Waller.
287 pages (enlarged type). Reprint of the 1899 edition
cloth $12.50

This book was first published the year after the Town of Flushing was incorporated into New York City (1898) and it thus deals with the entire period during which Flushing was a separate administrative entity.

It was written by the Rev. Henry Davey Waller who came to Flushing in 1889 as an assistant to the Rev. J. Carpenter Smith, rector of St. George's Church. Upon the latter's death in 1898 Henry Waller succeeded him as rector but by this time he had finished writing his 'History of Flushing', probably in collaboration with the former rector who had been gathering material for the book.

Flushing was chartered as a town in 1645 by the Dutch West India Company as the town of Vlissingen, the name of a town back in Holland. As the English took over New Netherland they anglicized the name to Flushing but it seems that the name could also have been derived from the "fflushinge Creeke" which flowed into the East River at that point. The book takes us from the time of the Dutch settlement, under Peter Stuyvesant, through 250 years of Flushing history, up until the end of the 19th century. It deals with events during four distinctly separate eras: the Dutch rule, the English colonial period under the Duke of York ("The Duke"), the American Revolution, and the post-revolutionary period.

Of particular interest is the Appendix which contains valuable documents, lists of earlier inhabitants, and other data brought together from many sources. The bibliography and the index at the end contribute toward making the book an important work of reference for anyone interested in the past history of Queens County.

Harbor Hill Books, P.O. Box 407, Harrison, N. Y. 10528

Historic White Plains.
By *John Rosch*. Preface by *Renoda Hoffman*.

A profusely illustrated history of the City of White Plains, originally published in 1939, with numerous photographs of now vanished houses and neighborhoods. The new preface, by the White Plains City Historian, tells the story of saving and moving the Purdy house, Washington's headquarters, and in various other ways updates the original text. New pictures of the Purdy house have been added. The book was republished with the cooperation of the City of White Plains. cloth $11.95

History of Westchester County from its Earliest Settlement to 1900.
By *Frederic Shonnard* & *W. W. Spooner*.

While drawing on the two previous works on Westchester history, Bolton's and Scharf's, which were essentially collections of town histories, the authors of this work present an overall view of the county's history, to be enjoyed as continuous reading. It is a scholarly and well-documented work, profusely illustrated, and is well suited also for younger readers. Reprinted from the 1900 edition. buckram $29.50

History of the Tarrytowns from Ancient Times to the Present.
By *Jeff Canning* & *Wally Buxton*.

The first comprehensive history of the Tarrytowns area, by two life-long residents of Tarrytown. It presents a well-rounded picture of life in this Hudson River community from Indian times to our own. Illustrated with rare early photographs many of which are unique and have never before been published. Thoroughly indexed. A new publication, 1975. cloth $12.95

Chronicle of a Border Town: History of Rye, 1660-1870, including Harrison and White Plains till 1788.
By *Charles W. Baird*.

In 46 chapters the author traces the history of Rye and vicinity from the Indian Purchases through the Reconstruction period. The individual chapters are devoted to such topics as *Town Matters in Olden Times, Mails & Newspapers, Rye in Connecticut Harrison's Purchase, The Boston Road, White Plains, Physicians & Lawyers, Slavery in Rye, the Revolution* — to mention only a few. A 105-page appendix contains an alphabetical list of Rye families. Truly a major source work for the history of lower Westchester. Reprinted from the 1871 edition. buckram $27.50

Harbor Hill Books, P.O. Box 407, Harrison, N. Y. 10528

The Spy Unmasked, or, Memoirs of Enoch Crosby,
alias Harvey Birch, the Hero of James Fenimore Cooper's *The Spy.*
By *H. L. Barnum.*

A facsimile edition of the first edition (1828), with a new introduction by *James H. Pickering*, Michigan State University, and an appendix: Enoch Crosby, Secret Agent of the Neutral Ground: His Own Story. — A fascinating tale of the American Revolution in Westchester County, the story of John Jay's peddler-spy who performed invaluable intelligence service for the American side. Crosby is generally regarded as the model for Cooper's spy-character, Harvey Birch. The introduction adds many new facts to our knowledge of the book and its author, H. L. Barnum. cloth $11.50

The Crisis of the Revolution: The Story of Arnold and André.
By *William Abbatt.* With a new preface: William Abbatt and his
  Historical Work, by *Jeff Canning.*

A reprint, in re-arranged form, of this extremely rare work, of which only 250 copies were published originally. Abbatt's writings span a wide variety of historical subjects, but the André-Arnold incident was of special interest to him. In this book, he follows Major André step by step on his fateful journey through Rockland, Westchester and Putnam Counties as the major schemes with the disaffected American general, Benedict Arnold, to deliver West Point to the British during the American Revolution. Abbatt provides detailed historical background of the persons and places involved with the capture, trial and execution of André, plus illustrations of many no-longer-extant houses and inns connected with the incident. 69 plates and 4 maps. Reprinted from the 1899 edition. cloth $16.50

General Orders of George Washington, issued at Newburgh on the Hudson, 1782-1783.
Compiled & ed. by *Major Edward C. Boynton.*
New edition, with an introduction by *Alan C. Aimone.*

The general orders issued by General Washington while headquartered at Newburgh during the final years of the American Revolution afford an interesting insight into the life and mood of the Continental Army as it spent its last winter in the New Windsor Cantonment. It was here that the first army chapel (The Temple) was built and the first U.S. medal of honor created, the origin of the "Purple Heart". This was the time of the "Newburgh Letters", written by disgruntled officers, and the famous "crown offer" which suggested that Washington take over as head of a limited monarchy. Reprinted from the 1883 edition, with added illustrations and a new introduction. cloth $8.50

A Two-Years' Journal in New York (1678-1680).
By *Charles Wolley.* Introduction & notes by *Edward Gaylord Bourne.*

A first-hand account of New York Colony a decade and a half after the English takeover from the Dutch. Charles Wolley, an English clergyman, describes the Indians of Southern New York and Long Island, as he found them during his two years' stay, their dress and customs, their hunting habits and their diet. His book was first published in London in 1701. Reprinted from the 1902 edition. cloth $7.50

Harbor Hill Books, P.O. Box 407, Harrison, N. Y. 10528

Anyone interested in the History of New York State will find this book a sheer delight. I heartily recommend it.
—Sibyl L. Golden (Review in *The Conservationist*)

Cloth $13.95

History of the Lumber Industry in the State of New York.

By William F. Fox

With an Appendix: The Roll of Pioneer Lumbermen.

22 full-page illustrations, map printed in four colors.

Originally published in 1901 as part of the 6th annual report of the New York State Forest, Fish and Game Commission, this is the first time this important reference work is offered as a separate book. It describes the development of lumbering from the time of the first settlers up to the end of the 19th century, dealing with such topics as: the first sawmills, rafting and raftsmen, logdriving, log marks, log railroads, sawmills and tanneries, to mention only a few. The 28-page appendix provides a table of first settlements and first sawmills, with dates of their establishments and the names of the builders. It is arranged by county and township.

There are 22 full-page illustrations from early photographs and a large folding map *in full color* giving a graphic presentation of the gradual settlement of New York State. This map, entitled *First Settlements in the State of New York,* (10 x 15''), shows the names of all townships, with dates of first settlements. It is colored in 7 shades, each indicating whether the area was settled during one of the following time periods: 1614-1700; 1700-1725; 1725-1750; 1750-1775; 1775-1800; 1800-1825; 1825-1900. — This map is available separately, printed on large paper, at $2.95.